RADICAL SELF-ACCEPTANCE

RADICAL SELF-ACCEPTANCE

The Spiritual Birth of the Human Person

ℰ⃝ℛ

James M. McMahon, Ph.D.

A Crossroad Book
The Crossroad Publishing Company
New York

The Crossroad Publishing Company
370 Lexington Avenue, New York, NY 10017

Printed in the United States of America.

Library of Congress Cataloging-in-Publication Data

McMahon, James M.
  Radical self-acceptance :   the spiritual birth of the human person
/ James M. McMahon.
   p. cm.
  Rev. ed. of: The price of wisdom. c1996, and Letting go of mother.
c1996.
  Includes bibliographical references.
  ISBN 0-8245-1821-7 (hc). — ISBN 0-8245-1824-1 (pbk.)
  1. Self. 2. Individuation (Psychology) 3. Individuality.
4. Separation-individuation 5. Separation-individuation—Religious
aspects—Christianity. 6. Mother and child. 7. Mother and child—
Religious aspects—Christianity. I. McMahon, James M. Price of
wisdom. II. McMahon, James M. Letting go of mother. III. Title.
BF697.M227—1999
155.2'5—DC21   99-15981
                  CIP

1 2 3 4 5 6 7 8 9 10 04 03 02 01 99

To Lijuan Niu McMahon
and
Lynn Marie Quinn

Contents

Introduction

On the southern part of Long Island there are many miles of Atlantic Ocean beach. My surfer nephew tells me that this area comprises one of the most beautiful beaches in the world—no faint praise from someone who has settled in Hawaii. My family loves this place. We were lucky enough to spend a week or so there each summer for many years. They were spectacular times.

Each year a newspaper article would appear warning swimmers about riptides, sometimes called sea pusses. Occasionally, due to an irregular constellation of sand on the ocean bottom, there would be a short strip of shoreline which didn't follow the rules of the rest of the ocean. Step into the water at this point and you might be whisked away out into the ocean in a split second. Fighting it was useless. In fact it was dangerous. The sea was not to be bested, and the swimmer who failed to acknowledge this quickly exhausted himself and was swallowed up. The newspapers warned us of this. They instructed us to look for the telltale signs of a rip, the discoloration and sandiness of the water, the small signs of turbulence. We were particularly wary of this because of our four small children. The water was always inspected before we set down our blankets and the digging with shovels and pails commenced in earnest.

The advisors of the signs and dangers of the sea puss always made the same suggestion, which was so hard to accept because it seemed to go against human instinct. They adamantly insisted that if you should get trapped in this bizarre undertow, it was essential to go with it, not fight it, and as soon as it had escorted you beyond the waves it would release you, guaranteed, and you could make your way back to the shore, or let the incoming tide do it for you. You would wind up on land unharmed, but perhaps some miles down the shore. To resist was certain death. And every year provided proof.

I learned a lot at the beach. I learned, for example, that when an enormous wave approached, it was best not to stand there and scream or even turn and attempt to drag my water encased legs to the shore. Many scraped bellies taught me this completely. But to this day, at the moment of truth,

I have an ever so slight resistance to putting my head down and diving into this gigantic wall of water. I do, and when I bob up on the other side, I am surprised that it truly worked. My survival by this means is a cause of wonder each time. Such is the power of human narcissism.

I want the world to work the way I want it to work, and when it doesn't I am miffed, and I try to force matters. I try to make it go the way I want it to go. The beach is such a wonderful teacher. I am convinced that anyone who spends a month on the beach with an open mind will be transformed. Far away from man-made buildings and airplanes and self-made notions of how the world works, or how we make it work, you can just sit and watch. Every single day, day in and day out, the tide comes in and out, in and out. Each morning light sneaks up on you. All life on the beach rustles. On the beach you can see it, hear it, smell it. It gets inside you.

And at night, sitting with your arms around your knees, a sweater between you and the rising winds, you let yourself be aware of the coming to an end of this cycle, the dimming of the light. All living things respond. After a few days, your mind is emptying. The power of the regularity and the beauty kicks in. Your heart begins to beat in rhythm with the waves, just as women who live together tend to menstruate at the same time. You identify with the sandpipers scurrying along the shore, wishing for them to slow down and relax. It is hard to be an atheist on the beach as the sun goes down. When you are on the beach it gets harder each day.

Nature always wins, and the wisest among us know that, and find ways to cooperate. But we are easily seduced by the idea the we can *do*, that we can master. It has been our *bête noire* from all time. Genesis tells us that we can have it all if we acknowledge our limitedness and leave to the transcendent One what is his. To not eat of the tree of knowledge of good and evil; to live with mystery; to learn humility—it seems to be our fate to repeat our mistakes over and over again.

It is not our fate, but it is our nature because we are fused with mother, our first transcendent. This profound connection with her leads us to believe, in the deepest of places within us, that we can do anything. Regardless of the health or quality of our relationship with her, our early "oneness" with her has left us with this kind of self-centeredness. We have overcome our terror by maintaining our childlike notion of her unlimited power and protection through all sorts of psychological tricks and deals. The stronger our fusion with her, the more central our secret pact with her, the more an underlying grandiosity lurks, even if we are manifestly self-deprecating. This is the "ego" that the ancients have been telling us about.

The drama we humans are born into is psychological as well as physical and rests particularly on our capacities to communicate with each other. Because of the enormous size of our skulls, we are born with relatively immature development of our bodies and nervous systems. As a result, we are totally dependent for an extremely long period of time. It's another of those peculiar dilemmas we humans seem prone to. Our skull must be large enough to house the most complex computer in the universe. As a result, the physical mechanics of the birth process demand that we come out of the mother prematurely, with an extremely limited capacity to get along on our own. If the rest of our bodies had sufficient time to develop so that we could become more rapidly independent, the skull would be too large to pass through the vaginal canal.

To compensate somewhat for this dilemma, nature has provided us with a face comprised of an enormous amount of muscles, more than any other animal, so that we may communicate our needs and discomforts as quickly and powerfully as possible. Ensuing is a subtle dance between mother and child, the baby employing all aspects of its emerging capabilities with each grimace and gurgle, and the mother receiving her offspring with every sense and sensitivity with which nature, life experience, and a good heart have equipped her. In the first hour after birth the newborn is alert and fixated on its mother, and the mother is mesmerized as well. They look at each other and form the most profound bond possible. That loving moment, so beautiful and so humanly moving, and so essential to our survival, contains within it the best about us and about life but also the greatest challenge each of us will ever face. From that moment the mother is taking her baby into a place not yet alive in her, and from that same moment the baby is watching with its entire being. The infant actually has the capability from birth to imitate its mother's gestures and expressions, and it does. After an hour or so of this, they fall off into deep sleep, exhausted both from the trip and from the meeting. How shall their hearts ever be disentangled?

Who would want to leave such a connection?

The prospect of surrendering some of our self-centered connection to mother is so terrifying—we believe that we cannot survive without it—that we passionately resist seeing it. We believe we must "know it all" to know anything. We believe we must "control" the world to be safe. We must be approved of and noticed all the time to be worthwhile. But real safety and the overcoming of fear are ours only to the extent that we are able to *surrender* to the universe, to trust the benevolent workings of a power greater than ourself. You don't even have to believe in this. If you observe with an open mind, you will realize it to be true. Observe. Sit on the beach.

If, in consultation with *your* higher power, you form certain clear but flexible *intentions* about your life, and if you let in the strength that comes from merely *observing* as honestly as you can just what your inner processes and behaviors are, and, most important, if you are determined to *radically accept yourself,* much of what ails you will just begin to disappear over time in the normal occurrences of life. There will be a shifting deep inside you, a releasing of your spirit. This change will surprise you. It will seem to occur "behind your back."

However you have stayed enmeshed, it is in accordance with your human nature. Just realize this and the healing will begin.

And this does not mean damaging your friendship with your mother. It means beginning to disentangle the strangling entanglements that have occurred over time, as if you were a fish caught in a net. By disentangling yourself, you will be free—free even to see her as she truly is, and to love her as a grown-up loves. She will be free, also, to go her own way. And both of you will be free to grow into the purpose of each of your lives, to return to who you truly are.

With separate hearts you will be able to love each other.

Each morning when I awake, I thank God for the first breath I attend to. I thank God for this day, for yesterday, for my sleep. I entrust myself to God's care as freely and with as much abandon as I can muster. And toward the end of my two or three minutes of prayer I say the following: "I love you, Jim, completely and without reservation. I accept you just as you are. I receive you joyously without any demand for change. I love you madly."

It is only in the last few years that I have been able to say this. It has been hard for me, the result of a long and arduous journey, one that is far from finished. Judging from the shocked reactions of those I encourage to affirm themselves in a similar way, the unbridled expression of love for ourselves does not come naturally to us humans—at least after the age of three or four or so. There is a horrific resistance to loving oneself, to accepting oneself, to *receiving* oneself just as one is, to allowing the joy that comes from a rich peace with oneself. Some of the refusal is within ourselves, the result of difficulties in our life, the failure of someone to convince us of our wondrousness. Some of our fatalism about the possibilities of happiness comes simply from the vicissitudes of being human, members of *homo sapiens,* a glorious but also faulted species of life. Some of it comes from our earliest cultural and familial myths. "Who says you are supposed to be happy?" we may have been scolded. Even Sigmund Freud, the father of psychoanalysis, was pessimistic, establishing as the goal of a good psycho-analysis the mere replacement of abject misery with ordinary unhappiness.

Who says we are supposed to be happy? Well I, for one, do. Happiness, even joy, even bliss, spring from ever-deepening wonder at our courage and beauty, which in turn results in a gentle sweet love for ourselves, love such as we might feel toward a baby. What I hope to demonstrate in this book is that dear love for ourselves is indeed possible. Not only is it possible, but it is possible in so profound a way that I call it radical self-acceptance.

But it is not magic. There are dark forces in us that strive to blind us to our worth. The appreciation, no less celebration, of our value is not spon-taneous as life goes on. Rather, it is the result of a journey, the journey of the spirit, a journey that comes after our biological birth and after our psychological birth as a toddler. It is in our *spiritual* birth that each of us can gradually recognize our uniqueness and the specialness of our vocation as persons.

In that recognition each of us takes the right and duty to ourselves to see the world through our own eyes, to recognize that no one has all the an-swers to the riddle of life, and that our perception is as valid as any other. Without getting on this Wisdom path, happiness is almost impossible, because the radical self-acceptance that leads to joy is actually a decision, a decision that can only be made by a free person struggling to lead his or her own life. We are humble as we accept this mantle of responsibility and mindful of all that we can learn from our contemporaries as well as the wisdom of the past. But our true wisdom is in daring to make the bottom line our own.

First we will look at what stops us from getting on the Wisdom path, the hindrances that the mere fact of being human place before us. There is profound resistance to such wisdom, and the first section of this book is devoted to that topic. Life is frightening, and we are all vigilant to find something outside ourselves that we hope will protect us from all our fears, especially the fear of death. The prototype for this, of course, is the relationship with our first "higher power," our mother. I become more deeply conscious as the years pass by just how powerful our first relationship, this love of loves, is, how beautiful and how challenging. For although this bond provides us with the strength to move forward on the journey to become our unique selves, there is an equally profound tendency to get lost in it. We often choose fusion with mother and subsequent surrogates over psychologically separating out into our true, unique selves. In this book I hope to spell out how that fusion operates in our daily lives and in the society around us as it propagandizes us.

Traditional theories of "separation and individuation" catch mere glimpses of the power and influence of the psychological fusion with our mother that characterizes each of our lives. The nature of our relationships with our caretakers has often left us with an unrealistic sense of what we are, indeed, capable of. The connection between insufficient or abusive parenting and a child's lack of confidence and self-esteem may be obvious. But being the apple of a doting parent's eye can be just as perilous to our emotional well-being. A parent's "smother-love" or starry-eyed devotion can warp our sense of ourselves and our abilities as well. We may find adult happiness just as elusive if we think we are greater than we are and fail to live up to these expectations. The result is often shame and unhappiness.

But regardless of the individual struggles each of us may have had with our parents, the main problem results from the unique spot we find ourselves in as human beings. It is inevitable that each of us gets stuck in some way in the mad love of the parent-child relationship. It is nobody's fault. We need no blame here. But understanding our unique experience and how it has formed us is crucial. Blame keeps us stuck; understanding, experiencing, and compassion liberate us.

How then do we heal and grow out into ourselves? Ironically, what seems to me to be the most productive way of helping ourselves and others is not so much to "change" but rather to "return" to what each of us is destined to be, were we not sidetracked by the vicissitudes of early life and development. In section two, then, I report on the spirit, that ineffable part of ourselves, present from the outset, which has a destiny in creating our unique roles in the transcendent unfolding of the universe. As much as life "throws us curve balls," and as tempted as we are to fuse with some "false god" that will make us feel safe, we forge ahead, you and I, to become the person we are destined to become. Throughout the lifetime struggle to wrest back our spirits from the grip of our early caretakers there are places in our psyches where both fusion and its opposite operate. This struggle is the focus of section two. What we need to do to liberate our spirits we may consider the "price" of wisdom.

All growing out occurs in relationship, whether it is with self, another, or God. As I said, none of us really needs changing. We need, rather, to jettison some ways we have learned to be, some attitudes and beliefs we thought to be essential to survival. When we manage this we naturally return to our true selves, which are perfect. Committed long-term relationships as well as other friendships are major opportunities to do just this. We will look at intimacy and relatedness and see that they are not only fun and wonderful in themselves, but also marvelous chances to drop the baggage of the past and to return to ourselves, to finish the unfinished aspects of our personalities.

I'm convinced that the only thing powerful enough to help us fully surrender self-destructive connections with our earliest caretakers is a relationship with a Transcendent, a Power greater than ourselves. Many people know this Power as God, although that name carries such negative connotations for so many that I almost hesitate to use it. The crucial thing to realize is that *we* are not that Transcendent, that there is a Power in the universe beyond us. However you negotiate this issue is up to you. But don't dismiss it out of hand. Such a dismissal is symptomatic of the very fusion with mother that has kept us stuck and unhappy. We will look at the relationship between spirituality and psychology and discover that there is no essential conflict here. Each is necessary for our growing out, and for someone on the Wisdom path they happily support each other. You will find in this section a simple technique that will enable you to look at something you are struggling with and make great progress in releasing it by yourself. You will discover the three crucial ingredients that are necessary for all psychological growth.

When you have faced the existential situation that all we humans have, and accepted that; when you have taken the steps to grow out into yourself that are suggested here, both by yourself and with loved ones and with God, you will be joyous. You will have accepted yourself completely and without reservation—yes, you will have accepted yourself radically. And that will be a good beginning! For we humans cannot learn these things permanently. It is our unfortunate limitation as a species. When it comes to psychological and spiritual truth, we can only "know" them for short periods of time. We can be enlightened for just one day at a time. Each day we need to practice if we are to remain spiritually limber. Great ballet dancers practice seven days a week. To keep at the level of fitness necessary for excellence in performance there must be no letting up. As those of us who have ever dieted or gotten physically fit know well enough, we grow out of shape more rapidly than we get into shape! So the third and last section of this book is a reflection on the ways we can maintain our psychological and spiritual fitness once we have "gotten into shape." All spiritual traditions have suggested practices. To maintain radical self-acceptance, daily practice is necessary. I suggest some ways that have been helpful to me and to others. You will find your own, for your own ways are more important for you.

I have organized this book in ways that make sense to me, and some will read it that way. Others will skip around, for what makes sense to me might not be the best way for them. It doesn't matter. What matters is that you form the intention to take the journey. I hope you dare to.

Part One

Resistance to Wisdom

Chapter 1

The Human Condition

෨ඥ

Today and every day the sun comes up, the tides come in and go out, the sun sets. Each day, as the impending light and warmth send their wake-up call to the earth, the myriad communities of insects, animals, fish, and fowl chatter and chirp and dance. In an omnipresent universal bazaar, all living things call out to each other, teach, establish territory, search for sustenance, procreate, and make music. Even underground in the cold season of waiting there pulsates and undulates an enormous energy, preparing itself for its explosion into appearance. In this neighborhood each day we rise, dress, and enter our personal bazaar unaware, for the most part, of the others. We assume a uniform for our work, and an attitude for our social contacts, an uneasy posture with ourselves.

Menses and menarche, erection and detumescence, life and death, birth and aging, loving and hating, mostly sad and sometimes glad, we roam the earth like feral children, lost in our consciousness. Awash in wonder, cowering in terror, we make a show of it. We dress the part and bravely manage the characteristics of our roles, playing first and foremost for ourselves, hoping to catch ourselves up first in the play if we are to engage, charm, and convince anyone else. This is life, after all, and everyone knows what that is, right?

We humans are in a spot. We don't know where we came from, we don't know where we are going, we don't know what the purpose of our existence is. We are faced with constant uncertainty and loss. We have little chance to rehearse. Yet we must perform, and do so with sufficient adequacy to stay alive. We demand perfection from ourselves and others, yet we are faced with constant insufficiency. The other day scientists announced that recent knowledge of DNA makes it possible to trace our ancestry back to Eve and Adam. The only problem is that one group asserts that Eve appeared 200,000 years ago, and another equally confidently maintains that it was 40,000 years ago. Oh, there was one other difficulty. Genetic reconstruction winds up placing Eve on a different continent than Adam. "They must have had an enormous phone bill," one scientist quipped. On that same day—and every day—forty thousand infants die of starvation, and the cities of the greatest nation in human history disintegrate in a plague of mood-altering drugs.

Each of us lives each day in this dizzying array of contradictions: scientific achievement and war; poetry and poverty; altruism and child abuse. We think of ourselves as the center of existence, despite warnings in our earliest literature about the folly of doing so. From the very beginning of consciousness, when humans first exchanged ideas about the dilemma of human existence, we realized that we were limited. Yet, at the same time, we have persisted in denying that reality. The more our scientific accomplishments support our grandiose illusions, the more we discover our limitations. Galileo looked out into the sky and discovered that, indeed, we are not the center of the universe. Darwin studied our origin and determined that we are on a continuum with all other life, not a breed apart, an insult we did not suffer lightly. Freud taught us of the enormous influence on our behavior of motivations far removed from consciousness; we cannot even claim clarity of intention about our ordinary, everyday behavior.

We humans are certainly in a spot.

And, if all this weren't enough, there is the problem of our minds being cluttered with all sorts of convictions based on decisions made in our earliest years, with little information and much terror. As I write, for example, I am aware of a great struggle. My spirit wants desperately to share these ideas. My demons—that part of me that wishes to stay fused with the past—have thrown up every roadblock possible in the past five years. Each time I sit down to write, a place in me gets activated—an old place, characterized, weirdly enough, by a desire to experience myself as lacking, wanting, short of the goal I have set for myself. It is a familiar place, almost like that of a former life—archaic, vague, hazy, sentimental, and very much alive. My desire to see the world through my own eyes, to have wisdom, is a big job for me. Despite many years of psychoanalysis, meditation, exposure to all manner of experiences and teachings in order to free myself, I am still riddled with old ways of being—with feeling states and behaviors that have reference not so much to the way things are but rather a world of the past created by me and sustained by me. In this world live my mother, father, brother, sister, and myself, relating to one another in unison and in tandem, at different ages and stages. I am an amalgam of their characteristics and my perceptions and distortions of them—of the truth about them and my lies about them—and my reactions to them—my fears and anger, and love and protectiveness, and betrayals and guilt. I wear their moods, beliefs, bodily postures, ambitions, and inhibitions. I am ready at the drop of a hat to re-create these early childhood scenarios with the unwitting adults who happen to stumble into my present life.

I am definitely in a spot.

On the other hand, through it all there are these moments when we experience immediate intimacy with ourselves, even as children. I remember when I was about nine years old. One Sunday afternoon in the fall none of my friends was around and I had nothing to do. I wangled twenty-five cents for the movies and a nickel for candy from someone and took off across town to the Burnside Movie Theater. I remember the walk very well. I was alone and I had a black plastic water pistol tucked inside my belt. I was on a very important mission. I don't recall what it was just now, but it was important and I was very focused. As I walked up a winding hill, looking for spies, I noticed those around me. I had no fear; I knew what I was about. I knew that I was with myself and the master of my destiny. I was very happy. Three hours later I adjusted my eyes to the sun as I began the journey home. The mission was over. The bad guys were gone. I was languishing with myself and the late afternoon light. It had been a good day. I was really with me and no one else. I knew me that day. I liked me that day.

There are three crucial realities that make being a human being so difficult. First is the length of time we spend as dependent children. There are mammals with a longer childhood, but not many. Second is consciousness, which is exclusive to *homo sapiens* and provides us with the gift as well as the danger of having opinions about what is happening to us throughout this long gestation. Our highly developed brain and nervous system make this possible, but at the price of limitations in what is, in other species, automatic or instinctual responses. From the very beginning we are observing, recording, and formulating philosophies about our experience. Since we are the first living things with a brain capable of self-consciousness, we are not necessarily so good at this; at best we are erratic and unpredict-able. Third, we are raised by adults who have had the same disabling expe-riences: a long childhood; chancy, self-created philosophies; and nurturing by people who were, themselves, faulted to some degree. We are raised by people trying to figure it all out who were raised by people trying to figure it all out, and so forth back to Adam and Eve.

Motherhood, the most generous and involving of all human activities, is also the most complex. The child knows nothing; the mother is still negotiating her relationship with her own mother. The possibilities for misfirings and miscues are practically infinite and, in fact, the best of child-hoods with the best of possible mothers leaves each of us with a lifetime of work to rediscover and maintain our spirits.

It is our nature to be faulted and limited. We tend to deny this, but our self-consciousness makes us aware of our vulnerability and thus we often feel terror. Our capacity for experiencing another person, of loving and loss, of needing, subjects us constantly to grief and rage. Terror, grief, rage— these are often our emotional states in childhood, and we must suffer them, for the most part, alone. Rare is the adult who is free enough from his or her own troubles, who attends to the emotional life of the child. The child has nowhere to go to flee these deep feelings. At the same time, while grappling with these emotions we develop the idea that we must be perfect in order to get love. Lord, have mercy on us!

The actual length of childhood is a subject of some dispute, but one thing is clear: it is much, much longer than we generally consider it to be. There seems to be an inverse relationship between length of life and the experienced sense of time. We all know that as we get older, the awareness of the passage of time is keener. Days, weeks, years, decades shoot by in the blink of an eye. As a child, it was much different. The weeks before the ending of school and the beginning of summer vacation were an eternity. The two weeks spent on vacation were timeless; whole dramas and rela-tionships were played out, partings and mournings and new relationships, crises, victories and defeats, pacts, new senses of the nature of existence, and still more partings and reunions. And Christmas! The interminable days until Christmas, with the excitement, mystery and toys, the prom-ised, dreamed-of gift. Time was forever in those days; it would never run out.

It's hard to determine just how long a particular period of time in our life seemed, but it is safe to say that the earlier chronologically it was, the longer it seemed to us. Being in the womb must have felt like eternity, and our peremptory discharge from that state, the universal involuntary eviction which is birth, had to undermine our confidence forever. Perhaps the experienced sense of time is a function of the enmeshment with mother, time moving more rapidly as our connection with her, at least in a physical way, wanes. What is clear is that, whatever happens in childhood, it is both chronologically long—say eighteen or twenty-one years—and more important, remarkably long in the psychological or experienced sense of time. What happens in those years is immensely powerful. We are totally dependent upon our caretakers for a very long time. These caretakers are physically larger than us and in complete control, seemingly all powerful and all knowing. What they say or imply or communicate, through words, actions, expressions, odors or whatever, is to be taken seriously, and this goes on for what is experienced, most probably, as hundreds of years. What in adult life is going to compare in influence to such an experience? What adult love or relationship, therapy or pedagogy can compete with influences of such intensity and longevity with these all-powerful, and apparently always correct, human beings?

Through all these experienced years we are aware, and unlike our biological progenitors, we attempt to make sense out of what we observe. In our aloneness we make decisions, powerful, binding decisions. We form beliefs, deep beliefs based on our necessarily limited (and simultaneously pristinely clear) vision, motivated often by abject terror, homicidal rage, and inconsolable grief as well as ecstatic bliss and joyous fusion. These "deepest beliefs," once conjured up, yield reluctantly. Just as we know of our faultedness, limitedness, and consequent vulnerability, real and imagined, we perceive the limitations and powers, real or imagined or overestimated, of our caretakers. As totally unprepared youngsters, we must make sense of all this each day.

We rapidly develop and learn to use all the tricks, conscious and unconscious, that our advanced neurological system has provided for us to lessen that terror. As infants and toddlers we get solace from our bodies. Where else do two-year-olds go for consolation when they are put in their crib? They have none of the sources of comfort adults develop. They cannot stop at the bar or use the telephone. But they can put their fingers in their mouth or play with their genitals. The body, then, becomes the locus of pleasure and contentment and some relief for the human. Much of our behavior later in life is an elaboration of this early attempt at self-soothing.

("That's *adult* entertainment?" my college student daughter once said to me as we drove past a "topless" bar.)

Later we develop symptoms, characterological rigidities or habits. We spin what I think of as main ideas, those deep beliefs that are formed in crisis and endure as profound motivating orientations throughout life. We enter into interpersonal conspiracies with those at home. Still later, we may become "true believers" of dogmas or gurus; we may become addicted to food, drugs, sex, money, work, power, and most of all, people—anything that we discover in the mad scramble of childhood that will give us some relief from our terror. And we stay enmeshed in mother.

All of life is a dialectic between staying with mother or becoming our unique selves. We begin life fused with mother, traumatically leave the biological fusion and replace it with a profound psychological fusion. We spend the rest of our days dealing with that. Yet from the moment of consciousness as we understand it, or even before, each of us is unique and processes the reality around us in a unique way. We have a spirit that wants, more than anything, to be free.

There are two great forces that pummel us for attention and influence. One is the force of life, that which transcends us and which infuses all things as we move forward inexorably through the cycles of life. It calls us to participate in life in our unique way. The opposite is the force of fusion. From the moment of birth, every bursting forth of spirit will be an ambivalent one. Spirit summons us to life and birth, yet each of us comes into the world in a big shock. It is our first important separation and shapes, in a sense, our various struggles to be born throughout life.

How do we know how to be alone after an eternity of oneness? The force of fusion beckons us in response to the surprise, the trauma, the terror of birth. In each subsequent birth of spirit throughout our life, fusion will be there to tempt us to stay with the mothering one, to latch on frantically to the breast as first we did with the relief of that first suck. In a sense, *psychological fusion* refers to all the ways we avoid the experience and awareness of aloneness. The prospect of being in relationship to our own self is unknown to us and terrifying because it is regarded as devastatingly lonely. We make the mistake of equating being alone with being lonely. By fusing ourselves with another we stave off the fear of aloneness (= lonely). But we shall see that aloneness is *not* loneliness. Aloneness can be joyous, while loneliness can fester in the midst of others.

We shall see that the antidote to loneliness is true relatedness with others, and that true relatedness to *self* is a prerequisite for that, and that *psychological separation* is a prerequisite for such relatedness to self. It is one of the dilemmas of being human that we have such an enormous struggle in coming to realize this. Rather, we tend to hold the same opinions and values as another—not as a personal decision, but rather to feel safe. We use the same modes of thinking, the same logic. Sometimes we hardly think at all, if independent thinking has been discouraged by those upon whom we depend. With respect to our emotions, we may allow ourselves to experience only the feelings that are acceptable and under carefully prescribed conditions, or we may rarely feel at all. Our opinions as to what it means to be female or male may be stereotypical; we may be critical of dissent.

In our interpersonal relationships we may tend to disregard others who are not in our family or group. With those important to us there is often the deep belief that another person's feelings or behaviors are contingent on *our* feelings or behaviors. We then tend to regulate our own feelings and behaviors as a function of the feelings and behaviors of another. Later we will look at this phenomenon more closely, but for now suffice it to say that *psychological fusion is the deep belief that there is an inexorable connection between our own feelings and behavior and those of another.*

Each time we become more ourselves—or, more precisely, return to the spirit we were born with and which we compromise in order to survive—there is a re-birth, a sort of death and resurrection. We die to an old way, a fusion, and we arise to a new version of ourselves, richer and more full of spirit. These deaths are not of our spirit but rather of the merger of ourselves with something other than spirit. In the case of our biological birth, the merger was a physical one, with mother; all the subsequent deaths, including the biological one, are also separations from some variation of fusion with mother. It is not death we fear so much. Rather, it is another separation from her, a final one, with no further chance of going back. It is the leaving of this dear friend about whom our life has, in large measure, revolved.

A few years ago I had a wonderful psychotherapy group. I had started it early in my professional career, and it had been in existence over twenty years. We had met all those years on the same night at the same time, and although there were no members who had been in the group that long, I had been. At this time there were five members, and they each had been in therapy for a long time. Most were no longer in individual therapy. They were very wise people and had shown great courage in exploring their lives. They worked so well in this group that I had little to do except to participate in it, myself, on occasion. From time to time I attempted to bring new members into the group, but the incumbent members were so far ahead of the newcomers that the novices would not remain. To be fair, the oldtimers resisted change as well. Finally I made a decision. I announced to the group that while I was not ending it, I would no longer introduce new members. They were stunned, because they knew immediately that my decision spelled the eventual end of the group. There was shock among the members and, after a period of silence, the subject turned to death. Each of us knew the jig was up. Like life itself, we could not go on forever.

In the ensuing months there was continual negotiation about the manner in which the death would occur. At the same time the interactions among the members became even more genuine and the topics more profound. I was amazed at this, considering how long and hard each had worked and how honest each had been. Yet, each had places that had not been tapped. There seems to be no end to the deepest beliefs we have that motivate our entire lives and yet are rarely communicated, even to ourselves. I encouraged them to reveal, in this final opportunity, aspects of themselves that they had never revealed to me or to one another or to another soul. Without exception, including myself, aspects of our most private selves surfaced and were shared.

One woman, speaking of her innermost beliefs about herself and her life to the spell-bound others, first used the word that I had been sensing about myself and others and now use freely. But at the time I felt it was forbidden to me as a psychologist. She said that it was her *spirit* that had kept her going throughout the years. Despite childhood sexual abuse, a seriously disturbed mother who dedicated her life to keeping her children from separating from her, and chronic illness that dogged her, she had never stopped moving forward, if only, at times, by the inch. She had been aware of this spirit for as long as she could remember. Each of us understood.

Yes, we human beings are certainly in a spot.

Actually, we are pretty good sports about it all. We don't know where we come from or where we're going. We must relinquish our first and most passionate love, mother, replace it with ourselves and face the eventual loss of that as well. We must deal with this despite many faults and limitations. We are raised by folks who are themselves quite limited; we have consciousness of what transpires and an intellect that prompts us to make interpretations to ourselves of all that is going on around us, and we are often wrong; we have no prototype in our experience for each stage of life as it occurs, and even our very instincts are disturbed by our conscious experiences and what we tell ourselves about them. We are surrounded by error and evil. Yet, we go on and manage to live and love. I see around me tremendous sacrifice and heroism. Daily there are miracles of compassion. The human spirit is quite something.

Despite all these strikes against us, our spirits desperately fight the powerful tendency to stay attached to, or enmeshed, in our early caretakers. We know in an immediate way that the task of life is to extricate ourselves from the directions of our earliest caretakers and to wrest from them some capacity to experience the world as it is, as we uniquely see it. I term this *wisdom. Wisdom is that understanding of reality which we accrue through our own experience—in those moments when we discard all influence and see the world through our own eyes.* We are always capable of moving into the place of wisdom. It can occur at any age and in any place.

In this Wisdom place we are separate from our influences. No one lives in our brain; no script is being carried out; the chronic affects of our past experiences are muted; no obsessive distractions remove us from ourselves. We are free to see what is there, to know a feeling, an impulse, a bodily state. We are free to think, to sort out the demonic conditioning from the veridical experiences, and through this lens of who we actually are at the moment, we see what we can see. At this moment there is no need for *faith* in a Transcendent. We can see before us the Transcendent, a power and energy beyond us and unknown by us. We are free at that moment of false gods: people and beliefs and behaviors that we learned could rescue us from our terror and grief. We see what is. There is no denial.

In this book we study the journey of the spirit, that fingerprint of a soul as unique as a snowflake. I try to tell the story of what that spirit is up against as it moves through life and of its struggles to maintain and express its uniqueness during its conscious life. I hope to encourage you to honor your Wisdom place. In this place lie awe, a sense of oneness with all things, a profound sense of responsibility for oneself—for one's co-creation with this mysterious Transcendent of what will be. Here also lies the potential for both evil and spirituality. We are free, and in a basic, irreducible way we must choose life or death. If we choose life, we can choose to have compassion for ourselves, to love ourselves—to have radical self-acceptance.

But first we must look at our mothers, for it is in the crucible of our love for mother that our spirit is forged.

Chapter 2

Our Love of Loves

ॐ

The most intense, profound, humanly absorbing experience each of us has had and will ever have is with mother. We all know this, but few know the depth of feeling of this involvement or the pervasiveness of its influence in all aspects of our lives. Always. Who can describe what mother means to us? We opened our eyes upon life, and she was there. From the earliest moment the infant sees its mother and imitates her. The first years of life are a passionate love affair between mother and baby. This is true of all of us, in every land, in every culture. Everyone knows this truth about love, from African griot to Shakespeare. The prototype for all love is HER. We all know this, but few acknowledge consciously the depth of feeling of this involvement or the pervasiveness of its influence in all aspects of our lives at all times and for always. No one is finished with mother. Your analyst, in his infinite wisdom, is not finished with mother. The priest in his pulpit, the guru in the lotus position before a thousand devotees, the Supreme Court justice writing a landmark decision, is not finished with his mother. No one is—ever.

The universal name for her is "mama," the first word spoken for most of us, the last for many. Those having experience with people of advanced age in institutions know the eerie sound of the call for mama in the darkness of the night. In a very real sense our entire life, the totality of our conscious existence, has reference to her. The other day, sitting in the park, I noticed a young woman, not more than twenty or so, chewing gum and blowing bubbles. In her care was a little boy of two or three, calling her mama. She was attentive and warm, but as she blew another bubble, I realized how little she knew about life and even about what she meant to that little fellow. Later I noticed him gaze at her when she was occupied with something else. It was a look of devotion and worship that he will seldom if ever give to any other. This young boy was deeply, madly, inexorably, impossibly in love.

The reason we all feel so strongly about mother is that we woke up to her, and believed from that moment, if not before, that she was *absolutely essential to our staying alive*. This was the deepest of beliefs. And we loved her for our lives. With her we first experienced terror and surcease from that terror. We have never forgotten.

I like to think that a reminder of this may eventually help us to put aside our differences. I will always cherish the image of the sister of Michael Rockefeller stepping on the dock in a primitive jungle fishing village. She had come in search of her brother, who was lost and feared dead. She stepped upon the dock in the cotton pants and shirt of her urban background. And an ancient woman, totally naked, breasts sagging, walked over to her and put her arms around her to comfort her. The sophisticated New York City girl, child of a powerful and wealthy family, broke down in tears as she accepted the compassionate mothering of this woman. This is the truth of our humanness, though we too quickly lose it.

We are all the same. It is the experience with motherhood, regardless of race or culture or economics, that binds us together; we have all had this profound experience. Through all of life, all of us, the most famous and accomplished as well as the more humble and deprived, in all parts of the world in every time, must make sense out of mother. All of us.

We are so familiar with the impact of mother, and it has so deeply moved us, constantly informing and regulating our lives, that we tend to take for granted its power. We may even deny or minimize its impact. But we remain connected to her to a much greater extent than we generally allow ourselves to know. The ways we are connected can be marvelous—the relationship with her is the prototype of all that is good in our lives—but they also are largely unknown to us. Unexamined, they may actually be limiting our spirits, even to the extent of mortal danger.

It is time to understand more of how this critical binding, unique to human beings and extending for what seemed to us hundreds of psychological years, influences us throughout life in all our affairs. The free person must study this special bond and come to appreciate its power and learn to recognize just where, because of the unique characteristics and faultedness of the human species, it has both enhanced and interfered with the development of each of us, and of humankind as well. It is time in our evolution to loosen our grip on the romanticized idyll of mother and child and see it for what it is: simply the most remarkable relationship in our life.

This will not be easy. As I have worked on these ideas, I have noticed tremendous resistance from people even to talk about the topic of mother, particularly about the need to separate psychologically from her. It seems the mere mention of the notion triggers deep and primitive fears. Even when working with psychoanalysts, it takes months in seminar for some significant loosening of the hold on mother. In these seminars I often start with vignettes that enable us to focus gradually on the power of the maternal relationship. Here is one:

> In the still of the night, a mother hears a whimper through her sleep. Soon there's a cry, the rattling of the crib, a swelling of complaint, a crescendo of sound far greater in size than its originator. The mother rushes into the room. The little girl is screaming, sobbing, gasping for breath in her agitation; all sphincters surrender, tears rush from her eyes, phlegm from her nostrils, drool from her mouth; the tiny creases of skin in her neck are moist. Her eyes hold a terror and a sadness, the deepest any human can imagine; her entire body from top of head to bottom of feet, front and back, right and left, is involved in a gigantic, cataclysmic keen. Her mother picks her up. There is immediate complete relaxation, perhaps a few minor, seemingly post-coital shudders. She is at peace....

And another,

> There are ten seconds left, time for one more play. The end fakes the linebacker and sprints to the end zone; the ball awaits him inches before his outstretched hands; he leaps and in the apotheosis of twenty years of training and discipline-honed physical and mental brilliance, he leaps, captures it and slams against the frozen turf, earning the six points ensuring victory. One hundred thousand fans are standing and cheering him. His teammates engulf him, lift him on their shoulders, this hero who has just provided them each with $11,000 for the day's work. He has guaranteed himself a contract in the millions of dollars. Forty million American men know him, admire him, envy him, talk of him. Millions of women are attracted to him. He is tall, powerful, healthy, sweaty, conquering. Scores of newspaper men and women surround him, taking his picture,

which will be in newspapers all over the world. The president will honor him at the White House. Heads of state know who he is; his Holiness, the pope, a few yards from the Pieta and the Michelangelo-decorated Sistine Chapel, has sneaked a peek. Fidel Castro has secretly watched the game. A microphone is shoved in the hero's face; the universe waits…"Hi, Mom," he says.

In class, everyone laughs with recognition. But our knowledge about our mothers is a compromise between our shared experience—as children of mothers—and the injunctions and special surreptitious "rules" that grew out of this seemingly eternal bond.

No one speaks much of this romance with mother. Yet, having completed a half century on this planet, I look around and am astounded at the extent of the involvement with mother of each of us. I used to think it was just myself, my particular difficulty in separation. Psychoanalysis implied that these things were stages, that the healthy, "genital" personality has outgrown such concerns and influences. Yet, as I observe myself and my peers and a quarter of a century of patients and public figures, it is patently clear to me that the relationship with mother persists throughout a lifetime and is the same from generation to generation despite our sophistication in nuclear physics and psychoanalysis.

There is a darling (and obstreperous) Irish singer named Sinead O'Connor. Twenty-five years of age, she has eyes that swallow you up; she sings like an angel; she expresses sadness and fear and even sweet anger that must steal the heart. Youngsters love her, and *Time* magazine wrote:

> Born in Dublin, O'Connor watched her parents split up "quite violently" when she was eight. Her brother responded to the domestic tumult by "fainting all the time." O'Connor's sister began having extensive conversations with strangers in bus stations. And Sinead turned wild. She was busted for shoplifting and sent off first to reform schools, then to boarding school. By the time her mother died in a car crash, her daughter hadn't seen her for nearly two years. "Her life never got better," O'Connor says, "and I suppose it was just as well that she died." In another publication she describes the frequent violent beatings she received from her mother. Yet she reaches the conclusion, "but she was the person who, I suppose, meant the most to me. If it wasn't for her, I wouldn't be singing. She *instigated* that." The first album was dedicated to her mother. [italics added]

To one who is noticing, instances of this mother worship are everywhere. Sitting in Madison Square Garden for a playoff game between the

Knicks and Boston I thumbed through *Hoop* magazine and saw the byline of David Dupree, the pro basketball editor for *USA Today*. The title of his article was "All-Star Forwards Barkley, Malone: Two Mama's Boys, and proud of it!"

"My mother's my best friend," said Malone. "She's always believed in me as a person. I could always talk to her about anything, even girls. My mom is my life."

Said Barkley: "If loving and respecting your mother and being proud of her makes you a mama's boy, then that's what I am. My mother stuck by me and supported me all the way. I think a lot of guys, when they're growing up, their parents don't support them like they should, but my mother was there every day, encouraging me. It made me try that much harder to make something of myself."

While we're speaking of sports figures, there's the phenomenon of Buster Douglas. Mike Tyson, as most know, is a concrete buttress of a man. He looks invincible, has acted invincible, and aficionados of the sport unanimously believed him to be an extraordinary prizefighter. Along comes Buster Douglas, an unknown, to do the impossible.

> Douglas had fought brilliantly, brutally, and in the 10th round had KO'd the seemingly invincible Iron Mike to become champion of the world in one of the greatest upsets in boxing history. Yet there in the ring stood the unknown, crying tears of sadness and jubilation, and paying tribute to his mother, Lula Pearl, who had died one month before. "I did it because of my mother," sobbed the David who felled Goliath, "God bless her heart.". . . A restaurant cook by profession, Lula Pearl was Douglas's best friend, his mentor and the one who taught him his earliest lesson in self defense. Growing up in a middle class section of Columbus, Buster was the frequent target of a neighborhood bully and complained about it one day to Lula Pearl. "My mother grabbed me and put me down," he recalls. "She said, 'He ain't nothing but a lot of talk. You'd better fight him—because you don't want to fight me.'". . . "From that point on," says the new champ, "it was like, hmm, it *works*."[1]

Some consider Sean O'Casey the greatest writer in the English language. His prose is like poetry, and it is hard to read very much at a time because of its sheer beauty. In the first of his six volumes of autobiography he describes himself as "the shake of the bag," the last child his mother would have. She had lost several sons, several previous "Johns," and he was to be the last. He describes his mother:

Forty years of age the mother was when the boy was three, with hair still raven black, parted particularly down the middle of the head, gathered behind in a simple coil, and kept together by a couple of hairpins; a small nose spreading a little at the bottom; deeply set, softly gleaming brown eyes that sparkled when she laughed and hardened to a steady glow through any sorrow, deep and irremediable; eyes that, when steadily watched, seemed to hide in their deeps an intense glow of many dreams, veiled by the nearer vision of things that were husband and children and home. But it was the mouth that arrested attention most, for here was shown the chief characteristic of the woman: It quivered with fighting perseverance, firmness, human humor, and the gentle, lovable fullness of her nature. Small strong hands, hands that could slyly bathe a festered wound or scour a floor—wet cloth first, then the brush soap-foamed, tearing the dirt out, then wet cloth again and, finally, the dry cloth finishing the patch in back and forward strokes and twisting circles of rhythmic motions. A sturdy figure carried gracefully and with resolution; flexible, at peace in its simple gown of black serge, with its tiny white frill round the neck that was fair and unwrinkled still. A laugh that began in a ripple of humor, and ended in a musical torrent of full-toned mirth which shook those who listened into an irresistible companionship.

And all this was seen, not then, but after many years when the dancing charm and pulsing vigor of youthful life had passed her by and left her moving a little stiffly, but still with charm and still with vigor, among those whose view of the light of life had dimmed and was mingling more and more with a spreading darkness; and vividly again, and with an agonized power, when she was calmly listening to the last few age-worn beats of her own dying heart.[2]

What man could feel more for a woman? What man, any man, I suggest, could feel more for a woman than for his own mother—and what woman as well?

Freud, you will recall, observed the intense passion that his patients felt in psychoanalysis toward both parents, but particularly the parent of the opposite sex. The importance of this discovery was not merely that there was such a phenomenon—I'm sure most people then as now acknowledged the flirtatious behavior of children toward opposite-sexed parents and considered it cute. It was the *intensity* of the feelings that was the shocker. The feelings they had as youngsters (this was believed to occur roughly around five years of age) were as intense and powerful as any they would experience toward any person in their lifetime. This was *passion* in its truest form. Freud called it the *Oedipus complex*, referring to the Greek myth wherein the hero, Oedipus, unwittingly kills his father and marries his mother. We are all aware of this phenomenon, although it is rare for us, as adults, actually to experience the feelings.

Psychoanalyst Matthew Besdine examined this phenomenon from the point of view of the mother. What was *she* up to in all of this? What did *she* get out of it? Besdine describes a particular kind of mothering, often characteristic of the mother of a hero of some sort. He calls such behavior "Jocasta mothering," after the mother of Oedipus. A "Jocasta mother" has an all-consuming preoccupation with her child who becomes, in a sense, a substitute for her own life. Typically the existential position of the mother is one of anguished loneliness, often caused or exacerbated by the loss of another child and the physical or psychological absence of her mate. There is probably an emotional predisposition in the mother for such fusion as well, as something about the child charms her. In any event, this constellation of factors is found in the background of genius and exceptional achievement.

> Psychoanalytic literature has explored the problems of Oedipus in depth. On the other hand, the part Jocasta played in quite unwittingly marrying her own son, finding her way into his bed, bearing him four children, and at last, hanging herself in shame and disgrace, is all too frequently overlooked or minimized. The lonely, affect-hungry widow, Jocasta played as significant a role in the inexorable unfolding of the Greek tragedy as did her unfortunate son. Her love for the new stranger, her son, played the contrapuntal theme to the loss of her husband. From Jocasta's point of view, the entire legend of Oedipus can be interpreted in a different light, and new conclusions drawn from it....
>
> Jocasta mothering has to be separated from the normal rearing process and the usual resolutions of the Oedipal complex. Jocasta mothering is a pathologic rearing in which the mother established an exclusive intimacy and binding closeness with her infant son in possessive, over-protective ways, injurious to both. A neurotic fixation develops in which the boy child cannot separate himself from the mother and identify himself fully as a man in relation to women; it also confuses the mother, so that all too frequently she cannot fully surrender her son in marriage. While there may be trends of this neurotic complex in all sons and mothers, when the normal is exaggerated, it becomes a pathologic entrapment for both.[3]

Besdine describes this pattern in many geniuses, including Freud himself. Genius seems to be enhanced dramatically by a particularly focused relationship prompted by mother. Freud's mother, doting and absorbed with her son, referred to him as "mein goldene Sigi." She had lost a child, as had Sean O'Casey's mother. Perhaps Sigmund and Sean had come to be their mothers' last hope for comfort. Besdine noted a similar dynamic in the life of Michaelangelo:

> No one knows why, but when less than a month old, Michelangelo was given out to nurse and remained at the home of a humble stone-cutter for ten years. The foster mother who reared him at Settignano had the deepest influence on his life, giving him the exclusive, intensive, binding, over-protective rearing I have come to call "Jocasta Mothering."
>
> The Jocasta mother, grieving over a lost child and hungering for affection, separated from her husband, either by her own design or by circumstances beyond her control, unconsciously seeks solace and comfort for herself in the love of her child. She draws her young son to her in despair and misery, but shocked by her own strong feelings for the boy and by his response, she also pushes him away. This trauma of closeness and distance, attraction and repulsion, increases the guilt of the boy child. It over-stimulates his sexuality, so that he longs and lusts too strongly for his mother. When she punishes him by pushing him away, she confirms his feelings of guilt and creates a sense of rejection. Michelangelo's sense of guilt and his distrust of all human relations had its origins in just such Jocasta mothering.[4]

The young Michelangelo, enmeshed in his relationship with his needy mother, developed deep beliefs about what was possible for himself. These were both negative and positive. He had to be loyal to his mother and yet feared engulfment so that intimacy with women was extremely frightening. His passive father made the danger of her submerging him seem to be a real possibility, which presumably led to guilt and ambivalence in relationships with males. Yet the adoration of his mother, the continual, exclusive experience of the powerful madonna communicating endlessly that he both could and must accomplish great things, contributed in a most significant way to Michelangelo's extraordinary achievements.

Having spent so many years studying the subtleties of human behavior, I am skeptical about psychobiography. Broad strokes about humans are disrespectful and dangerous. They assume that we are capable of knowing more about each other, from a distance, than we actually are. Yet there is no doubt in my mind that something like this *could* happen and probably does all the time. Genius, or exceptional accomplishment, is not explained by a doting mother, but it certainly doesn't hurt. We are all controlled by our experienced possibilities, and to have the most important person in our life, our personal goddess, telling us constantly that we can and must do even the seemingly impossible can do a lot for us.

Recently a book by a young self-improvement entrepreneur, Anthony Robbins, caught my eye.[5] The book jacket beckoned, promising astounding results.

> *Unlimited Power* is a revolutionary fitness book for the *mind*. It will show you, step by step, how to perform at your peak, while gaining emotional and financial freedom, attaining leadership and self-confidence, and winning the cooperation of others. It will give you the knowledge and courage to remake yourself and your world.

Robbins's story is certainly an amazing one. At twenty-five years of age, without a college degree, he was a self-made millionaire, conducting training programs for industry and the military at stiff fees, happily married and living in a "castle" overlooking the Pacific. Each year thousands were led by him in walking barefoot over burning coals, the so-called firewalk.

His book is an amalgam of enthusiasm, common sense, inspirational ideas, and neuro-linguistic programming (NLP)[6] self-help strategies. He clearly has a big heart and lots of energy. How has he accomplished so much? I suspect the most powerful ingredient in his success was revealed inadvertently as he described his teenage aspiration to be a sportscaster.

When Tony was fourteen, Howard Cosell visited his hometown, pitching a book at the local bookstore. The young Robbins decided to find out what it took to become like Cosell, and so he got his mother to drive him downtown to the bookstore and wait while he inveigled himself through the crowds to talk to Cosell. The punchline, of course, is that Cosell gave him the interview. The real significance to me in this story is his mother's cooperation and encouragement. How many mothers would let their fourteen-year-old boy stay home from school and then chauffeur him on such a mission? Mrs. Freud would, of course, and Michelangelo's stepmom!

Elsewhere in his book, Robbins alludes to his mother's marital difficulties and losses. There's a good chance that Robbins learned a powerful lesson about the necessity and possibility of overcoming impossible odds. He possibly had the most empowering coach in the world, his mother, preparing him. Whether others will be as successful utilizing his strategies without such a powerful personal coach is doubtful. From Michelangelo to Buster Douglas, when Mother's on our side, the impossible often is done. On the other hand, when Mother is against us, even the probable is often impossible.

Genius aside, our ordinary lives give evidence to the pervasive results of this seemingly infinite and eternal bonding. As we begin to attend to it, we will see instances all around us. It has also been documented in the laboratory. For twenty-five years, Lloyd Silverman and his colleagues devised ingenious techniques to measure, quantify, and verify in the laboratory key principles of classical psychoanalysis.[7] They used a tachistoscope, a device which presents visual stimuli so rapidly that the observer is not aware of seeing anything intelligible. Yet a large body of research demonstrates that the stimuli are, indeed, registered somewhere in the mind. Changes in various kinds of behavior, physiological and otherwise, have been measured and recorded, apparently as the result of being exposed to these "unseen" stimuli.

Silverman and his colleagues presented a picture of a man and a woman merged at the shoulders like Siamese twins, followed by a verbal message, MOMMY AND I ARE ONE. Their subjects were not consciously aware of seeing anything. The results were startling. In 1985 they presented their research in a key article in the prestigious journal of the American Psychological Association, the *American Psychologist*:

> Evidence is presented for the thesis that there are powerful unconscious wishes for a state of oneness with "the good mother of early childhood" and that gratification of these wishes can enhance adaptation. The main data that support this thesis come from experiments in various laboratories employing the subliminal psychodynamic activation method with over 40 groups of subjects from varied populations. These studies have reported that the 4–millisecond exposure of stimuli intended to activate unconscious symbiotic-like fantasies (usually the words MOMMY AND I ARE ONE) produces ameliorative effects on different dependent variables in a variety of settings.[8]

Just what were these "ameliorating effects"? In *Psychology Today* Virginia Adams described Silverman's work:

> Although you are conscious of seeing nothing more than evanescent glimmers, astonishing things may happen to you after you have been exposed to them a few times. If you are a schizophrenic or a depressive, your symptoms may fade for a brief period of time. If you are a student, your grades may improve. If you would like to slim down or stop smoking, you may find it easier than before to resist the temptations of food and tobacco.[9]

It seems the mere *idea* of oneness with mother, even if we are not conscious of thinking that idea, affects us profoundly!

Silverman's work is enormously important for a number of reasons:

1. It demonstrates the presence of an unconscious wish and thus supports both the notion of the unconscious as well as that of unconscious motivation.
2. It demonstrates the presence of a pervasive, if not universal, desire for union with the mothering one.
3. It informs us of the healing power of such fusion. The mere eliciting of the fantasy resulted in clear, if temporary, improvement in adaptive behavior.

I suspect that there is a relationship between this universal longing for mother and certain other universal tendencies, such as prayer and meditation. Both the healthy behaviors of aerobic training and the self-destructive ones of addiction may have at their base this same pervasive longing for mother, which may be represented and symbolized by chemical, mood-altering conditions of the brain. It is especially interesting to me that after trying many other stimuli which were designed to elicit responses to various other postulated impulse and wish states consistent with classical psychoanalytic theory, the only one that had consistent results was the stimulus MOMMY AND I ARE ONE. Oh, the power of mother!

We humans have made so many strides in all areas of existence. So many advances. So many improvements. But in our basic human concerns, there is little change from the very beginning of recorded history until the present. When it comes to the power of mother, the instinct to reproduce, the urge to protect our territory and to dominate others, the need to relate to a Transcendent, the first communicators of all societies and cultures presented these basic human experiences in myth and dogma. Today, just about as much is known about these issues in the most primitive tribe in the rain forests, untouched by modern civilization, as we know in our most august universities (although both societies are smug and protective about their own point of view). The terror at separation from the mothering one is so profound that the most "sophisticated" of us have as much trouble as the witch doctor. Even psychoanalysis, which opened the discussion of psychological separation and individuation, has great difficulty actually dealing with it. When Otto Rank, a member of the Vienna Circle, the founding fathers of psychoanalysis, posited it as the central issue in life, he was roundly condemned. He most clearly understood our unique human problem—and it frightened everyone. We just don't want to deal with the meaning of mother to us and to look at the deepest ways we stay attached to her.

The problem we psychoanalysts have here is just another instance of the *universality* of the difficulties all of us humans have in dealing with mother. It is known that poor, disenfranchised, adolescent girls frequently have babies early in life without regard to financial security or even a reliable man to help. This occurs not out of the need for the comfort of the sexual embrace so much as from the realization that *mothers are powerful.* No matter what blows life deals them, another human being will be bonded to them in the most powerful human relationship possible, one which they probably know firsthand from their experience of their own mother. The less advantaged and more tragically deprived people are, the more overt is the power of mother. In such a setting it is an honor and a symbol of status to defend the mother's honor, even if it results in the shedding of blood or even the death of self or a fellow human being. Mother worship, sadly, does not inevitably support life.

But it is not only in the ghettos that mother is the operational principle. It is true of each and every one of us. A few years back newscaster Maria Shriver sat at a table conducting an interview with a Russian woman. The woman, a traditional housewife, was also the manager of a major industrial plant. This double role prompted Shriver to ask the woman what could be done about the lack of power of women in Russia, shown by their having executive jobs but still having to manage a family. "Power," the Russian woman drew up sharply and answered. "Power...I put the food on the table. That is the power."

There are, of course, other relationships that have a profound impact on a person's earliest experience of the world. Father, of course. But I wish to emphasize what I feel to be the *most* profound relationship each of us has, that of mother and child. Even father gets a great deal of his power by association, as it were, with mother.[10] Our exceptional gifts, our special difficulties—just about all of who we are and what we do—bear the imprint of the relationship with mother. And for the most part we are terrified of knowing the truth about it.

Child psychologist Louise J. Kaplan eloquently describes the process toward awareness of Self during the first three years of life.[11] She elaborates Margaret Mahler's breakthrough in describing what she refers to as the second birth, the *psychological birth*, of the human infant.[12] Although the basis for the separated self is established in the first three years of life, Kaplan points out in the final chapter of her book,

> In every adult human there still lives a helpless child who is afraid of aloneness. When the conditions of social life are oppressive and antihuman, the adult is as alone in the world as a helpless child. This would be so even if there were a possibility for perfect babies and perfect mothers.

But there is no possibility for perfect babies and perfect mothers. And even if social life never became oppressive and antihuman, our very nature and the psychological realities that emanate from that nature and the nature of our caretakers and others around us through life make our quest for coming fully out unto our own selves a lifetime task.

Yes, mother is the Power; Mommy and I are One; she is our first Transcendent. And it takes a lifetime to sort it out, to wrest our spirit back and learn to love her simply for the fellow human being she is.

Chapter 3

The Eternal Conspiracy

෨෬

Stephen Levine, author of *Who Dies*[1] and other books, is an American Buddhist whose development in compassion has led him to work with the dying and those around them. From time to time he leads workshops, or days of recollection, for those whose death is imminent, those grappling with grief, and those whose work it is to help the dying live. These are moving, profound experiences in which several hundred people meditate together and, with Stephen's guidance, explore their grief and heal. I have spent many days this way, and they have changed me.

The first time I was at such an event, after a brief meditation, Stephen asked if anyone in the audience had experienced the death of her child. I was aghast. Twenty minutes into the day he inquired about what is probably the most tragic event a person can know. Twelve women raised their hands, and what followed was an exquisitely touching and beautiful expression of motherhood. With Stephen's compassionate and skillful encouragement and guidance, each spoke of the events of her child's death and, more important, of the life of the deceased child in the hearts and the minds of the mother, each and every day, from that moment on. They were helped to accept, let go, release the guilt and shame and remorse that inevitably follow so profound a loss. In the process I witnessed the intensity, the almost unspeakable depth and beauty of the love between mother and child, the grief beyond understanding in such a loss. One mother described her child as having been part of her, and that part had died forever. Others spoke of their deceased children with a knowledge and depth of understanding that amazed me. It reminded me of a patient who described her relationship with her child as spiritual. "I know when she is hungry, even if she is in a different room." When it was time to wean her child, this woman was exquisitely sensitive to her baby's reaction. She spent weeks "listening" carefully to her, making sure she was ready to let go of this part of their relationship. She, herself, was getting ready to let go, for her child's separation was hers as well. No one leaves another without the other's struggle. This is poignantly true of each step of the child's struggle to become who he or she really is.

Years ago, in a psychological separation seminar I conducted for therapists, one of the members illustrated this complex interaction in a paper she wrote.

> I am going to explore the concept of separation in the mother-child relationship from two different aspects. One, from the viewpoint of a daughter, the other from the vantage point of a mother.
>
> …The child may feel such intense feelings of abandonment in the process (of separation) that it is experienced almost as if it were a death.
>
> The mother of this…child usually suffers from the syndrome herself. Having been unable to separate from her own mother, she fosters continuance of the symbiotic union with her own child. She encourages this dependency in order to maintain her own emotional equilibrium and becomes threatened with her child's emerging individuality. She cannot deal with it and clings to her child to prevent this separation. She then further discourages moves by the child toward individuation by withdrawing her support.
>
> Seen through the eyes of a daughter, I can understand the entangled yoke that my sister and myself shared. Unconsciously, but in a methodical manner, my mother arranged to pit both of us against each other. The feud was between us. We each sought to be the better daughter. We tried in this way to incur approval and love from mother. Mom was home free.
>
> It was always difficult for me to say "no" to mother. An incident in point occurred about five years ago when my mother requested that I purchase the apartment that she was presently renting so as to guarantee that she had a permanent residence. Because of my guilt, my misconstrued sense of responsibility and my inability to deny her for fear of her disapproval, I agreed to do so. During the period that I was proceeding with the legalities of the transaction I felt angry, depressed and helpless. I knew that I did not want to own an apartment in Florida but felt too guilty to refuse. With the support of my therapy group, I was able to get a clearer picture of the dynamics of my behavior and clearer insight into my feelings. Consequently, I was able to verbally say "no" to my mother regarding the purchase. This, for

me, was the beginning of my freedom to do what was best for me and to realize that I did not need my mother's approval in order to exist.

Almost by definition, I followed to some extent the same pattern with my own children. Although I didn't utilize the same techniques of having the children compete with each other, I managed to work out my own formula for fulfilling my own personal needs.

My youngest child, a son, suffered the most. At a very early age, possibly at age two and even at age three and four, he was unable to leave me to play with other children. Nursery school was equally difficult and painful for him. He clung to me. Although this was frustrating and embarrassing, there was a part of me that was being fed. I was important and needed. His feelings of abandonment at any move towards separation were so real and painful that separation from me to go to nursery school could only be accomplished by friends physically removing him from me and putting him into a car and driving away. The look of panic and fright on his face as he was driven away is still with me. It should be noted that abandonment feelings comprise not one feeling but a combination of several others: depression, anger and rage, fear, guilt, passivity and helplessness, emptiness and void.[2]

The writer went on to describe the struggles that ensued over the next few years. She faced these problems and sought help for both her son and herself. The result of her courageous honesty and bold action is that each overcame this impasse and went on to have rich and rewarding lives. I have not seen the writer for ten years but I did have the opportunity to meet with her son. He is a wonderful man, happily married and a parent, himself.

The mother concludes her open and searching report:

The insights that I have gained have carried over into my relationships with my other children. I have tried to create an atmosphere of acceptance and respect and to initiate openness and directness. They do not seek my approval nor I theirs. They are all living away from home and maintaining themselves both financially and emotionally in an independent manner. Our relationship is close and affectionate.

It is so easy to blame the mother for whatever goes wrong in development. It is commonly thought that there are some people who have such minimal constitutional stability that any withdrawal on the part of the mother would cause problems. Even in those people where the mother's withdrawal appears to be the main cause of arrested development it may look as if the mother could have behaved differently. It assumes that she had a choice and could have acted in another manner. Nothing could be further from the truth, for indeed this kind of mother is caught in the same bind with her own mother that she reproduces with the child. It is not a choice or decision on her part. A patient has to become aware of and express the hostile feelings towards his mother....Eventually, a healthy acceptance comes to exist and the patient can...see his mother as a whole object—with good and bad—and, as a result, accept responsibility for his past as well as his present.

The relationship between mother and child is the most powerful human engagement possible. Within it lie all the possibilities of human wonder and grief. Witness the brave woman who wrote the above. No one is to blame. Psychological separation is a "no fault" event. Each of us has the same task in life: to wrest ourselves back from this powerful engagement with our earliest caretakers. This does not mean that the engagement has been bad. No one of us has failed to benefit, in some fashion, from our earliest caretaker. Typically, there is much to save and cherish. But in the intensity of this early engagement, and our consciousness of it, there was ample opportunity for our spirits to get lost—and for our mother's as well. From this point on, remember, no blame, just understanding, feelings, and, hopefully, compassion and love. In all human things we are faced with the same dilemma: we are able to do it better than most other species; we have the capacity to soar, to make something new where nothing has been. Yet at the same time, ironically, we are flawed. Our consciousness, the length of our dependency, the flawed nature of our caretakers, all conspire with the power of the universe to render us, in Ernest Becker's stark phrase, "the gods who shit."[3] So, too, with mothering.

Our unique situation results in a relationship with mother which is so intense, profound, complicated, passionate, loving, hating, touching, exciting and grief-ridden, and of such long duration as to make the time after childhood, the rest of our lives actually, a period of recovery from childhood itself.

I struggled hard to write this chapter. Yet in a way, it's the easiest. It is so close to my life, something I have been reflecting on and experiencing, speaking with others about for a long time. But as I write, my stomach is upset. I have virtually locked myself in a room, forbidding myself to go out until I complete it. It represents such an important step. I can feel the conflict, and I want to escape it any way I can, and I have many ways, but for some reason today is it. For in writing this book, and particularly this chapter, I am surrendering another piece of my fusion with mother, the part that says I should never speak my mind, particularly to strangers. Worse, I am making *public* what is so private. I am speaking of the relationship that began in the womb when, in reality, Mommy and I were One.

From the moment, whenever it was, that I had the first experience of Self, it was in intimate connection with mother. This has been true of all of my development, and it was so for a very, very long time, made even longer by my child's conception of time. What a relationship I was in! And somewhere in me I want to stay in it!

One day I was determined to understand more about my relationship with my mother. She was dead and had been for some time. Yet, I sensed her working in me, and I wanted to be aware of this. I planned to run around the reservoir in Central Park and to spend this solitary time thinking about her. It takes me a long time to run around the reservoir, so I had plenty of time. But I couldn't! It was like my early forays into meditation. Each time I intended to think about her something else popped into my mind. "Oh, look at that beautiful tree," "Don't forget to pick up milk," "What a beautiful woman," "Is it going to rain?" It was impossible for me to focus on my mother and what transpired between us and what she was telling me even now. I guess she was telling me not to think about it!

Thinking about mother is a very hard task for all of us. Oh, we have ideas about her and little speeches and memories we tell each other. But actually thinking? Trying to understand what it was actually like between us? It is rare. It is as if we have made up our minds and that is that. She is bad, she is good, she loved us, she preferred my sister, or whatever.

Sometimes we idealize her. British psychiatrist Ann Dally writes eloquently of this. She describes idealization as

> a feeling of love towards something or somebody towards whom one actually has feelings of both love and hate. The hate is ignored and so kept from consciousness. The love is unrealistic because it is separated from the hate with which it is actually inextricably connected. Thus it becomes illusory, in that it is supported by distorted or falsified perception which is used unconsciously to prevent the hate from becoming conscious. If it is pointed out that hate is actually present alongside the love, angry reactions are liable to be provoked.[4]

When we are not denying who she is or over-idealizing her, or yearning for her, we are often blaming her. Part of the reason that parents are denounced so much is that we don't want to leave them. If we can complain, vilify, regale ourselves and whoever will hear with their faults and crimes and misdemeanors against us, we live with them. This is not to say that we should deny who our mother was and what transpired between us. On the contrary, it is crucial to know clearly who she was. Blaming her, denying the truth about her, or idealizing her are just strategies to avoid that knowing. She's just a human being, after all, like everyone else, even like ourselves! To separate psychologically means to know her and all our feelings about her. Ultimately, as we grow in understanding, we will also grow in compassion and forgiveness, even gratitude. And we shall work toward psychologically separating, not because our relationship with her has been bad but rather because growing out into self is what we—each of us—are destined to do.

But we do not want to know. Knowing would mean we can no longer see her as the madonna with no faults or as the witch-ogre who ruined us beyond redemption. Knowing, truly knowing, would render her just another person, a scared little girl, as puzzled and often overwhelmed by life as we. Mother? That wouldn't do. We wouldn't have a mother then, a parent. We would be orphans. A sixty-five-year-old man came to see me one day, in tears and agitated. His ninety-five-year-old father was dying. "He's frightened," Joel said. "I can't stand to see him frightened." What Joel—this accomplished, vigorous parent and industrialist—couldn't stand was no longer to have a strong father, to be on the verge of being without a father altogether. No, we don't want to know who they are, these fallible human beings we call mother and father. For to know that would set us free from them, and that prospect is terrifying.

Tom, a thirty-two-year-old banker, came to see me because he was unhappy in his marriage.

T: I think I'm going to have to fly out to California next week; my father may be getting sick....He's lost fifteen pounds in the last couple of weeks.

J: How old is he?

T: Seventy-seven....He's getting up there....everybody's gotta die I guess....Maybe it's getting to be his time.

J: Has he been sick?

T: Nah....He's got arthritis and diabetes and stuff like that but he's an old warhorse—made of iron...like, indestructible.

J: What does the doctor say?

T: Doctor?…Are you kidding? My father wouldn't go to the doctor, doesn't believe in them…thinks they're all a bunch of quacks.

J: How do you feel about it?

T: Well, we all have to go.…I was thinking about it on the way over here.…What is my feeling about my father dying? He's had a good life.…We all have to go some time.…I'd miss him but my life would be pretty much the same.…And then I ask myself, what if it were my mother.…How would I feel about that? That's a different story.…I don't know how I would deal with that. It's funny.…I hardly ever see her, but knowing she's alive is important to me…reassuring. If I didn't see her for thirty years but I knew she was alive, I'd feel safe, secure…but those same thirty years if she weren't around…that scares me.…It's like being an astronaut and being dropped on the moon and the spacecraft leaving you behind.

Every human being knows that feeling. It is not restricted to those with a "disturbed" upbringing. It is universal. All of us have endured the shock of birth; the lonely terror of unintentional neglect in infancy; leaving mother's breast, her touch, her presence; going to school…leaving, leaving, leaving. Some of us have had apparently ideal childhoods, and yet we feel it exquisitely; others seem to survive the worst with optimism and courage. But all can relate to Tom's feeling. She was our life; she was us. It is terrifying to move away, and the terror remains throughout life. It is not crazy to know this terror. It is natural.

Each step we make to move away, prompted by our spirit to become more our unique self, is a struggle. Typically, a move toward psychological separation is followed by resistances so profound and persistent that demonic is the only word for them. Success is followed by self-sabotage or reverting to old, familiar behaviors. I think of it as a "call back." Each time we move ahead, a place within beckons as we struggle to stay on the new path. It reminds me of the two-year-old struggling to free himself from his mommy's hand only to look over his shoulder longingly and yearningly when he succeeds. Sometimes he catches himself up short and runs frantically back. We, too, yearn all our lives to move forward, to grow out into our potentiality. Yet, successful as we might be at it, there is still grief, a residual sadness that comes upon us here and again, sometimes when we least expect it, often at the very moments of our greatest successes. And sometimes, in some manner, we run frantically back.

It is not just fear that trips us up. The love between mother and child is real. *It is the model for all other love relationships.* Leaving mother is leaving the greatest love relationship of all, the first and the most powerful, and the one we believed and desired would be forever, and forever special.

But the terror is real, as well. From the very beginning we have been fused. Also from the beginning, we have known the impetus of spirit, and we have been aware of these powerful forces at odds within us. Fear and desire for security kept us fused with mother in the first place. We bend that way always. Spirit keeps us growing out into our unique selves. It determines how we shall affect the universe. Such is our destiny and our responsibility. It is the expression of something that transcends ourselves, the very life force of the universe. The self is that part of us which manages this struggle. It is buffeted about by both tendencies and tries to work things out. This dialectic, this moving forward and backward, continues throughout life. The sum total of the push-pull of separation-fusion and the awareness of self engaging in this struggle at any particular time is the "person," the self in its uniqueness.

Some do not separate far from the mothering one. Some seem to take off early and travel far with little looking back. Most of us zig-zag back and forth. A truly wonderful path is a steady, consistent progression in the direction of psychological separation and freedom. For some, the progression may be slow; it may not seem to get very far. Others may have strong tendencies to slip back into old, fused ways when the going gets rough. There are even those who have no intention of going anywhere, and whose steps forward are so half-hearted that they never get off the block, much less out of the neighborhood. Some may be so afraid of leaving that they fight desperately even the steps others may take toward liberation.

Fusion manifests itself, as we shall see, in our *thinking* and *feeling* and *behavior*. It shapes just how we are in the world and, most important, how we process the world both within and around us. It affects our relationships, our understanding of life. Certain deep beliefs, born in fusion, comprise the organizing principle of an entire lifetime. Our one and only life may be lived almost as in a dream or as a role in somebody else's play if we drown in fusion. This is very important business. (We will look at this closely in the next chapter.)

Add to this the social context in which we must function. From early on the psychologically fused state is idolized. Even when it comes time to move from the family and go out into the world to form a family of our own, the message of fusion is clear. At the end of a course on psychological separation, we decided to bring in music that illustrated this propaganda, in the direction of either separation or fusion. From the "golden oldies" to the present, 90 percent of the songs had a fusion theme: "You are my reason to live"; "Can't live, if living is without you"; "My one true love"; "What'll I do when you are far away"; "It had to be you."

Even at those moments when our biological destinies propel us, almost without our awareness, to leave our parents behind, we carry with us the seeds of reconstruction of this former way of life—even in our romantic relations, for each stage of growing bears this insignia. She helped us leave the embryonic bliss of the womb. When we had to leave the breast to see better the world about us and indeed ourselves, as a touch different from the rest of it, she made it safe. When we got control of our bodily functions, becoming a member of the universal society of the toilet trained, she was there guiding and encouraging. When we stood and could see, even to the horizon, she encouraged us and kissed our boo-boos and stifled a tear, her own, that her big boy was growing up.

Then she spiffed him up and left him out in the "real world" for hours at a time. She welcomed him home and listened with the interest of the deeply in love to the vicissitudes of his day. As he moved away somewhat, in his discovery of his maleness, toward his peers, and made the decision to renounce his old ways with her and accept the necessity of being like his dad, she let go. Each day, each way, each step of the way, she was there encouraging and struggling to let go herself. These were deep feelings both were boiling in. The little boy described above, hysterical at leaving mother to go off to school, is the more accurate representation of what is going on inside than the "little trooper" society tells us we should aspire to be.

Even when we ostensibly shut out mother to experience and experiment with our sexuality; even when we allow ourselves to care for a person of the opposite sex, researching gingerly the strange blend of care, lust, and need for validation that romantic love often is, the prototype even for this is our relationship with her. The first romance, for boys *and* girls, is with mother, and it is this romance that is the model of exclusive, monogamous, undying—as well as potentially obsessive and addictive—coupling that often characterizes our future love life.

Mother loves so beautifully, completely, and unselfishly. She is so accepting, and for so long. The child worships her in return. How are they supposed to let go? How do they release this "life grip" on each other?

In the most ideal mother-child love the mutual letting go, which must be done for both to continue their "coming home to themselves," is one of the most painful of all human experiences. In it lie the seeds of all future comings together and partings, the stuff of anguish that we all know these to be. We deny this is so and sentimentalize it. We can sing "You are my reason to live" about someone we scarcely know. We can fall into the depths of despair about the ending of a relationship with a fellow human whose presence on this planet was unknown to us a short while ago. But mother, our very lifeblood for so long, our life companion through the first tragedies and challenges of our lives, we can joke about.

First and foremost, the relationship with mother is a human one. There are two persons involved here with needs, desires, capacities for love, fears, and insecurities. All that is possible in all subsequent relationships is in this one. No relationship will be so trusting, so emotional, so intimate, so passionate. And when it comes time to break the bond of exclusivity, the loss involves grief beyond understanding. The passion that characterizes the sharing of the mothers who have lost children to accident or illness is actually true of all mother-child bondings, but we are able to *deny* its power if the other person is still physically before us.

When we love, we give a part of ourselves to another and receive, in return, a part of them. When that love ceases in that form, the mutually transmitted selves die; they cannot be returned. When we lose anyone we have loved, our heart is permanently etched with that person and a part of us dies. Our selves can regenerate, but this takes time and can only occur in the ether of mourning and pain. If too much of ourselves has been given over, terror may be the result, because we feel empty, devoid of being.

Even when this is not the case, the anguish is enormous. When we have loved we enter a domain that I can only describe as that of *concern*. Is it possible to *care* and then be separated, psychologically, from the cared-for one? It is not just the biological terror and grief at loss that I am speaking of. Rather, it is the peculiarly human problem of coming to terms with the *meaning* of it. How can care stop? We have experienced it. How can care stop? It feels like a violation of human nature. Though we may not have the words for it, those of us who have not deadened ourselves to grief experience this anguish each time we love, and lose, a beloved.

The pain is so great at the prospect of leaving mother, our greatest love, that we tend to deny it, to minimize it, not to fully feel it. Consequently, we never fully separate. The problem is not merely the pain of loss, though that is monumental, but a human existential dilemma, a particular kind of guilt at leaving—perhaps "leaving behind" is a more precise way of describing it—someone we have loved so deeply and fully.

Yet, when we separate from our parents, it is only to put our input into ourselves. Who we are at any moment of separation is actually the result of our loving and struggling interaction with them. We grow as a result of all relationships, and certainly this one. There is much we have taken from them that we can never separate from, nor should we. Those aspects of them that enhance us we can joyfully maintain and thus, in that sense, we do not leave them. More precise, perhaps, is that we *complete them* in ourselves through the creation of our lives. And, of course, we can always love them, in the special way that only psychologically separated people are able to do; that is, to love the other *as he or she actually is*, as other. We need to hold hands through the generations.

The price of full existence and freedom, the decision to be who one actually is, is terror and grief. We need to fight constantly the entirely human tendency to fuse with someone or something in order to avoid these feelings and to yield to the archaic but comforting memory of the special oneness with mother.

The fusion comes about in several ways. As we have seen, the way we humans enter the world and spend the first years of life on this earth, so intimately bonded to our nurturing ones, makes profound fusion an inevitability. There is no way to avoid it. For all of us, in addition, there has been some degree of disturbance in the nurturing process and consequently some additional amount of fear. Some children are perhaps genetically more fearful. Some parents are more troubled or have unusual pressures on them. Typically, decisions are made to cope with this fear, and typically they involve a stronger tendency toward fusion.

Then, of course, there is the matter of the real love we have been speaking about. We tend to be like those we love, to join with them, yes, even to fuse with them to some degree. This is a natural process. In childhood this is even more intense, for all the reasons we have spoken of so far.

Finally, there is the issue of specialness. As we were attended by our caretakers, particularly mother, there was this delicious feeling of specialness we will never have again, at least that way. Probably the bottom line of the trouble in adult matings is coming to grips with the reality that there are two children in the relationship trying to become adults, not one child, special to one parent. This sense of specialness is also natural, an unavoidable sense as we experience the ministrations of our upbringing. And it is not just the "omnipotence" of infancy that I refer to here. The sense of specialness develops in a more profound, invasive way psychologically throughout development. It may have originated in infancy, but the flesh and blood of it—the nuts and bolts, so to speak—are nurtured in the day-in and day-out experiences of timeless childhood. As I sat in the linoleum-floored kitchen of my childhood on lunch break from elementary school, eating tomato soup and a bologna sandwich and listening to Kate Smith on the radio while my mother bustled around me, I was not conscious of the likelihood that no monarch ever had been attended to with such focus. We deny this to be the case, and fusion is the deepest denial.

So we resist wisdom and yearn to return to that love affair with mother. We have given her our spirit; it was the only thing we had. We did it out of love; perhaps out of fear; perhaps out of lust—all the human capacities for involvement—and when the wrench occurred, it came with an awful ache. We are left, I believe for all time, with a yearning and a longing, and a kind of loneliness that we sense fusion can overcome. In our separated spirits there is a membrane that no one can ever fully penetrate, but mother did. The whole world is mourning.

As Margaret Mahler has taught us, at age three we experience our second birth, our psychological birth. We become and see our separateness. Lurking below that awareness, though, is a deep longing for Mommy. It never fully leaves us.

This is the eternal conspiracy—that each of us secretly protects a special relationship to mother. "You are my reason to live," "Can't live if living is without you," "My one true love," all have deepest reference to mother. We harbor and nurture a specialness—that we are mother's one and only (as we once were); that we are *central-to-her* and she, in turn, *central-to-us*. This is the EGO that the spiritual teachers have spoken of throughout history. This is that part of ourselves that is fused with mother, that believes we are *especially* special, that makes us, secretly, better than anyone. We are the best, even if that means being best at being worst. Yes, this is the part of ourselves that believes that we are, in our specialness, God.

We rush around our day's business, speak with each other, laugh, nurture somewhat, and even make love. Yet we are all isolated in an essential way. We all harbor this "secret," and thus we lead parallel lives, never fully reaching out to the other, unwilling or unable to seek a true equality in which all yield this delusional mother-fusion, this "divine" specialness, and see us all, mother included, as truly equal co-creators with the principle of life. *This requires yet a third birth, a spiritual one, in which the adult comes to the full embrace of spirit as part of Spirit.* The irony is that to be truly special, in the sense of the development of our personhood, our unique blend of self and spirit, the genius of our own original way of being in the world, we must relinquish, at least from our end, our specialness to mother. To be a person we may retain much of mother, but not that.

This demands courage, generosity, and a love that we humans are quite capable of but which requires a transcendent reach, and a willingness to look at everything upside down, to challenge everything we know.

Chapter 4

Fusion

ℰↄ🙡

When we speak of one person being "fused" with another we, of course, do not mean that person A is identical with person B. The closest there is to this is the symbiosis between mother and child *in utero*. Even their bond is not identity. From the outset each is a separate entity both physically and—albeit embryonically—psychologically, though there is profound dependency one upon the other. The more *dependent* a person is on another, the greater the likelihood that the dependent one will tend to mimic the other. Young children will give youthful versions of their parents' attitudes. Is it an accident that the opinions of children voiced in school regarding the events of the day are just about identical to those of their parents? The depended-upon person is viewed as nearly omnipotent and this view is reluctantly abandoned, although, as in adolescence, it may be colorfully attacked.

No human is ever entirely free from some degree of fusion, either with a parenting one—what I term "vertical enmeshment"—or a contemporaneous reconstruction—what I term "horizontal enmeshment." We are all fused to some degree with others from the past and in the present.

There are certain benchmark events in becoming physically and psychologically separate and self-contained. Physical birth is followed by Mahler's "psychological birth," the "terrible twos," when "no" becomes the banner of separated self. Shortly thereafter, there are relationships with grandparents, baby-sitters, children, and other adults. The move from home to school, so poignantly described by my former student, overnight stays at Grandma's, at friends' houses, perhaps summer camp—all of these events

39

make psychological demands on both child and caretaker. Finally, there is puberty and its tempestuousness. The development of sexuality provides a dramatic drawing away from family into self as a bridge to connection with another. Soon there appears a self-created reality outside of the caretakers' home. As the old joke about adolescence goes, "As soon as they're fit to live with, they live with somebody else."

As this drama unfolds over roughly two decades, it is characterized by the constant shuffling back and forth between physical and psychological independence, psychological separation,[1] and temporary returns to a more childlike dependency. Each physical stage of separation is made possible by physical readiness, reality expectations, and parental cooperation, and each prepares the way for the increasingly separated self to both experience itself and then act on the world. All three of these conditions—readiness, expectation, and cooperation—are necessary for such trial and error to occur in a relatively safe environment.

There are many stops along the way, and the young persons feel and believe many things about themselves, their world, peers, and caretakers throughout this journey. Some of these points of view of the child are nearly universal, coming primarily out of development, like the "cockiness" of the toddler, or the "omnipotence" of the nursing infant, or the "arrogance" of the teenager at some period. Some are more idiosyncratic, a function of temperament and the psychological experiences of a person's unique, brief life.

To complicate this even more, things are not always as they appear. The dimension of confident separated self, a clear idea of self-identity, is a gradually emerging phenomenon and can be deceiving. Its genuine accomplishment does not necessarily coincide with its manifest expression in any particular instance. The more provocative of us may actually have been quite insecure, and those appearing more dependent and clinging may have found quite distinct perceptions of self and others that are held to with fierce separated conviction. And then there is the sometimes puzzling phenomenon that a physical step forward is often followed by a return to old familiar ways of being.

It is as if the dialectic between separation and fusion for the first two decades of life is a dry run, a trial for the work that must be done for the rest of our lives in making our selves truly, solidly, unambiguously psychologically separate from our early caretakers despite the residual fusion that will always remain in all our relatedness. We have been emotionally and psychologically tied together with another human being for so long and so deeply that it is a constant challenge to change and separate more into ourselves. We are constantly in relationship, even in our most alone times.

We begin life fused with mother, biologically symbiotic, incapable of functioning, even physically, on our own. When this is ended abruptly and dramatically and somewhat traumatically by birth, we develop the deepest of human relationships with her in our childhoods, which seem to us to go on forever. Then we must relinquish *this* intimacy as well. We must give up this anchor, so that our spirits, timeless and mysterious, pushing for expression, can find their way in the world. The journey is always ambivalent. We are reluctant to leave and quick to return to fusion with mother.

Psychological fusion takes place in the following intrapsychic processes:

- thinking
- feeling
- understanding and forming opinions about the nature of reality
- developing values
- behaving

When a person is fused with another, these psychological characteristics are interfered with by inhibitions of some sort generated in relationship to the other, present or past. Thus he may not be able to exercise these capacities at all. He may not be able to think originally or allow himself to have any emotions or only certain ones. He may not feel free to understand the world through his own eyes. Rather, he may actually "see" what he has been instructed to see. He may automatically and unthinkingly accept the values of another. His behavior, what is possible for him to do, may be profoundly limited by another. In all of these essential qualities of uniqueness, he feels beholden to another's prior judgment. He is not free to be himself. He is not free to love and accept himself.

But in addition to these "compromised" intrapsychic functions, there is a major psychic flaw characteristic of the fused person. The fused person believes his functioning, both psychologically and behaviorally, to be *essentially intertwined* with another and that, therefore, *the welfare of the other is contingent on his functioning.* Everything he does is experienced as a heavy burden, for in a basic way he believes it to be the cause of the way others think and feel and behave.

To the extent we are fused, then, we are limited by having the very way we see the world, our opinions and values, thoughts and feelings and behavior, proscribed by others *and*, equally as devastating, we are constricted by the deep belief that however we think or feel or behave we *essentially and inevitably* create powerful reactions in others. In effect, we control their behavior. Consequently we are responsible for them. We must be very careful! We are not really free to be ourselves.

I must say it over and over again: the tendency to fuse is exclusive to humans. It is, indeed, our central problem, and it stems from the uniqueness of our mothering. The very capacities for awareness, reasoning, and problem solving, which make possible our magnificent accomplishments, are the very characteristics that lead to what is often an enormous liability: our tendency to "fuse" with another when it would be better to let go. Thus, we humans are challenged to accomplish a special kind of letting go that no other living thing need do. We call this *psychological separation*.

What follows is a deeper examination of how this entirely human tendency to fuse originates. Then we'll study the ways it manifests itself in adult behavior, both in its individual expressions and in the overall way we organize our lives. My hope is to help the reader get a deeper "feel" for these goings on in himself or herself and in others. Then we'll speak of what keeps these archaic tendencies in place, often protected by seemingly impregnable fortresses of defense. Finally, we'll discuss the conflict that ensues in every one of us when these crusty fusions conflict with the life imperatives of our spirits. A simple conceptualization of personality will make more visual what we are up against (Figure 4–1, p. 53). This visual framework will provide the context in which we will look at the vicissitudes of the struggle between stasis and growth throughout life. It will encourage more space in the profound desire to grow into ourselves that lies in everyone, however dormant.

Let's begin at the beginning, in the infant's embryonic understanding, in psychological terms, of what is transpiring between her and mother. Melanie Klein, pioneer in the field of child psychoanalysis and a contemporary and student of Sigmund Freud, created a profound and permanent alteration in psychoanalytic theorizing about development. Perhaps it was because she herself was the mother of three that she grasped, in a particularly sensitive way, the crucial nature of this early mother-child bond. She suggested that all the dynamics of the family, as Freud described them, actually occurred much earlier in the life of the child. In fact, the most significant events that would influence the person's future were happening as he suckled his mother's breast. "The first external source of anxiety can be found in the experience of birth," she wrote. "This experience, which according to Freud, provides the pattern for all later anxiety-situations, is bound to influence the infant's first relations with the external world."[2]

Klein went on to provide a map of the murky and thorny terrain of the intrapsychic land of the infant, a terrain that will forever mark a person's psychic functioning and connect him or her with mother. She wrote:

> Throughout my work I have attributed fundamental importance to the infant's first object relation—the relation to the mother's breast and to the mother—and have drawn the conclusion that if this primal object, which is introjected, takes root in the ego with relative security, the basis for a satisfactory development is laid. Innate factors contribute to this bond. Under the dominance of oral impulses, the breast is instinctively felt to be the source of nourishment and therefore, in a deeper sense, of life itself. This mental and physical closeness to the gratifying breast in some measure restores, if things go well, the lost prenatal unity with the mother and the feeling of security that goes with it. This largely depends on the infant's capacity to cathect sufficiently the breast or its symbolic representative, the bottle; in this way the mother is turned into a loved object. It may well be that his having formed part of the mother in the prenatal state contributes to the infant's innate feeling that there exists outside him something that will give him all he needs and desires. *The good breast is taken in and becomes part of the ego, and the infant, who was first inside the mother now has the mother inside himself.*[3] (Italics added)

Klein's description of the various events, internal and external, that may influence the nature and characteristics of the fusion are mesmerizing, and should be explored, but they are not the main point here. What is important to grasp is the reality of the fusion itself. The details of how a person negotiates the fusion, particularly from a psychoanalytic point of view, is not our task. We seek to know the power, passion, and terror that motivate fusion, so that we may better know what each of us is up against and can recognize the residual adult versions of this fusion in our present life and create ways to grow out into the world.

Most animals have a very short infancy and childhood. Animals that run in herds typically expect newborns to be ready to move with the herd in a matter of hours. Even mammals with a somewhat longer period of dependency are typically left abruptly by mother at the time that nature dictates it is time for them to fend for themselves. There may be emotional reactions to this, but the demands of survival plus the animal's biological readiness make this possible.

Not so with us. We are enormously dependent, virtual cripples, for a very long time. We are unable to communicate verbally for years. But communicate we must and we do, all the time, with the numerous facial muscles nature has blessed us with, our gurgles, our odors, even our temperatures. Mother has to put aside, in large measure, her ordinary, logical, adult communication skills and get into the communication of her baby. It takes a lot of attention, a lot of heart, a lot of good will. It is very intense.

The intensity continues for a long time, perhaps never to end. Is it a surprise that as a nineteen-year-old Korean woman was pulled out of the rubble of a collapsed department store after sixteen days without food or water, she said three things: I am naked. I want my mother. How are the others? In the shadow of death her shame demanded attention; after that, she spoke of the most important person in her life, mother; and finally, she demonstrated her identification with the others, a truly beautiful quality nurtured, in all probability, by her Eastern ethos. From her mother's breast, through all of her nineteen years, and forever, she will be negotiating her relationship with her mother. MAMA is the first word we all learn, and it is the same in most languages. It is also the last word many of us will utter. For all her nineteen years, this young woman, this miraculous earthquake survivor, has been making sense out of this most wondrous of relationships. For during all these years she has been forming deep beliefs about what she surmises mother is feeling, what her facial expression means, whether mother loves her, or loves her enough, or approves of what she does and who she is. Unfortunately, we are often wrong about these conjectures, yet we sometimes build our whole life upon them.

This, then, becomes the task of life: to disentangle ourselves from the enmeshment with mother that has been our experience from when we first "woke up," for we woke up to her. At birth we began, and from then we have continued to separate—from the breast, her smell, her smile, her touch, her voice, her grace. Lured by reality and prompted by his spirit, the child instinctively, tentatively, sallies forth into the world. In an approach-avoidance dance he moves back and forth between mother and world, seesawing this way and that with his self as the fulcrum and the shift in direction the result of the increase in anxiety when he has moved too far either way. Nor does this process end with childhood.

Wisdom is that understanding of reality which we accrue through our own experience—in those moments when we discard all influences and see the world through our own eyes. This accumulation of wisdom is a lifetime process and a process separate from "knowledge" or "insight" or learning the "right way to be" through psychoanalysis or pedagogy or any other influence....Wisdom comes at all times in life. Much of it is developed in childhood and adolescence, when protected by the umbrella of parental approval, we can see what we can see. The struggle between parental injunction and personal vision is clearer in these years. Even when we accommodate our behavior to the power of the authorities, we know what we are doing and why we are doing it. Even if beleaguered we, at least, have a sense of self.

At that time of life when we begin the physical steps of separation, during young adulthood, during the stage of intimacy, the capacity for transferential distortion becomes apparent as a sign of the waffling that ensues with great velocity between our own perceptions and those of former authorities. No longer sheltered by that "umbrella" of parental protection, the injunctions that we more clearly opposed (or wisely cooperated with) take on a new potency as we are faced with the anxiety of life on our own. Our own perceptions tend to yield to parental injunctions and to the projections of these onto the world in the service of our security and the delusional reestablishment of the primitive notion that this enmeshment will save us from death. It was one thing to fight against our parents for our own perceptions when we "knew" they would protect us against death at any cost. It is another to fight them when we are on our own. The temptation to hold on to them and their "protection" is very strong and it takes the form of transferential distortion and the abdication of our own individual and unique capacity to perceive and understand our worlds.

And so we stop seeing and knowing in our own right. When our lives are not working well we look to get help and guidance, although the temptation to get it in a transferential way, i.e., in a way that does not give obeisance to the necessity of our own separation, is very strong. Even in those modalities which deal with the content of separation, such as psychoanalysis, the very structure of the procedure is antiseparation, albeit necessary, as it most often is, at the time.

All of the insight of psychoanalysis is a stepping stone to the solitary insight a person must make. This is why the period after psychoanalysis is so important. It is during this time, when opened up to novelty through psychoanalysis, the person must reintegrate these insights into new, fresh, *personal* knowledge which is wisdom. Until this point his or her insights have been based on interaction with the wisdom of the analyst.

In a way all socialized knowledge must be relearned in a personal way for it to be wisdom. This is a very problematical task. It demands, among other things, the willingness and capacity to put aside consensual validation to explore reality on one's own terms and come to grips with it on one's own, risking at once the censure of others and self during this unchartered course and at the same time the possibility that one's own solution not be "as good" as the consensually validated one. This truly demands courage but it is a necessity for true humanity. It is far better to be you than to be "right."[4]

What an irony! As we get older we may lose wisdom! Actually, as we move through life, we are challenged to regain wisdom, and when we accomplish this as adults, it is for real. But there is constant and intense pressure not to.

Psychologically separated or not, however, our behavior belongs to each of us, and as much as we may want to abdicate responsibility for ourselves, we cannot. Nature, the ultimate authority, holds us responsible for ourselves, and there is no escaping. We can deny, repress, even lie, but the truth is that our life is our life and no one can really live it for us. We will be the major recipient of the consequences of our behavior, psychologically separated or fused, conscious or unconscious.

In all that we do we have choices, though we may not be entirely aware in every instance. In fact, the capacity for awareness, or, at least, the sincere desire for consciousness, is itself a separation stance. We can choose to attend to the nature and demands of reality, the world around us, the inner promptings of our spirit, what we need to express to complete ourselves; or we can attend to an edition of the world that is someone else's, a caretaker's, obeying what the other would have us do to make us safe.

Our emotional life can be the natural, spontaneous result of our interactions with the world or our understanding of it; or it can be a jerry-built system of old "familiar" emotions designed to keep us in an archaic place. The affects we experience can give us crucial information about the world; or they can obscure the true nature of reality by having reference to the past as if it were the present.

We can feel what we need to feel, see what we see, think what we need to think about the nature of reality, what needs to be done, what we believe about things, and take actions that express ourselves and meet the demands of nature; or we can feel old, "chronic" affects or nothing at all, perhaps discharging affect in "mood" bursts, acting impulsively to rid ourselves of painful affects, further anesthetizing ourselves.

We can intend to think clearly and objectively regardless of what is happening around us or inside us. Or we can think obsessively or not at all. We can deny, "not know," think in routinized and stereotyped ways, have opinions that others gave us, not discovered or evaluated by ourselves, not "owned" by us.

For example, I sometimes wake with things on my mind. One day recently I awoke thinking about a friend and some troubles she was experiencing. I hadn't heard from her for a while and I was worried. I felt sad and slightly depressed. That same day I heard that an acquaintance was writing a book. I was aware of feeling slight anxiety. These two things resulted in my feeling on edge for some time. Finally, I sat down and observed my experience. I was aware of the feelings I just described. I was aware that just having these feelings, in itself, disturbed me; I was feeling somewhat self-critical. As I noticed this I made *the intention of accepting me* as I was. I determined that I was not going to increase my discomfort by dumping on myself. I was going to be compassionate. I reminded myself of my determination to accept myself no matter what I was feeling. When I did this, it occurred to me that I was feeling *responsible* for what was happening to my friend. I really had nothing to do with her circumstance, had shown love and support and availability to help in ways that I realistically could. The feeling I was experiencing was really what is referred to as *codependent*. I was fused with her in this instance, making her reality my reality, feeling as if her feelings and behaviors were a function, in some mysterious way, of mine. Similarly with the colleague who was writing. I placed him inside myself in an old fused place where my brother and I fought for my parents' attention. I don't ordinarily feel so competitive these days, but this particular man and I have a history in which I had often been fused with him. I saw that I am vulnerable to being "called back" to this old way of being, which has reference to an even older way of being. I became aware of what was going on and accepted the feelings and myself. I knew I would be off-center for a little while, but that if I didn't do something self-destructive to remove myself from those feelings, they would pass in time, as feelings do, unless we keep stoking them. My ever-ready tendency toward fusion was in operation but my spirit was in charge of my behavior that day and I went about my business.

Most of the time we are in a struggle between the part of us that wants to return to our essential selves, which I refer to as the spirit, and that frightened part of us that wants to hold on to our connections with our caretakers. These connections are in those deep beliefs, those chronic affects, those "actings-out" that are demonic in their intensity and motivation, determined to keep us from moving toward a greater destiny. We may look at any particular piece of behavior and understand it to be an expression of spirit, or its opposite, a fearful homage to a past security—a sort of micro-fusion. Each of us does this from time to time, and there are periods in our overall movement toward becoming our true selves that we rest in considerable fused behavior. We are all, as I once heard, works in progress.

If this tendency to fuse remains a pervasive way of dealing with fearfulness, what results is a sort of "macrofusion" wherein the major thrust of a person's life can be considered as imprisoned by largely unconscious imperatives and fearfulness. Upon close scrutiny this can sometimes be seen in persons who give the offhand impression of having a firm grip on life. It is most probably true of those men and women who, after a lifetime of apparent success and accomplishment, commit some deed that topples them from the heights to disgrace. The headlines of each day's newspaper illustrate such people. Here are a few examples of chronically fused lives from my personal experience. I've put them in the form of vignettes.

> In the case of Seamus, the chronic affect he lived with as a child was shame. There was no way out of this that he could see. He was shameful if he made a mistake but he was also shameful if he did anything well. Anything that he did that wasn't a response to a direct order from his parents or some parent-surrogate, overtly or covertly delivered, was an occasion for his shame. So he had the task of trying to excel and fail at the same time, in order to maintain the chronic affect of his childhood. He unconsciously desired this because he wanted to be a good boy and also because he loved his parents very much and wanted to please them. He couldn't fail too much because they would be embarrassed and also because his spirit wanted to protect him. But he couldn't succeed too much because they always cautioned him about being "a big shot." He was fearful he might lose them. His spirit was always tripped up at the crucial juncture. He became a master at seizing failure out of the jaws of success.

The effects of these deepest beliefs and the manifestation of chronic affect may refer to *present* people or situations (*horizontal enmeshment*).

They may also be experienced directly, in connection with people or events of the past (*vertical enmeshment*).

> Arnold is the best man at his brother's wedding and says, "I never want to be the best man at anyone else's wedding now that I have been one for my brother." On the face of it, this sounds like loyalty and love and it is, but really, it is a response to Mom, who has told him that you can't trust anyone but family; that it is a dangerous place out there. Arnold, who feels insecure in his relationship to her, in reaction to her own difficulty in loving him, accepts her views because he is trying to find a way to please her. Her envy toward her husband, a successful public servant, gregarious and well liked, though always struggling financially, prompts her to communicate to her son that he will have "special entry" to her by being a wealthy businessman (as opposed to her public-sector husband) and not "giving it away" to strangers decades later. His "family devotion" is an example of vertical enmeshment and his controlling, his "buying" of his relatives, is horizontal enmeshment. He has a deep belief that by earning enough money and meting it out to his family, he will be guaranteed their love. He does not succeed in this but does manage to "corrupt" several of his children. His own lack of psychological separation (the ultimate loyalty to Mom) has resulted in total enmeshment with his spouse and a barely controlled alcohol addiction (which has resulted in his being forced to take "early retirement"). He has no friends and appears ten years older than his sixty years. When he is not thinking about when he can "safely" take a drink, he is obsessing about the lives of his grown children and interfering in them.

Regardless of how much a person accomplishes in life, no matter how different from his origins the externals of his life may appear, many persons stay connected to their caretakers by managing to create situations that will result in bathing in the chronic affects of their earliest childhood world.

> Maurice is a fifty-year-old physician. He has a Park Avenue practice and lives in a beautifully appointed apartment on Manhattan's historic and affluent Upper East Side, in which he shows off his art collection. He has a beach house in East Hampton. Yet, when he came to see me, Maurice was miserable to the point of suicide. By means of an adroitly self-destructive business deal, he had managed to arrange himself on the brink of bankruptcy. Through the increased use of drugs and alcohol and compulsive sexuality, his health, relationship, and profession were threatened. He was filled with terror, trusted no one, even carried a pistol to protect himself from the dangers he felt were stalking him. Although the externals of his

life were dramatically different from those in which he had grown up, he had managed to maintain the *affective state* of his childhood—chronic affect. He was worried about money, preoccupied with persecution from outside enemies, unable to have loving contact with another human being. In short, he was a very good boy who had never left home; he carried his parents' anxieties with him. He lived in the chronic affect of his youth, dissociated from all his own feelings about his parents. This sophisticated urbanite had never psychologically left the linoleum covered kitchen of his poor Brooklyn childhood, with all the fears, beliefs, attitudes, and expectations of his lonely and abusive childhood. Yet, he would rather die than know the truth. Almost. His spirit prevailed, he dragged himself into my office, and with great courage he fought to know the truth.

This final vignette describes a man who also acted out a great deal to avoid his feelings and not know the truth. But he had many "deep beliefs" that tyrannized him and kept him frantically running in an ill-fated search for security.

Tomas, the lover of a patient, is a loving, creative, and adventurous person who has devoted his life to helping others and has great talent in doing this. His role in life has been to be the savior of an extended family who had to move from one country to another, one culture to another. Tomas managed all this with great agility. But Tomas was not to own his very spirit, although the ethos of his culture provided for much blustering and bravado along these lines. He was a "real man" and could posture with the best. In reality, he was an indentured servant. He was slave to all the reincarnations of his mother, who had taught him that he would be loved for his service, and consequently safe. She was not so good at actually providing this love and appreciation, but she was a wizard at holding out the promise.

Tomas, approaching sixty, is still trying to find the right formula to achieve this goal. Despite a heart attack, ulcers, and compulsive smoking, his days are long and stressed in his attempt to support and govern a large and unappreciative family and other people as well. There is no end to his sense of responsibility. It is as if he were codependent with the world. His friend reports that when they walk down the street together, he is continually telling her to step aside if he vigilantly perceives someone who may want to pass. He engages in this behavior constantly and regardless of the significance of what is transpiring between them, to her upset. And this is the tragedy of his enslavement to the deep beliefs of the past. While Tomas is compulsively being mother's good boy, he is unrelated to those who really love him. You see, he is not supposed to love and relate—to anyone outside the family of his childhood. So he is condemned to live his life recreating the family who didn't love and appreciate him and ignoring those others who are eager to love him for his many wonderful and loving characteristics.

In contrast to these lives, when we are committed to the full development and expression of our true selves, we struggle, aware or not, to think our own thoughts, feel our own feelings, and form our behavior based on our unique perceptions of the nature of reality and our understanding of what needs to be done. It helps to think of the psychological person as comprised of three forces: self, spirit, and ego. *Self* is the immediate consciousness of unique identity. It includes all the characteristics of what Freud referred to as ego. The ego, as Freud used it, is not our common usage. We generally mean "self-centered" by the term. This is closer to the way I use it. The Freudian ego[5] refers, rather, to all the functions of the mind—motor control, perceptions, memory, affects, thinking—that are involved in helping individuals negotiate the environment, particularly in getting their instinctual needs or urges satisfied. I include all of these wonderful human capabilities in my meaning of self. Self, thought of in this way, is a miracle of life. It is both expressive and receptive. Self is both the person acting, and, at the same time, being aware of self.

Spirit is the embodiment of the life force. It is an aspect of the power beyond the self: God, Tao, or, the term I prefer, the Transcendent. We share this spirit with all living things. The term Transcendent embodies the dimension I believe to be crucial to this power; namely, that it is something beyond and outside of ourselves, something that preceded our persons and will outlive them, something that has properties that transcend what we alone have, yet carries no extraneous or metaphysical connotations. It is a notion mostly defined by our *relative position* with respect to it, not by any ontological characteristics that we impose on it. Paradoxically, those human qualities that the Freudian theory of personality would subsume under id—the instinctive, sexual, sensual, biologically imperative aspects of ourselves—I would include under spirit. Spirit encompasses our myriad, magnificent, uniquely human capacities, both psychological and physical, our passion, our creativity, our movement toward growing out unto ourselves. These profound pushes, incidentally, are part of our very nature and thus are natural, not supernatural, and no extra-terrestrial vision is necessary to explain them.

As we separate more and more psychologically, we discover more and more of life and reality. There seems to be no end to what it is possible to know and understand. Reality is infinite; each of us is engaged with a piece of it at any moment, but there is always more to find and explore. It is spirit that moves us in the direction of infinite reality. It is what and who we are as human beings and, as such, spirit acts on self and energizes and motivates it toward life. When we discuss the nature of change, we will see what it is like for us to "bump into" a new dimension of reality.

Ego, in the way I use it, refers to influences that also impinge upon self but originate in early fusion between mother and child. Just as spirit urges us on and out into the vastness of the new, ego wants us to remain where we are. Ego wants us in the psychic ambience of the specialness of our relationship with mother. There is tremendous force and power in these tendencies, demonic in intensity. They fight the thrust of spirit fiercely.

I understand ego as a blinding attachment to self, a self which, in psychic reality, is enmeshed with mother. There is a range of rigidity in this enmeshment. Merely feeling good about ourselves is, at the outset at least, related to the celebration of our being by our caretakers. But then there is a switch. Those of us who were not so celebrated, or who were celebrated in a random and unpredictable way, who were not listened to and noticed sufficiently, often have reacted to the anxiety engendered by this treatment with an excessive fusion with the mothering one. This frantic attempt to "hold on" leads to an excessive ego, one that must defend itself at all costs and can never be criticized. Such persons are cursed with the self-imposed demand for perfection, at least for the eyes of others. All of us fall somewhere within these parameters.

Each of us is made up of self and the knowledge of ourselves. This self is constantly being torn between demonic influences toward fusion with mother—ego—and, simultaneously, a push toward psychological separation and identification with the Transcendent, whether acknowledged as such or not. This is spirit. The "person" is the eternally unique expression of that struggle as it ensues, at any moment, within self. Figure 4–1 is a graphic representation of this dynamic.

Life takes place in the moments of conscious awareness of the state of this dialectic in our interaction with the world about us. We are truly alive

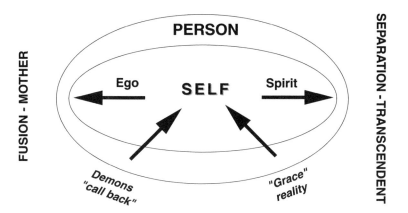

Figure 4-1: The Psycho-Spiritual Makeup of the Person

Demons "call back" refers to the inertia and tendency to return to old, fused ways of being, particularly when we are moving forward into previously proscribed areas or making rapid strides in growing out into ourselves. "Grace" reality refers to the phenomenon that the universe seems to cooperate, often in mysterious ways, when we are moving forward, doing what is "right" for us as opposed to acting out or yielding to call backs.

and living when we can become aware of our affective state and become free to think, when we are able to observe and ponder what is happening inside and outside of ourselves at each moment, and when our spontaneous activity reflects this consciousness.

Here is what's at stake: the battle between our push toward growing out into the persons we truly are and the seemingly demonic pressures to stay connected in some manner to our fusion with our caretakers will decide the quality and value of our lives. We are really speaking of the extent to which our one and only life will be ours!

- Do you want to live your own life?
- Do you want to act spontaneously?
- Do you want to free yourself from fear?
- Do you aspire to be all you truly are?
- Do you want to find your unique vocation?
- Do you want to put your unique input into the universe?

- Do you want to know and love and be known and loved by a fellow human being?
- Do you want joy to be a familiar inner atmosphere?
- Do you want totally to accept and appreciate yourself?

Of course! But you may feel it is impossible. Or you may believe that the amount of work it would demand is beyond you. Actually, the problem is one of understanding—understanding fusion. Few of us have any real knowledge or awareness of how that works in us. Even the belief that nothing can be different is probably a fusion-born belief.

We often choose not to be so conscious and awake, and fusion is the culprit. Psychological fusion stems from fear. We are afraid of life on our own; we are afraid of disobeying the injunctions of our parents. We are enjoined from acting spontaneously, for such behavior would indicate an independent relationship with self. It would represent separateness. Much of the time we live in fear of awareness, in fear of knowing our finiteness, our limitedness, our finality. We hope that by staying enmeshed with mother, we will magically stave off death. No wonder we dread psychologically separating. Who can blame us?

As a result many of us never really get to know ourselves. We live the lies that are expected. Instead of fighting to know who we really and uniquely are (our spirits) and fulfilling our calling in life, we tenaciously hold on to archaic "deep beliefs" that often remain unexamined and unchallenged. We continually create situations that enable us to maintain chronic affective states. We act out scenarios of the past.

The real tragedy is that fear of becoming who we really are keeps us fused to what we believe will keep us safe, and we are willing to sacrifice our very lives for that safety. But it doesn't work! Not only does staying fused with another not protect us from danger, real or imagined, it actually puts us in jeopardy! *Freedom and safety come not from fusion but from psychological separation*! Only then are we free to become who we truly are and seek out our vocations as part of the transcendent nature of things. In becoming part of the transcendent nature of the universe there is no danger.

This is not impossible. It is not even complicated. It *is* mysterious, though. It means each of us has to search inside for our spirit and form the intention to become ourselves. Most important, and even more difficult, is to begin to consider relinquishing our ego, or at least to loosen its grip on us a bit. How to do this? There are no mechanical answers, but many helps are given throughout the rest of this book. Each of us can start at any place. There is no best time, and it is never too late. No particular preparation is necessary. We just need to find that intention. Many find it in deep pain. However it is found, we need to form the intention of becoming ourselves, begin to observe ourselves and how we function, both within ourselves and in the world, *without trying to change ourselves or anything else.* And most important, we must strive toward total self-acceptance as we begin this journey.

Part Two

Return to Spirit

Chapter 5

Psychological Separation

ℬℭℛ

In a review of a biography of Charlotte Brontë in the *New Yorker* a few years ago, I was struck by this statement:

> A Danish biographer I know once described his vocation to me by saying, "I track the process of individuation to the point at which it fails." That excellent definition of biography suggests why some glittering, eventful lives are in fact repetitive and depressing, and why some chaste, deprived lives, like Charlotte Brontë's, are riveting. It's the drama of individuation which gives biography its suspense, and cuts through the trivia of a life to its vital mystery.

Psychological separation refers to all the ways that a person, yielding to spirit, pushes outward in the eternal continuation of birth toward the light of the Transcendent. It is the way each of us fulfills our unique destiny.

Yet working with many persons and taking a good, long look at my own life and the lives of those about me have confronted me in the deepest of ways with the pervasiveness of psychological fusion and the relative rarity of the person struggling toward psychological separation. James Baldwin once said, "The world is held together by the love and passion of a very few people."

In the past we have considered indications of fusion as pathognomic— a sign of a "disease" process. We have distanced ourselves from this and tried to categorize those unseparated behaviors we could not ignore as "mental illness." This helped us deny the pervasiveness of these issues in our own personal and professional life. It was those "not-me's" out there that were the problem, the "not-OK's" who failed to separate psychologically—not me!

The reality is that psychological separation is the unusual state—not fusion! A person may not have psychiatric symptoms (at least that we can see), and may, in fact, look to all the world like a "perfect" specimen but, in actuality, be the least psychologically separated of any of us. The very behavior we have ascribed to his mental health may be an example of such profound fusion that his spirit is strangled. Witness the periodic reports of "solid" citizens who go on a rampage—sometimes killing their own parents! *We are all fused.* To recognize and accept this is the beginning of the release of our spirits in our one incarnation of consciousness. It is the opportunity to heed the call of our unique vocation and become who we are and do what we are to do.

Walking through Central Park one day, I saw a dog, poised, then exploding toward a squirrel. The squirrel scooted up a tree; the dog assessed the situation and his eye caught another dog some distance away. He loped rapidly over to this leashed potential playmate and, after sniffing out the situation, loped back to the tree and his old friend, the squirrel. Then he noticed a flock of pigeons some distance away and headed for them.

He was totally absorbed in life, this animal, "knowing" what to do next and throwing himself into it with complete focus. (His "master" ran about, meters behind, frantically calling the beast's name, to no avail; the dog was obviously heeding a higher call.) It was beautiful to watch. It is at moments like this that I realize how limited we are. The development of our consciousness, our long childhoods, and our flawed caretakers have so seriously damaged our doing what needs to be done according to the laws of nature; we can do so many more things than an animal, but in the basic things we are disabled—amazing!

Then there's the matter of purpose or meaning, the reality of the impending closing of the light, and coming to terms with that. A little knowledge is a dangerous thing, they say—we are damaged once again. Of course we deny; of course we fuse and remain fused; of course we look outside ourselves for explanations; of course we look for people of wisdom, of course we watch TV all day long. We blame each other; we wage wars; we constantly try to reinstate those moments of idyllic bliss when the gods incarnate, our parents, were in our presence and protected us. Of course we permit abuse and suffering if that is part of the deal. Of course we hate our parents for betraying us by winding up as mere humans. Of course we create God in our image and likeness.

We must each make our own way and find what provides joy much of the time; that is the way of nature; that is our tail wagging. It is a total mystery, a humiliating reality. It can be fun, though, and taming our ego makes the ride smoother.

The *sine qua non* of joy is knowing as deeply and fully and completely as we can that we are OK. We are not perfect, because it is not possible for humans to be perfect; we are flawed. It is our essential nature. One of the signs of this is our demand that we *be* perfect! That dog is perfect and is not concerned with the question.

We need to accept our flawed selves and have compassion for ourselves. At those moments when I manage this, I know that I feel loving and tolerant toward all my sisters and brothers, whom I know to be in the same boat. Then I am able to do my vocation, and while I am not crazy about ultimately losing awareness, I can live with it, even, at moments, seeing in it a task I must accomplish. At times I even experience the bittersweet humility that accompanies the realization that my purpose is to yield graciously to the will of the Transcendent.

To do this I must be on the road of psychological separation. I must be wholeheartedly committed to being who I am in its freest and fullest form. This is why I have written this book, for I know that many of you will identify with me and use some of my experiences and thoughts as support and encouragement in your own journey. You will also create more experiences and thoughts that are even more appropriate for you, and maybe you will let me know about them!

Psychological separation is wresting our lives back from the grip of our caretakers. The reason to do this is to become, in a sense, more like that dog. Of course, we are superior in many ways to other animals. We are capable of love and compassion; we can influence our destinies. But the dog has an advantage because there is so little that comes between his perception of what needs to be done and his doing it. Our ability to make decisions about right and wrong, our impulses to share and care, enable us to transcend the capability of an animal. Yet, sadly, what most often motivates our behavior is lust and greed and rage and fear and faulty judgment and inhuman feelings and violent and horrific behavior. These are the offshoots of fusion and its compulsion to deny and control and protect itself, destroying all that gets in its way.

Psychologically separated persons are free. They will never move to the world with the absolute instinctive spontaneity of the dog, but, unencumbered by ego-protecting, demon-ridden fusions with caretakers, they have a chance to do the right thing according to their lights. They are in the *Wisdom place*. They see what *they* see, know what *they* know, feel what *they* feel, act the way *they* see fit to act. In so doing (and here I borrow a theological term), they "co-create" with the universe. They put their absolutely unique imprint upon the world. They do not merely carry out the word of their parents.

Psychological separation is realizing that our psychic destiny is not *essentially* intertwined with anyone. As dependent children the existence and actions of our caretakers, particularly the mothering one, was experienced, and was indeed essential to our well-being and even our survival. As psychologically separated adults, we realize that we are sufficient for survival unto ourselves. Whereas in our childhoods mother was central-to-self, as adults we are central-to-ourselves. Nor are we, nor do we aspire to be, central-to-someone. This is a scary notion but, as we shall see, the more independent we become, the more we are actually capable of giving and receiving love, the more love there will be in our lives. Psychological separation does not relinquish love; rather, it enables us to abdicate the fear that underlies the belief that a particular one *must* be in our lives for us to get enough love. A person may be special to us and incredibly dear, but as a psychologically separating[1] adult, no one person is *essential* to our existence.

Complete psychological separation is not possible or even desirable. There are many things we take from our parents, and from others as well, that enhance our spirits and are joys. Psychological separation, in the way that I use it, is the *natural* tendency or movement of each of our spirits to be who we truly are, unencumbered by hidden deep beliefs, chronic affects, injunctions, or habitual ways of being that either drag us down or make impossible our destinies during our conscious, physical life on the planet. Psychological separation is about the paradox that we must leave some in order to return to ourselves so we can love others (even if these others are the same!). It hardly ever demands that we physically leave a person. It almost entirely refers to our *internal* relationships with others, and finally to ourselves, and ultimately to something Transcendent. Psychological separation does not mean we must leave anyone or anything, including parents, although this is our fear, and in many instances the psychological meaning to us of struggling to be ourselves. It does refer, however, to ceasing to solve the problem of mother by staying a child. It implies a commitment to knowing exactly who our parents are and that may mean, for a time, terror, and perhaps, at a point, forgiveness.

Psychological separation is to be in the service of our own life. It is to know deeply that we are enough, that we are the executive of our own psychological attributes.

These attributes are thoughts, emotions, judgments, perceptions, and the integration of all these into purposeful behavior. To the extent that these capacities are relatively free from the injunctions, identifications, introjections, and projections developed in relationship with a caretaker of childhood, or perpetuated by involvement with present-day, transferential "incarnations" of a caretaker, we say we are psychologically separated.

Psychological separation also refers to more complex personality characteristics. There are life scripts or patterns that we may be carrying out in reference to family dynamics. Our beliefs, opinions, and values may be unthinkingly, or out of fear, the same as, or rebelliously opposed to, those of our caretakers. How much fun do we deserve? How sexual should we be, how spontaneous, how creative? How hard, or little, shall we work? How should we raise our children? How have we formed our religious attitudes and opinions? How important is health? Should we let each person decide about these things or, if we are "right," is it our responsibility to impose our judgments on others? What does life mean? What, if any, is our purpose? Are we free to determine this ourselves, or do we take the opinions of some authority, living or dead?

But the crucial dimensions of behavior in which the fusion-separation drama plays out can be reduced to three: *thinking, feeling,* and *behaving.* Let's look closely at each.

Thinking

A number of years ago I made a naive discovery. I found out that thinking has little to do with intelligence. I found this out from two sets of experiences. The first occurred on a cross-town bus on a Sunday afternoon. The bus was less than half full. Passengers were by themselves for the most part, and apparently absorbed in reading—parts of the Sunday *Times*, books, magazines, bus schedules. It appeared to me to be the kind of reading that serves the same purpose as watching the floor numbers on an elevator—a way of getting out of the present experience of being with strangers, a way of isolating, of excluding. All of a sudden two folks boarded the bus. Each dropped a token in the machine and moved toward the rear of the bus. They were in their late twenties, I would say, totally engaged with each other and the conversation they were having. The volume of their speech was a little louder than usual on a Sunday cross-town bus and, in contrast to the guardedness of their bus mates, they made little attempt to hide the content of their conversation. She was wearing a dress; he, slacks, sport jacket, white shirt, and tie. They were a little pudgy, and there was something slightly off about the color matching of their outfits. Eavesdropping on their conversation, it soon became apparent that each was mildly retarded. They were arguing:

He: You should have stuck up for me; I don't know what to say to her.…You should have told her.

She: She's your mother.…I have my own mother.…I have to take care of my mother.…You have to take care of yours.

He: But you're better at talking than me; you should have told her (*angrily*).

She: (*assertively and looking right at him*) Look, she's *your* mother…you have to learn to take care of her…to talk to her.…It's not my problem.…Don't yell at me because you don't know how to do it.

The rest of the bus was silent; the passengers seemed engrossed in their reading materials. It was as if this event were not taking place. There were a few more go-rounds on this issue, and then it was dropped; the couple fell into a more neutral topic. Something seemed to have been resolved without a tear in their relationship. What flabbergasted me about this was the amount of thinking that was going on. Neither of these individuals had great cognitive skills. Their memories weren't the best; they spoke slowly, ponderously, as if searching for words as they exerted effort to stay focused on the topic. Both were full of emotion and this informed their dialogue but didn't disrupt it.

Their discussion brought to mind Thoreau's report of his conversations with some of his "guests" at Walden Pond. He describes a simple man:

There was a certain positive originality, however slight, to be detected in him and I occasionally observed that he was thinking for himself and expressing his own opinion, a phenomenon so rare that I would any day walk ten miles to observe it, and it amounted to the re-origination of many of the institutions of society. Though he hesitated, and perhaps failed to express himself distinctly, he always had a presentable thought behind. Yet his thinking was so primitive and immersed in his animal life, that though more promising than a merely learned man's it rarely ripened to anything which can be reported. He suggested that there might be men of genius in the lowest grades of life, however permanently humble and illiterate, who take their own view always, or do not pretend to see at all; who are as bottomless even as Walden Pond was thought to be, though they may be dark and muddy.

Further on,

Half-witted men from the almshouse and elsewhere came to see me; but I endeavored to make them exercise all the wit they had, and make their confessions to me; in such cases making wit the theme of our conversation; and so was compensated. Indeed, I found some of them to be wiser than the so-called *overseers* of the poor and selectmen of the town, and thought it was time that the tables were turned. With respect to wit, I learned that there was not much difference between the half and the whole. One day, in particular, an inoffensive, simple-minded pauper, whom with others I had often seen used as fencing stuff, standing or sitting on a bushel in the fields to keep cattle and himself from straying, visited me, and expressed a wish to live as I did. He told me, with the utmost simplicity and truth, quite superior, or rather *inferior* to anything that is called humility, that he was "deficient in intellect." These were his words. The Lord had made him so, yet he supposed the Lord cared as much for him as for another. "I have always been so," said he, "from my childhood; I never had much mind; I was not like other children; I am weak in the head. It was the Lord's will, I suppose." And there he was to prove the truth of his words. He was a metaphysical puzzle to me. I have rarely met a fellow-man on such promising ground,—it was so simple and sincere and so true all that he said. And, true enough, I did not know at first but it was the result of a wise policy. It seemed that from such a basis of truth and frankness as the poor weak-headed pauper had laid, our intercourse might go forward to something better than the intercourse of sages.[2]

The same year that I observed those hard-thinking lovers I happened to be teaching graduate students in clinical psychology as well as candidates in a post-doctoral training program in psychoanalysis. These were clearly very intelligent individuals with great memories, a storehouse of information, and exceptional cognitive skills. Yet I found among a surprisingly large number of these folks a disinclination to actually think. Oh, they could throw information around, all right. They could spout names and dates and theories and theorists, but when it came down to actual thinking, many were unwilling or unable to risk an opinion. If I asked a class the most important factor in eliciting psychological growth, I could easily get a "printout" of the most sophisticated theories on the topic, but few would venture their own opinion. It really was like pulling teeth. I took to forbidding the use of the name of anyone else in their answers but soon rescinded that because it made the students too anxious.

Part of the reason for this was that these high academic achievers had been spoiled by the emphasis on information and performance in our educational system. Another part was because they were so darn smart they had become lazy; they knew they could get by simply by regurgitating the vast amounts of data they had accumulated and so easily stored. Yet another part of the reason was that high academic achievers are often motivated by pleasing their parents—an unseparated behavior in itself—and so they are often still looking to bring good grades to Mommy for her approval. It was the good grade, not their capacity to think, that was rewarded. (In fact, many folks who insist on thinking run into all sorts of problems with the institutions over the years and often do not make it to this level of accomplishment.) Most of all, I believe, was that as smart and accomplished as these people were, many still had an *inhibition* against thinking for themselves. They could use their good minds in the service of something that was acceptable to their family and society, but they had never engaged in the task of psychological separation that would make their thinking processes autonomous, in the service of growing out into their unique selves.

So I discovered that year that there was no necessary correlation between intelligence and thinking, and that we often make the mistake of equating the two. We consider those who show flashes of wit and have a good store of information to be smart and good thinkers. We assume that those who seem limited in intelligence, especially with regard to information that they can show off with, can't think well. Sometimes this is the case, but just as often, I suspect, it is the opposite. The capacity to think clearly and powerfully depends on the extent to which one is in the process of psychological separation, and that depends more on qualities such as courage and spirit than intelligence.

Taking over our own thought processes is the absolutely necessary key to psychological separation. It is the beginning of freedom from the bondage of fusion, our fixed ways of thinking, feeling, and behaving. This begins with taking a good look at our life. There is in each of us, simultaneously, a strong, relentless push forward into ever-emerging life and an equally powerful desire to stay where we are, or even to go backward. To intend to separate psychologically, we must strive to examine our opinions about everything in life, to question our philosophies, to become clear where *we* stand with respect to everything. This is a tricky task, because many aspects of our philosophies are unarticulated, even to ourselves.

A patient of mine, as she began to grasp how deep and extensive her shutting down about her family and her father's alcoholism was, said to me:

> My *thinking* was even controlled—not merely my behavior—but my thinking. I couldn't think that the alcohol caused his problem; he even had alcohol in his sick room at the hospital! I would work to make money to cover up for him. Once he wrecked the car and I worked to buy wheels for the car so he could get to work. "I'll take care of it, Dad," I said, and later on in life I would rage, "How could he do that to me?"

But we can begin to get in the mode of separated thinking. This does not mean that we are never confused. It means, rather, that we are ever vigilant to our personal integrity and honesty about our thinking, feeling, and behavior, and are open to change. Sometimes I think that certainty is our *worst* characteristic. Certainty locks us in. We begin to defend the truth of what we believed yesterday instead of being attentive to the truth of the moment, which may clash with the truth of yesterday.

For example, a man finds that he is not interested in sex. He can have many reactions to this, all of which can have implications for psychological separation. He can be depressed, criticize himself, or he can, perhaps, rationalize that "sex is overrated." Take the latter. This may be a legitimate, "owned" philosophy. How to find out? Either alone or accompanied by some sort of ombudsman of the soul—a therapist, a counselor, someone trained and devoted to the individual's path through life—he can try to determine what he actually believes about sex. If he has difficulty even thinking about this, that is a sign in itself that he is operating in terms of someone else's opinion. Undaunted, he may continue to struggle to think about this, wresting his attention back as his mind wanders, using the realization of his distraction as further evidence that something is operating to keep out of awareness what *he* has decided he needs and wants to find out. He has formed the *intention* to learn the truth about his sexuality. Thoughts begin to come. What is sex? What do I know about it? Where did I learn what I know? What was it like at the beginning? What am I feeling as I wrestle with these questions? When was it good; when not so good; when not at all? Who influenced these things? Just what is overrated about sex? with an acquaintance, a friend, a loved one? one or many? as a personal profound discharge regardless of the other? with the same sex? What do *I* really believe? What is *my* position? Will I fight for that even if the unseparated emotional demons put up a whale of a battle?

The raising of these questions is not designed so much to bring a logical, rational answer or solution to this man's "problem" as to get to the totality of his person, free from the constriction of conviction, so that *his* truth will be freed up to move forward. Some weeks later, he finds himself thinking about all the messages he has received about sex, including the one that he should never think about it! Thinking about it is sinful, touching himself is sinful. His father's reticence about sex returns to him, his mother's disgust. He reexperiences the lonely shame of his adolescence; his "salvation" in the church, which "forgave" him and accepted him as long as he promised to work hard to not do these "dirty" things again—and to not fool around with thinking for himself. He notices his final resolution, to allow himself the pleasure of sex only when burdened with lifelong obligations or when defining himself as a sinful child or "under the influence." In short, sex was to be in his life as he perceived it to be in the lives of his parents.

There are certain key characteristics of thinking that give us a clue to when we are on the separation path. To begin with, healthy psychologically separated thinking takes place in the *present* and attempts to solve problems that are on the cutting edge of the present and the future. We are able to mull over in our minds the consequences of a certain course of behavior without having to take the risk of the behavior itself (although sometimes we actually have to do something to get crucial information).

Fused interferences with this thinking process can occur at several junctures. For example, there can be a disturbance in the "appreciation" of the consequences of our behavior. Some people "just don't learn from their mistakes," we say. This means that the result of a particular behavior is at odds with what a deep belief dictates it should be. The deep belief, a not-to-be questioned conviction from the *past*, serves to interfere with the *present* thought process. So the consequences just "don't register." They are denied, repressed, and stored away in the prison of enforced unconsciousness. The most dramatic example of this is in the addictions or any compulsive behavior a person driven by deep beliefs must do, regardless of repeated bad consequences.

Then there is the actual injunction not to think. "You think too much, that's your problem" is something a person might have heard repeatedly. But often the injunction is much more subtle: punishment, withdrawal of love, and threats of abandonment associated with autonomous thinking. The thought processes grind to a halt. Sometimes this affects academic performance. Thinking of any kind is done away with. Such persons are cognitively blank, neuter, even though they may be quite intelligent. Sometimes the academic or problem-solving functions of thinking are retained. They may learn that it is permissible to use their good mind in the service of an overall deep belief, or fusion with a parent and a parent's deep beliefs. But they are not to think for themselves; they are to be *good* children.

One of the joys of my work is to watch people as they recover from these enmeshments and cautiously, timidly, and hesitatingly experience a rebirth of their capacity to think independently. They truly come alive, for inhibitions against thinking always lead to deadness of spirit. And they are always accompanied by inhibitions against feelings.

Feeling

Feelings are profound epistemological events. In addition to providing the color and excitement of living, they also give us vast and valuable information about the world. Our feelings are often considered merely to be "reactions," consequences of what happens to us; they also, however, prompt behavior. In the therapy business we used to promote the "expression of feelings." The opposite of "expression," in this metapsychology, was "repression," and we all knew that was not good! It led to symptoms and constrictions and unconscious behavior, often of the negative kind.

But there is an additional and much more important stratagem of feelings: the simple *experiencing* of them. Thus, while repressing them or "stuffing" them is not helpful, unthoughtful, impulsive "expression" is also not helpful. At its least harmful, it dissipates the affect and obscures the information it may have provided. Sometimes it makes us feel good, but our knowledge of addictions teaches us that feeling good in itself is not enough. The "feeling good" needs to be the accompanying affect to behavior that is psychologically separated and in the service of spirit. It generally needs time for the spirit to eke its way toward wisdom. The "you're the bad guy, I hate you" approach might be momentarily satisfying, like the use of a drug, but it is a missed opportunity. To sit with a feeling, to let it sink into the completeness of our person, to milk it for all its meaning, to let the spirit be the final arbiter of action, whether conscious or not, seems better for us.

So the constriction of thinking is accompanied by the constriction of affect (or the premature discharge of it), and since these two profound human characteristics are constantly interacting, we are indeed complicated and limited beings. Our thoughts may result in feelings; our thoughts may result in behavior that may result in feelings; our feelings may lead to thoughts. There is a constant interaction among thinking and affect and action (and I include under the category of action "doing nothing" as an option).

When there is interference with thinking and affect, there is a cutting off of ourselves from the possibility of novelty. Remember, thinking and affect and action take place in the present, on the interface of the present with the future. The present is merely the future of a moment ago. This is where life takes place—excitement, spontaneity, relatedness, self-awareness, and joy, to name a few. These are the stuff of life and are infinite in their possibilities. Psychological separation is what makes it possible for us to interact freely with the world.

There are many modes of interference with *productive* thinking, all of which serve to cut off the experience of the full range of our feelings. We may be "thoughtless," for example, having little conscious awareness of what we do or say or feel. Not that the demons of such individuals are quiescent; far from it. These are the "bulls in the china shop," folks who often wreak havoc with the feelings and lives of others and, when confronted, respond with a blank stare, apparently empty of any awareness of their acts.

Others are filled with cognitive activity that is called thinking but is in actuality the compulsive spin-off of fear mediated by either guilt or worry, depending on whether the obsessiveness is about the past or the future. A person may constantly worry about what is going to happen in the future;

another may ruminate guiltily about some transgression. Neither is living in the present. The present is obliterated by this pseudo-thinking. There is no room for true emotion.

Another variation is the person whose fear activates a deep belief about danger and persecution, which results in constant rumination about the nature and locus of the threat and how to cope with it. Her thinking may be very efficient as she figures out others' motivations and scopes out the world for the possibilities of danger or punishment (some of which she may have arranged by her prior behavior) but she, too, has removed herself from the present reality. Such a person often does not see the forest for the trees. Her fearful obsession keeps her so focused on the "danger" that she is unaware that she is driving eighty miles an hour and is in real danger of losing her license (not to mention killing herself or someone else).

Others may use thinking obsessively to control affect. These are the super-neat, organized folks. When this is to excess, proper affective inter-action with others is impossible. Such a person's affect may be so con-stricted that he fails to receive important information about what is going on about him. His desk is perfectly organized and his reports are on time, but he may be unaware that people around him are uncomfortable and would rather not be in his presence. His timely report may leave out a crucial point that could only have been gleaned by the capacity to interact affectively with another, or to use his own emotions to understand accu-rately the meaning of some event.

Of course, there are also those whose inhibition against thinking may lead to hysterical, mindless fluttering through the world. The demons are active here as well, and when the consequences of this "mindless" behavior are pointed out to the person, she often responds with a pseudo-affect, an emotionality that prompts the bystander to think that this person is a truly feeling individual. Actually, the opposite is the case.

Whenever there is a problem with thinking there is a problem with feeling! It may not seem that way, but it is so. All the ways the demons conspire to interfere with our thinking also interfere with our emotions because affect is the greatest epistemological tool we have! If we know what we feel and accept that reality, we are on the road to knowing what is, and this is exactly what the demonic forces of fusion do not want. They want us to deny. They must keep us out of the present. Incidentally, this is what transference is all about. All humans have the tendency to react to new significant relationships as if the person with whom they are now relating is a crucial individual from childhood. We tend to understand what this person says or does through the prism of the past. We may transfer onto him or her feelings that we have had toward significant persons of our past. This tendency is another way of not psychologically separating, of staying fused. *Transference is the most profound psychological mechanism that we employ to keep us out of the present.* It is the antithesis of experiencing and appreciating novelty. The study of our transference can be a wonderful opportunity to examine where we are fused but unexamined; it is a strong tool of fusion, for it depends on nothing but our own private psychological processes. Not only do we *think* of the past as in a guilty rumination, but in the throes of a transference reaction we are psychologically *living* in the past.

Of course, living in the present involves a relationship to the past as well as to the future. We must learn from the past. It is also good to have sweet memories. And we must inform the present with our long-range plans and goals. We must take care that our present moment doesn't seriously damage the future. But these are psychologically separating thoughts and feelings *in the present.* The cognitive activities described above are disturbances in our thinking capacities and are designed to get us out of the present.

When I have had a good day writing, for example, it is not unusual for me to find myself coping with compulsive critical ideas. "Is this really any good?" "Such and such a chapter neglected this and that." I feel a sharp emotional pain—the *chronic affect* that resides in me and leads to thoughts and feelings of shame and tries to get me to stop thinking and feeling. If I have spent time composing sentences to communicate thoughts I have developed over the years by living my life, noticing, communicating with patients and others, reading, meditating, recording, and organizing, is this not in itself a good thing? Even if it never amounts to anything more, it is still not an activity that deserves self-abuse. A more psychologically separating fellow might even permit himself a modicum of joy at having expressed himself, especially when this act flies in the face of his household gods who importune, "Never think for yourself!" Even louder, the demons shout, *"Never let anyone know you have a good thought about yourself!"*

Happy, joyful, self-satisfied ideas and emotions are in conflict with the deep ideas and perhaps even the main organizing idea of my life. The chronic affect of these ideas spews out like a leak at a poison gas factory. Each time I do something inconsistent with these ideas I can expect an encounter with my fused "truth squad," which is going to take me to task one way or another. A patient of mine refers to her self-torture as the "Annette police." I have learned over the years that I can count on these attacks and that they are full of hot air—paper tigers, as the Chinese would say. Still, the purchase of joy for me is not cheap; more and more these days I pay the price.

These chronic affects are always in me and provide a certain familiar "feeling tone." They tend to color the spontaneous eruption of affect stemming from a good experience and, together with deep beliefs, want to tip the balance in the direction of maintaining enmeshment by once again not knowing or perhaps acting out. But psychological separation works toward the availability to our awareness of the full range of feelings from joy through anger to grief. And it teaches us to love ourselves while we are having any of these emotions.

Behaving

Acting out is a way of leaving the present and of not knowing. It is a behavior, often involving some short-term pleasure, which distracts us from knowing the truth of the present. At the same time it often expresses, symbolically, an aspect of the unconscious main idea of our life.

Denial is choosing not to know. We may even choose not to know that we are not knowing. But the fact that we work so hard not to know, and to avoid knowing that we are not knowing; the fact that we will fight with all our strength any attempts to help us see that which we do not know, suggests to me that we really *do* know, somewhere, everything there is to know. Every experience we have ever had is stored in our brain, and this includes all its aspects: smell, temperature, and so on.

We also know when we are not feeling, and even when we are feeling too much. Excessive emotionality and especially excessive pain are often in the service of denial. But the realization that we know what we are doing doesn't influence our doing it to any significant degree. This knowledge is generally unconscious (and we are keeping it that way), reinforced by armies of demonic resistances, deep beliefs, and chronic affects. When we do not know what we are doing, we are under the control of the deep beliefs of our childhood and the chronic affects that accompanied them at the time and that became frozen in place.

Acting out is a good example of how we know what we are about, even in our most mindless behaviors. The classical analysts taught us quite correctly that a symptom serves both to keep the conflict of the individual out of conscious awareness at the same time that it is a "partial expression" of the conflict itself. If a person is in "danger" of having the truth come into awareness or of feeling something painful that he might have to explore, he might strongly tend to act in a way that will distract him. This act is designed both not to know and not to feel. It has the added fused "bonuses" of removing him from the psychic present and symbolically discharging some of the conflictual energy. If he gets drunk, high, acts out sexually, screws up his job or relationship, gets in trouble with the law, hurts himself physically, to name a few of the options, he has the added fused "dividend" of suffering later. This keeps him further out of the present, further isolated from his true self, more deeply ensconced in suffering—suffering is always a non-psychologically separating experience—and sets him up for further acting out in a never-ending spiral of self-destructiveness.

All the ways we employ not to know or feel, not only the more dramatic ones, eat away at our spirit. They involve us in an energy-draining vigilance and cut a wide protective swath in our persons. They take enormous energy, which is no longer available to life. They unnecessarily excise parts of self, interfering with productiveness, spontaneity, capacity to know, relatedness, creativity, self-awareness, and joy.

The psychologically separating person, on the other hand, notices that the world works in an ever-expanding consistency. When I am in a Wisdom space, I recall things from the distant past that are just what I need in the present. The world works because the world works, and to the extent that we are in the Wisdom place, we merely notice that which has been in front of our noses all along.

If our thinking is riddled with narcissistic, ego-protective rationalizations, we do not notice that the world works, and we even blame the world for the chaotic state of affairs in our own. Such a person "knows" the motives of others without any data. Nothing is remembered that does not have reference to her self-centered agenda. She acts out a great deal because the tension is so great; her entire cognitive system is set up not to know certain things she fears to be true about herself. She cannot patiently bear the affect, which will provide new information as needed, and which, like the flow of a river, will change into new affect all by itself, the way of nature. Rather, something must be done about it in a controlling way, and what is done is generally vastly inferior to what nature, or the Transcendent, will accomplish by the very nature of things.

The fused person is imprisoned in fixed, stereotyped, actually quite limited modes of thinking; affect that is either muffled, chronic, or explosive; behavior that is unconscious and designed to not know and symbolically to perpetuate a dead, old, loyal agenda and drama of the past. Such persons are dead before their time and dangerous, too, to themselves and others. For acting out is an omnipresent impulse, and judgment is impaired.

All spiritual teachings, from the beginnings of recorded history, have been trying to get humankind not to "act out" (as has psychoanalysis). The psychologically separating person, on the other hand, has a thought or an experience, conscious or not, and this is accompanied by a strong feeling. He experiences this feeling; he knows it is to be borne without much thinking, certainly not with acting out. Often the feeling changes by itself. A new feeling, perhaps a thought comes, and life goes on. He may leave it at that, or he may examine the feeling, particularly if it has some quality, such as intensity, that he wants to learn more about, or perhaps eventually release. He observes, thinks about it when the affect is no longer present, at least in its intensity. He mines it for its epistemological value. Perhaps it prompts him to address a certain issue in his life. He makes a plan by thinking and effectively carries this plan out. His affect is appropriate to his perception and his understanding. Its main value is *what he can learn from it.* Sometimes it can be fun, too.

Extreme pain in circumstances other than tragedy, and especially the *chronic* affect of pain or suffering, is always fused. The *experiencing* of this pain (anxiety, depression) without acting out, without "fighting it," is crucial to psychological separation. Both the pain itself and our ways of coping with it are means of staying connected with the past and must be observed in themselves. Most strategies at separating (or growing or maturing, however it may be conceptualized) deal with the results of the pain, the symptoms, but do not encourage the pain itself. Each of us must be encouraged to accept it, to observe it.

To know the pain is to cease being intimidated by it, to realize that it is attachment. Accepting pain acknowledges that we are OK, even when we feel "bad." Acting out or yielding to the impulse to do something not in our best interest is the same as being unable to say no to someone intimately involved with us when he or she asks something of us that we don't want to do. In this situation, however, the person is residing inside us. Acting out is not growing; it is returning to mother, in whatever way we believe will keep us safe. It is refusing to be ourselves. It is, as a patient of mine told me, refusing to live life "walking with yourself."

The repetitive cycle of not knowing, not feeling, and acting out must be stopped at the juncture of behavior. Knowing in the present is the beginning, the abdication of denial; feelings must be reclaimed. Our fused patterns of "doing" the world must be gradually released. There will be mourning in this process, a real withdrawal accompanied by much sadness, but the pot of gold at the end of the rainbow (it *is* a rainbow because even the first tentative steps toward intention, observation, and acceptance bring sweet results) is joy. When Freud said that the most we humans can hope for is to move from misery to common unhappiness, he was too early in our understanding of the evolutionary purpose of psychological separation to have benefitted by the reality that the affect that accompanies psychological separation is joy. *Happiness is our birthright,* and I will accept no less a goal for any of our work on this planet than this. *We are destined to be as happy as a rose is beautiful or a sunset breathtaking.*

When we start on this path, in a rather short time we feel peaceful, as on a dull summer afternoon in the country, bright and green, with healing warmth and cooling breezes. Worries start to slip away. This is the closest thing to timelessness that we will ever experience, though the moment itself may slip quickly away. Nothing seems to upset us, yet nothing excites us much either. There is a curious silence, a oneness with all around, and at the same time a faint loneliness. We are so new at this that we are a little shy. We are in a new place, in someone's garden, someone we do not yet know well.

Psychological separation is a process; it is never completed. As we live more and more in the Wisdom place, we will experience the full range of emotions. They will often be intense, but they will pass. They no longer linger when their reference is gone. They can be experienced, communicated, and learned from, remembered, or discarded.

Our thinking will be logical, rational, the "secondary process" thinking referred to by the classical analyst. We can perceive, remember, reflect, try out solutions, be accessible to and informed by affect but not overwhelmed. Impulse is subservient to but not strangled by judgment. We have sufficient confidence in the safety of the world and the integrity of our own functioning that chances can be taken. We can step out into the unchartered, because we know so well where we are and trust the universe to support us. Acting out is rare because we would never want to miss any of our experiences, even the painful ones. We know that they, too, are ours. We are alive, happy, generous, and appreciative. We are ourselves.

Now our relationship with our parents dramatically changes. I think it can be summed up by the sense of no longer being afraid of mother and father. Psychological separation has nothing to do with physically leaving or cutting off contact with anyone unless that is what we decide is in our best interests. The work of psychological separation occurs internally, in the intrapsychic organization of the self. There is no need to cut off contact with our parents. Rather, we simply cease to relate to them as if we were children. In the best of all possible worlds, our parents will always have a special place in our hearts, a place of gratitude, compassion, and love. But we no longer need to be their needy children, looking to them for approval. Recently, I had this interaction with a patient:

Joe: I no longer react to my bosses, my friends, and authorities as if they were my mother and my father.

Me: (*The thought popped into my head.*) Some day, perhaps, you will no longer react to your mother and your father as if they were your mother and your father!

In group therapy one day we reflected on what our lives would be if we were "neutral" about the opinions our parents held about us. Everyone laughed at this "absurd notion." We *all* strive for mother's approval and notice, and the manifestation of this is the dramatic presentation we call our lives. And most of us are strikingly unaware of this, unaware of who we indeed are.

The more primitive a culture is, the stronger the bond to the mothering one; the more emotionally disturbed a person is, the greater the fusion. (Consider the schizophrenic person on the street; with whom do you think he or she is engaged in dialogue? Sometimes I try to get a sense of the suffering of the schizophrenic by imagining myself waking up and hearing my mother's voice. Then all day I would be in conversation with her or a delusional surrogate. Can you imagine?) The less criticism of mother is tolerated, the less individuality is permitted. The more a society is organized in parent-child modes, the more violence is tolerated as the only "solution" to a violation of stereotyped ways of behaving. And self-knowledge and self-awareness are profoundly discouraged. Is it surprising, then, that we know so little about ourselves and tend to look outside for validation and approval?

There are tremendous resistances to taking over responsibility for the regulation of our own self-esteem. We've spoken of many of them. We want to avoid the pain, the fear, the "disloyalty," the "ethical" guilt of leaving someone who has loved us so deeply. Psychological separation actually makes real love and relatedness possible, but it *feels* like abandonment, it *feels* like aggression, and that is disorienting. Every step we make to move from the need for the approval of mother to an independent self-approval is disorienting and sad. We have to face the finality of our life as well. No one around us seems to want us to engage in this struggle either! Society conspires to sabotage us. Why should we bother? And how in heaven's name do we do it?

When we make the move to detach from the mothering one, who is to take her place? Upon whom (or what) are we to rely for the safety and well-being that we counted on her for? Who will provide for us physically? Who will take care of our emotional needs, make us feel secure and safe? Who will make us believe that we are good and consequently deserve to feel happy? The "psychological birth of the human infant" and our knowledge of physical and psychological development suggest to us that as nature takes its course, we are able to do this automatically, and we teach this in our textbooks as a theory of "normal" behavior. Except that nobody manages to do it.

The trouble is we know too much! We are filled with sadness at leaving the one we have loved so much and for so long. We have had this eternity of dependence, and we have serious doubts whether we can negotiate life on our own. We are terrified. We have consciousness, so that we are deluged with questions about what it all means. Our minds, conscious and unconscious, are inundated with unresolved conflicts, deep beliefs about the nature of reality, some helpful and some not. Because of this consciousness and our long childhoods—and our naturally flawed parents—we are limited. Not only are we not perfect, we are scarcely prepared to negotiate life on our own at all, and we know it! Our capability prompts us to ask, "What shall I do? What does it all mean?" And our limitedness makes it impossible to answer the questions. What shall we do? In the midst of all this confusion we must grapple with all these puzzles about

ourselves. Our society tells us we are ready. Yet we are a mystery to ourselves and we are frightened.

Finally, of course, if we are separated enough to make this an independent inquiry, we must ponder the imponderable. Is there a God? a Creator? In a sense, this question stems from our peculiarly human admixture
of greatness and limitedness. Our ability to pose it attests to the ability to
notice and make some sense out of how things work. And so we use the
same categories and constructs to approach that which transcends us all,
that which by its very nature is unknowable. Yet we try to name it—through
the prism of our faultedness, our limitedness. Our pride commands us to
understand, to solve the puzzle.

Our awareness and the poignancy of death make grappling with it inevitable. Our spirit seeks reconciliation with Spirit. This is what spirituality is—the *search* for reconciliation, not some "solution" determined by
someone or some organization outside ourselves. It is the engagement with
the *magnum mysterium* that makes us spiritual creatures, and we all do it,
even the most committed unbeliever. We make this quest. It is our nature,
as much as it is the dog's nature to chase squirrels. Our first transcendent,
of course, was mother, and we are bent throughout life with the tendency
to stay connected with her in some way. She is our first god, and part of us
wants to keep it that way.

Our ego demands that we solve this problem in a satisfying way—a way
that we can understand! Often we join the "religion" of science or some
belief system that enables us to hold on to the grandiose ego-mother fu-
sion-denial. We want to hold on to the greatness of humanity. We live on
a planet hurtling through space at forty thousand miles per hour. We are
suspended in the universe, spinning around in a galaxy, each of us held
onto earth by the mystery of gravity. The whole thing works perfectly,
more perfect than anything we humans have ever been able to accomplish
on our own, more reliable, more predictable. What arrogance, what hubris, what insanity it is to demand to understand it!

Each confrontation with our limitedness, each "ego-busting" discovery,
has failed to convince us of our proper place in the universe. Copernicus
discovered that our planet is not the center of the universe but rather a
satellite. Darwin pointed to our humble origins as a species. The king, the
warrior, the priest—all may look back to a primordial ancestor, the snout,
the failed fish who, out of necessity and with great reluctance, staggered

out of the air-starved bog to stand up in search for air, leaving the more accomplished and efficient breathers to their slime. Freud suggested that rather than even being the center of our own personal universe, we are more like the rider upon the horse who, when the beast lunges to the left, cries out "turn left" to convince others and herself that she knows what she is doing, that she is, indeed, in charge. What assaults on our self-centeredness! But we are not dismayed. We keep on demanding the impossible, to be gods ourselves despite many lessons to the contrary. It is no wonder that we humans do not take readily to the notion of a Transcendent.

If the world works so well, and we are so limited, is there not something that transcends us? In my view the awareness and indeed the relation with such a Transcendent are natural and normal. I think that when left to our own devices we seek the Transcendent. I used to think that this search was necessary to help us separate from mother. Now I believe that it is not that we must discover the Transcendent so that we may leave mother, but rather that the innate, natural awareness and experience of the Transcendent are obscured by our tendency to remain fused with her. Relationship with the Transcendent is not a supernatural thing, something above the plane of the physical and psychological. What it transcends is our *psychologically fused state*, our relationship with the "false god" of fusion and its acolytes: addiction, dependency on others, and grandiosity. It restores us to the natural Tao-like reality of what is, and this can only be experienced in the Wisdom place of psychological separation. So we separate out into a relationship with the Transcendent. "If you would be saved, sell all you have, leave mother and father and come follow me." The letting go of mother-fusion, with its accompanying self-centeredness, naturally leads to an intuitive connection with something transcendent. Surrendering to this (or should I say, "returning") is the only way we can truly separate. This is, indeed, *the spiritual birth of the human person*.

There is a tendency to see the errors in concepts that were developed in the past by people in search of understanding and to conclude from this that all attempts at understanding are superstitious. If we applied this standard to science we could be just as dismissing. We must use the language of our time, and this language is always limited. We are dealing with something infinite, and our knowledge of it will always be limited. The important thing is the process. When the search is on the right track, it is generally accompanied by *joy* and *radical self-acceptance*.

How we approach the Transcendent will be explored in the chapter on the relationship between the psychological and the spiritual. Suffice it to say here that there is a natural interplay between them, and that they support each other. Contact with the Transcendent can encourage psychological exploration, and psychological exploration can lead to clarity and a natural movement toward the Transcendent. It is a real adventure.

Another word about our limitedness. When this truth about our natures is accepted and the natural awareness of the Transcendent experienced and accepted, then the fun begins, because our natural limitedness is nothing compared to the self-imposed limitedness of our fusion. When that fusion is yielded, we are in touch with the greatest power there is, that of the universe, that of life itself. What we, even in our limitedness, are capable of is mind-boggling, but the accomplishment of this is not an *achievement* but rather the *expression* of our uniqueness (more about that distinction later). Wilson Bently, the photographer, photographed over five thousand snowflakes in his lifetime. None was identical with another. Fingerprint experts are able to determine the differences in the prints of identical twins. We are unique, and to the extent that we free our spirits from mother-fusion, we contribute, by our essence, to forming the universe as it will continue to exist for eternity. Each drop of sweat, I am told, ultimately reaches the ocean, and our uniqueness lives for all eternity.

There is nothing to "believe" here. It is enough to know that we are part of something greater than ourselves; that there is more to know; that *we* are not God; that there is a greater language in the universe, and that we can get to learn more of it. Some resolution with the Transcendent, some humility, seems to be necessary for our spirits to be free.

The ultimate psychological separation (and spirituality) is total self-acceptance. When we have separated from mother, we are free to accept and approve of ourselves. We no longer need the approval of anyone.

So, psychological separation is, finally and ultimately, the self-regulation of our self-esteem. It is the determination, the intention to disengage from the compulsive, addictive behaviors and feeling and thinking that result in mood alteration, positive or negative, through achieving the approval of another, past or current, living or dead, physically present or absent, external or internal. It is freedom; freedom to live our own life, to love freely, and to relate to another and others.

Every one of us suffers a weight of self-criticism and pain that we are only too quick to dump onto another. Watching TV news, my impression is that most of the broadcast time is given over to determining "who is to blame." If we don't know at this moment, the viewer is consoled: "An investigation continues!" The history of ideas is filled with these encoded criteria of behavior. The truth of the matter is that psychologically separating persons do not need an external criterion for their behavior. They are close to nature, the Transcendent, and they intuitively know what is right.

Those who hid the Jews during the Holocaust at great personal danger and inconvenience to themselves were at a loss to explain their behavior. They didn't feel it *needed* an explanation. "It was the right thing to do." They knew. Contrast this clarity with those whose professions are to tell people what their behavior should be. They were the first to accommodate to the Nazi regime. A Papal Concordat was signed. With the poignant exception of Dietrich Bonhoeffer and a few comrades who broke with the organized church in protest, Lutheran church leaders made an immediate agreement with the Nazi leaders. The more subtle arbiters of human ethics, the psychotherapists, also made peace with National Socialism. Geoffry Cocks, in his fascinating book *Psychotherapy in the Third Reich*,[3] makes the case that even though the largely Jewish psychoanalysts were forced to leave or worse, "psychotherapy enjoyed a prestige and influence unknown to the profession before or since." Under the Nazis, psychotherapy enjoyed a heyday!

The studies of people who helped the Jews provide no clear reasons why they did so. They may have been members of a church or not, Nazi or Communist or anarchist. All of them, though, were described as exhibiting two somewhat vague characteristics: 1) prior to the war they were considered to be people who thought for themselves; and 2) they all seemed to have a humanitarian bent. Contrast this with the battalion of pot-bellied, middle-class, and middle-aged men, having no particular political point of view, who were drafted to follow the fighting troops into the hamlets of Eastern Europe with the express purpose of exterminating the Jews. They were to put a gun to the back of a person's head—child, woman, or man—and pull the trigger.

These were ordinary men—shopkeepers, pharmacists, ordinary people. The night before their first assignment they were given a way out. Their commander, himself terrified and sickened, stayed locked in his house on the first day of the initial massacre. He informed his troops that if it was too difficult for them to carry out this duty they would be given different work. Few availed themselves of this opportunity! In fact, throughout the war there is little indication that anyone was censured in any way for failing to kill Jews—for absenting himself from this duty. Yet those who refused were extremely rare, rarer even than those self-possessed persons who risked *everything* to do what they considered the right thing.

Psychologically separating people *know* the right thing, and they strive to do it. And they know they are good, the way they are supposed to be. They know that they make mistakes. That it is human nature. They correct them. They apologize. But by and large, they don't lose their self-love. And they would never make their self-regard contingent on the opinion or motivations of others!

Some criticize those who seek their own truth, who "follow their own drummer," as being selfish and self-centered. Perhaps they are speaking of those who are truly narcissistic, individuals pathologically fused with mother who give themselves permission to run roughshod over their peers. But truly separated individuals are kind and loving, inclined to be sensitive and responsive to others. These are the persons who risked their lives to aid the Jews. Becoming oneself is an expansive thing. Such persons are appreciative of life and generous back toward it.

In the next chapters we will follow the journey of the psychologically separating person. We will look at the various ways that hindrances can be engaged. We will examine the relationship of the psychological to the spiritual. We will see how a long-term intimate relationship fosters growth. We will study just what psychological change is and learn some simple mechanisms to generate these changes in ourselves.

Chapter 6

The Nature of Psychological Change

✄ ℭℜ

All of life is recovery from childhood, particularly the mother-child relationship and what happens to us as the inevitable consequence of being human as well as the particular vicissitudes of our unique experience.

Change is return—return to spirit, to nature, to the Transcendent. It is not becoming something else; it is un-becoming something and becoming ourselves—a return from the false god of mother-fusion to the true divinity of the psychologically separating spirit of each of us.

Paradoxically, change does not occur when we go at a problem head on. Eastern approaches to growth, the "paradoxical intention" theories of the Gestaltists, the insights of Viktor Frankl, all have instructed us that to change something, we must first not attempt to change anything at all. This approach has not caught on much because it is at odds with our egos, the consequence of the delusions of unexamined mother-fusion. Psychoanalysis has had trouble here because it has relied so heavily on intellectual functioning, on making the unconscious conscious. The main instrument of change in psychoanalysis is the "interpretation," and the main work is the analysis of the resistance to the repressed memories of childhood, the return of which will result in insight and consequent freedom to make new and better choices.

There is great value in psychoanalysis, but it often comes a cropper in that its understanding of psychological change relies too heavily on the egocentrism I have been describing.

My observations have led me to consider three central and crucial factors to be operating in all psychological change:

- Intention
- Observation
- Radical self-acceptance

First and continually, we need to be helped to keep the focus on what we want to change, to examine it, be committed to it. Observation is the study of our actual behavior as it occurs, without any particular attempts to change it. This can be done by vigilance, by psychoanalysis, by meditation. Most critical is the constant, unrelenting challenge on our part and the part of therapists to the self-criticism that constantly barrages us.

We humans always seem interested in changing ourselves. From the time of conscious awareness someone has been telling us to change, to improve. We go to school to change and learn. Our religious institutions are forever prompting us to do better. We are admonished to forgive others but rarely reminded to forgive ourselves. Rare is the authority that hasn't held up before us the ideal of perfection. By now we too may be willing carriers of that message. We may be urging change and perfection on others. Certainly in the early moments of the day, when the first light sneaks into our rooms, we are often troubled by some nagging notion of something we have failed to do or be, probably something even deeper. We drag ourselves out of bed gamely to have another shot at it. To make ourselves better today. To change.

As children we naturally aspired to the next step. There is a strong urge toward mastery. It is our spirit prompting us to unfold. What a paradox it is that as adults this natural impulse toward unfolding, generally accompanied by so much joy in childhood, gets perverted into a demanding, self-critical abuser. It often comes disguised, this punishing demon, as the helper, the encourager. But it is a fraud. It is not a friend. It seeks not joyous self-expression but the creation and perpetuation of a chronic state of regret. Its mission is to keep us in the delusional belief system that to change, to become better, will make us happier, when its actual motives are to keep us fused with the parental experience of striving to improve in order to achieve parental approval, to be acceptable, to be "good enough."

So we must approach this topic of change very carefully and tenderly. We must begin by questioning the very notion of change. We must start with the dangers involved. We must look at where within us this change is to occur. We must question why we must change at all. Then perhaps we may begin to tease out the factors in ourselves and our lives that may profitably be relinquished. Of course we must maintain loving self-acceptance throughout the whole process or else we are up to something suspect, something other than change.

After all, what is it that we change? It is not who we are. We are who we are, have always been, and will always be, though the forms that our selves take are not always known to us or perhaps even understandable. Still, the self develops many characteristics or character traits in its journey of consciousness. Many of these traits are in the service of fusion, and we may decide to yield some of these as we become stronger and braver and more willing to leave mother to search for the Transcendent.

We speak of changing ourselves or changing others or being instrumental in the changing of others. But what is it that is changed that results in different behavior or affective tone? What about the man who is afraid of making friends with women? He would like very much (he thinks) to marry, settle down, and raise children. But he is terrified of meeting women. He breaks out in a sweat every time he speaks with a woman. He generally avoids such situations, but should he find himself in one, or courageously force himself into such contact, he is a wreck. He tends to rely excessively on alcohol or drugs to calm him down and supply a feeling of confidence. He gravitates to women who challenge him less, but then he finds them less interesting and consequently less suitable for him in the long run. What needs to be changed here?

The locus of the problem lies in the man's deep belief that he is insufficient, not acceptable to a woman with whom he might fall in love and consequently find essential to his existence. Because he cannot satisfy this hypothetical woman (mother?), he believes she surely will abandon him in one way or another. This elicits terror, which is a natural result of another deep belief—that he literally will cease to exist without this woman once she has become so essential to him. The locus, then, is in his beliefs and their attendant terrors, which lie in the self. Compensatory and defensive behaviors are encouraged by the demonic motivation that has as its underlying purpose the maintenance of fusion with mother. His spirit is neutralized and his self is inundated with self-deprecation, which is encouraged by his demons. Thus his poor feeling about himself goes unchallenged, and the problem is reinforced.

Remember, the unique problem we humans have is that we have developed incorrect deep beliefs and affects that close us off from the prompting of our spirits. Consequently, the natural, inevitable unfolding of spirit into person has been blocked. Our ultimate goal will always be to restore ourselves to our natural functioning, to become who we are, our true selves. Our true selves never need to be changed. Just the opposite: our true selves need to be liberated. Even "orthodox" psychoanalysis understood this right from the beginning. Strachey, in a very important article in 1934, states,

> There is, after all, nothing new in regarding a neurosis as essentially an obstacle or deflecting force in the path of normal development....The final result of psycho-analytic therapy is to enable the neurotic patient's whole mental organization, which is held in check at an infantile stage of development, to continue its progress towards a normal adult state.[1]

So if our friend decides to change and consults a psychotherapist, the first thing that must be done is to attempt to understand what he wants changed and why. Simultaneously, we must begin to help him restore himself to a condition of self-love; to help him understand that he is stuck "in the grip" of something and that this is entirely natural and a very human phenomenon. We need to help him to change his faulty belief system, in which he sees himself as *being* a problem rather than *having* a problem. This will not be an easy task. We humans do not suffer relief from pain lightly. There may actually be an increase of symptomatology in order to maintain the inner atmosphere of pain. Or the opposite could happen. There may be a "flight into health." He may get "all better." This is a sort of chameleon-like defensive strategy designed to get the observer off track. As soon as the observer stops telling him about the nature of reality as he, the observer, sees it, our hero will revert to old ways. Or he may make impossible standards of behavior so that he will always "fail" and consequently remain ensconced in the familiar inner atmosphere of suffering.

In an atmosphere of unrelenting love and acceptance, the therapist keeps observing and communicating these strategies. Little by little the person's deepest belief system is affected. The notion that he must suffer to be loved is relentlessly, albeit gently, challenged. Slowly the familiar affects of fear and the depression are interrupted by puffs of relief, of peace, occasionally by hints of joy. The "problem" is often not so important or has evaporated.

There have been many approaches to change. We have ordered ourselves to change; others have ordered us to change; psychoanalysts have
told us that to have insight will free us to change; Gestaltists have told us
that to fully experience and express our feelings will lead to change; the
cognitive therapists teach us to "think" our way into right living; the bio-
energeticists have promised that a direct attack on the bodily manifestations of our conflicts will set us free. Viktor Frankl's notions of "paradoxical
intention" suggest that the best way to change is to attempt to change
nothing at all; Buddhists, similarly, have advised the loss of self to meditation and the Sensei.

What is it that we change? And how do we do it? Let me share with you
what I have noticed. To begin, I emphasize again the danger in self-attack
and abuse the moment we begin to think of changing anything about
ourselves. If there is something we want to change, or if we are experiencing pain, *we must strive toward compassion toward ourselves as a beginning*.
If we are stuck, we must infuse ourselves with massive doses of self-love.
This is hard because it seems to be our nature to attack ourselves when we
are down. Beliefs that we are supposed to be perfect—as defined originally
by someone or some standard outside ourselves—are unthinkingly made
our own. This, in itself, is often a large part of the problem.

One of the greatest occasions for self-abuse is the belief that we "should"
be able to change things by ourselves and that it is some kind of a character
fault if we cannot. So on top of where we are stuck, we add another layer of
pain and fear. All this is based, of course, on an incorrect notion of the
nature of humans. We are limited. We are flawed. It is natural for us to
make mistakes. It is natural for us to form deep beliefs that at a later point
may cause us difficulty. It is our nature!

So it is important to approach the situation with great care and tenderness. It is also important to remember that, whatever happens, *we* will be
doing the changing. Whether we go it alone (and a great deal can be accomplished this way, as we shall see) or ask the help of a professional
caregiver, we are still the ones who will be doing the changing. It is all up
to us. We may expose ourselves to individuals or groups or circumstances
that maximize our chances for growing out into some behavior, but the
locus of change is in our self. Change occurs when we readjust the balance
between the influence of the demons and that of our spirit. There is a
strong temptation to see the help as coming from someone else and to lose

sight of the reality of who really is in charge at all times. We are. Reaching out for help itself is a profoundly independent act. Ironically, we must be cured, in a sense, before we seek the cure. The job will be completed when we realize this.

To change our self involves shame. It involves the shame that prompts us to believe there may be something intrinsically wrong with us because of our "shameful" behavior or because of the abuse we received at the hands of others when we were dependent persons. We had little choice but to react to that abuse with felt shame. But there is also the other kind of shame, that which ensues from the very experience of our limitedness, the kind of ontological or existential shame that abuts our faulted lives. To aspire to change reminds us of this and reinforces this shame.

For all the reasons we have discussed so far, we know there is an enormously strong tendency to remain fused. And despite the complaints we may have about our childhood, there is a realness about that time of our life that never gets fully transcended, an inevitability, as well. We could do precious little about most things regardless of our frustration or determination. We learned that this is the way the world works, and we learned this over a very long time, hundreds of psychological years. Things were the way they were, and there was no changing them (though we could try), and there was no escaping either. Perhaps there was a certain comfort in this inevitability and predictability.

The concepts of freedom, creating our own environment, and leaving a self-destructive situation were unknown to us and, in a sense, still are. We have few prototypes for such behavior. This is why change is so difficult for us. On the deepest, perhaps "cellular" level, we do not believe change is possible. It is like discussing psychological separation with a toddler or computers with an aborigine. At our core, change and psychological separation go against our deepest beliefs and experiences. Yet our spirit challenges us to try. This dilemma I believe has been the theme of the earliest human literature: *How can we transcend our psychological fusion when we have deep beliefs that doing so is impossible?* We have conjured up all sorts of gods and theologies to help us manage this, because we know deep inside that not transcending it is death in life and an unspeakable grief.

To change is to return to our natures and Nature, God, the Tao, the Transcendent, what is. It takes place in a deep, often unconscious part of ourselves, and it is not the result of our throwing our egoistic wills at a problem. It is more like surrender, abandoning the ego-fusion motivated patterns of thought and feeling and belief that have kept us isolated from our spirits and what is.

If I had to select one word to describe my vocation, I would choose *teacher*. Every aspect of my work—therapy, supervising, writing—is pedagogy of one sort or another. The word *doctor* actually means teacher, but not a teacher in the sense of imparting to or demanding of the pupil. Rather, as in all good education, the teacher searches for ways to help the pupil get in touch with his or her innate tendency toward growth. In medicine it is said, "The doctor treats but nature (God) heals." As I became aware over the years that psychotherapy tended to be much too intellectual (the mind being the reflexive agent of our hubris), I paid attention to the ways others taught in other disciplines.

I watched Pablo Casals teach his master class on television on Saturday mornings, and I read about Benjamin Harkevy, the great teacher of the Philadelphia Ballet. More recently I came across F. M. Alexander's technique for postural realignment. Before I read anything about him or by him I took lessons with Betsy Gaw, a gentle teacher who helped to excavate my top-heavy ego-laden head from between my shoulders and taught me to move it forward and up, delicately. After my session with her I wrote this note:

> Yesterday I had my first Alexander session with Betsy Gaw. She is a kind and related and competent lady who gave me a very good session. As I lay on the table and she was doing her stuff I kept on thinking about intention and acceptance. She gave me the instruction to let myself be aware of my inner processes at the same time as I listened to her. I thought that this in itself was an acknowledgment of reality because this is the way it is; there is always an inner process paralleling our awareness or responsiveness to that which is around us. I was in an interesting state in which I hovered between sleep, awareness of the relationship between intention and psychological change and responsiveness to her directions which were, basically, to be aware of body and to "intend" to have the body move in the direction it naturally inclines toward, not by forcing it by direct action or will, but merely by intention. It was a marvelous experience and I was excited because it felt I had bumped into something important for my growth, both personally and in my work.
>
> Parenthetically, although I was in a very emotional state that day, at the end of the session I was relieved of any concern save that which was hap-

pening at that moment; I was fully absorbed in the present activity, a wonderful activity. As I type this I have the thought that it would be wonderful to have Betsy observe me typing and help me do it right. I have been much more aware of my head and also, even as I type, aware of wanting to do everything "as nature intends."

The Alexander technique is the most gentle and delicate of procedures. As I received the teaching, I knew that this was what I was trying to do in psychotherapy. There is such great respect for the person. The person is never admonished to do anything, merely to stop doing certain things. There is great trust in the innate sense of the human organism to right itself; upon study of physical and mental habits, it is gently suggested that the person say "no" to these faulty habits. Faulty habits are not defined arbitrarily by the teacher but rather by what works for the organism and what does not. It is a remarkably healing experience.

In *The Use of the Self* Alexander explains certain principles of his approach. Using as an illustration a teacher trying to help a person improve his golf game by keeping his eye on the ball when preparing to swing, he reveals the mistakes we make in trying to change:

> To the question why he continues to take his eyes off the ball, in spite of his intention to follow his teacher's instructions and in spite of his "will to do," the answer is that in everything he does he is a confirmed "end-gainer." His habit is to work directly for his ends on the "trial and error" plan without giving due consideration to the means whereby those ends should be gained. In the present instance there can be no doubt that the particular end he has in view is to make a good stroke, which means that the moment he begins to play he starts to work for that end directly, without considering what manner of use of his mechanism generally would be the best for the making of a good stroke. The result is that he makes the stroke according to his habitual use, and as this habitual use is misdirected and includes the wrong use of his eyes, he takes his eyes off the ball and makes a bad stroke. It is clear that as long as he is dominated by his habit of end-gaining, he will react to the stimulus to "make a good stroke" by the same misdirected use of himself, and will continue to take his eyes off the ball.[2]

"End-gaining" is, of course, what we have been speaking of when I urged caution about setting goals and suggested tentativeness in forming intentions to change. On the bodily level, Alexander discovered what the "paradoxical intentionists" knew and I always intuitively appreciated—that the best change often occurs when we decide to change nothing at all. Alexander points out that the moment we have an end result in mind, a whole set of psycho-physiological expectancies are activated. We love these reactions because they seem "right" and "familiar" to us. This is why change of any kind is so difficult.

> On the other hand, the use of his mechanisms which would involve his keeping his eyes on the ball during the act of making a stroke would be a use entirely contrary to his habitual use and associated with sensory experiences which, being unfamiliar, would "feel wrong" to him; it may therefore be said that he receives no sensory stimulus in that direction. Any sensory stimulus he receives is in the direction of recreating the familiar sensory experiences which accompany his faulty use, and this carries the day over any so-called "mental" stimulus arising from his "will to do." In other words, the lure of the familiar proves too strong for him and keeps him tied down to the "habitual" use of himself which "feels right."[3]

One night in my therapy group, Buddy was speaking of his fear that a project he has been working on for fifteen months would be found wanting, that he would not receive a promotion, and that his career would be permanently thwarted. This would be due, in his obsessive view, to the length of time he took preparing this project, some factors he inevitably missed, plus the "fact" that he made a mistake in staying in this position when he was offered a lateral move two years ago. The individual who moved into that slot has progressed better than he has, and Buddy is suffering deeply, convinced that he made a stupid mistake.

Tess, another group member, responded to him. She said that he was playing an old tune, that he kept on worrying about doom and gloom when in fact he was doing very well. He must be getting something out of this worry, she suggested. Granted it was painful, but it was also familiar. Buddy concurred—and began to berate himself for his not having been able to change this trait despite years of therapy. He pointed out that his father always found something wrong with his performance. If he achieved a grade of 95 percent, his father would demand 100 percent. His father always had his eye on what was lacking. Buddy was correct in his historical understanding. Tess was also right in her observation that this was a familiar theme and a familiar affect. But how to change it? "No matter how I try, I can't seem to make this better," Buddy anguished.

To get back to our analogy with the Alexander method. Buddy's suffering is a good example of the individual's desire to *feel right* in gaining his end. Buddy was not really aspiring to end his suffering. He was aspiring to have his report praised, to get a raise, a promotion, and so on. If pressed on the issue of suffering, he would reply that these accomplishments would make him feel better. This, of course, is not the case. None of his other many accomplishments had such a happy outcome.

Buddy is an end-gainer and, as such, wanted to accomplish his ends while feeling his old familiar feelings. He needs to be helped to focus on what Alexander calls the "means-whereby," the activities that lead up to an outcome, whatever that outcome might be. Twelve Step programs refer to this as taking the right action and detaching from the outcome.

In operating this way there will be some discomfort, because it is unfamiliar. It is at this point that the battle is joined. The tendency is to employ "will power," an old familiar strategy that is bound to lead us to failure and its attendant regret, the familiar chronic affect of the "bad child." Will power, as Alexander points out, is the use of himself that is misdirected. So what does Buddy do? Tess has made an astute observation. And Greg, another group member, has told him he is wonderful and successful and that he should know it. (Buddy loved that, by the way, because it enabled him to get into a symphony of "yes-buts," by which he could drag out infinite data regarding his horribleness.) Buddy himself was capable of analyzing his behavior until the cows came home and engaging in a little parent bashing at the same time, which enabled him to bathe in his old, familiar victim affect. Ah, the good old days.

Just as Alexander instructs his students to say no to the misdirected but familiar physical movements that make it impossible to get the desired end results, I told the group members that they must say no to any self-critical statement they make about themselves at any time. They must be vigilant about this. There is no reason that they, I suggested, should *ever* abusively criticize themselves for *anything*. Evaluate their behavior objectively? Sure. Regret a behavior, even feel remorse or sadness about something they have done? Perhaps. But never hostile criticism. If they don't like something they have done, they are to have compassion for themselves. When they notice that the objective evaluation of their behavior is tinged with criticism instead of compassion, they are to say an adamant "No!" Then they are to say, "I love you, (Buddy, Tess, or Greg)."

The group was stunned. You would have thought I had instructed them to do something outrageous, like stripping naked and walking outside. But perhaps that is what I did. I instructed them to strip themselves of their old, familiar ways of dealing with themselves, to say no to these ways, and to replace them with a statement of unconditional self-love.

Let's round out our analogy with Alexander. Basic to his theory is the notion that the relationship between the head and the body is the primary controlling factor in improving the performance of a movement, task, or activity. Primary means (1) *most important* and (2) *the first in the sequence of events*. Alexander believes that as he helps a student say no to the faulty ways he holds his shoulders and neck, the head will naturally be released. I allow my neck to be free in such a manner that I *delicately* move my head forward and up and allow my *whole* body to follow. From this primary principle, the entire organism, as one unit, begins to function properly. Automatically, without awareness, our golfer would keep his eyes on the ball and his stroke would improve.

What is the *primary* factor in psychotherapy, the most important, the first in the sequence of events? *Radical self-acceptance!* No one ever changed anything while in the midst of self-hate and self-abuse. This is why there has been so much unsuccessful psychotherapy. This is why shame has been ignored as psychologist Helen Lewis has taught us and you shall see in the next chapter. As she listened to the psychotherapy tapes for her research, she heard *in vivo* the development of rage and shame in the very setting dedicated to the release of suffering. "Successful" cases came unglued and patients returned armed now with psychoanalytic jargon with which to abuse themselves.

The other day a patient of mine complained that she was seeing spots before her eyes and was worried that there was something seriously wrong. This is a woman who has made wonderful changes in her life, but each time she gets rid of one seemingly impossible situation she develops another to replace it. I asked her if she had consulted a physician (I had heard of these spots before, incidentally, in another quiescent moment), and she replied that she had not, that she was afraid lest she discover she had a brain tumor. After a pause she began once again obsessing about the spots, how if she had a brain tumor it would ruin her life, all would be for naught, and so forth. I replied that she should check it out with a physician and that until she did it was pointless to talk about it. She lapsed into silence and after a few minutes told me that if she couldn't talk about what she wanted to, she might just as well leave; she had no more to say. Upon encouragement from me she told me that what I said is what everyone says to her, and it makes her feel like a real jerk. I was just like everybody else, and if she were able to go to the doctor's easily she wouldn't be coming to see me. She wasn't enraged and out of control, as she had been in the past. I realized that I had shamed her, and I told her that. We spoke of her shame and what she tends to do with it, and after we had explored that I apologized to her. In my impatience I had lost sight of the importance of helping her say no to her own self-criticism. In this instance I had compounded the problem.

In psychotherapy the primary controlling factor is radical self-acceptance. To try to help a patient rid herself of a behavior that she feels terrible about, without first ridding her of shame and guilt and helping her learn to say no to the knee-jerk, self-abusive but *familiar* ways of dealing with herself, is bound to fail and unnecessarily extends treatment. It can even lead to a therapeutic *folie á deux* in which the faulty pattern of behavior is repeated in the therapy endlessly and without analysis. But what I am encouraging takes a long time as well. We are fighting against hundreds of years of faulty beliefs and affects, which are held to tenaciously because they are *familiar*. To do something different doesn't feel "right." There is enormous inertia. We are struggling against an infinity of influences and loves and loyalties and fusions. It is miraculous that we change at all. Certainly any movement toward the reclamation of the true self must be accompanied at the beginning and always by radical self-acceptance or it is doomed, and we are doomed to remain fused with our caretakers and miss our only opportunity to be truly with ourselves.

Maureen, the woman I just described, had a bout of insomnia several months ago. At the time nothing seemed to help her; she would miss days of sleep at a time. She was growing increasingly desperate. One morning she called early and left a message that I had better do something, perhaps suggest a doctor who could *really* help her. After an initial irritation I realized that she needed me to reassure her that I would be with her and that she was feeling very frightened and lonely during the night. I mentioned this in a supervisory seminar that I led and one of the students commented that perhaps Maureen needed the assurance that I would help her over this difficult time. She suggested I should indicate to Maureen that while I couldn't actually solve the problem for her directly, I would be there for her and would do my best to help her. I wouldn't abandon her no matter what.

I told Maureen this when I saw her. I made some suggestions about how to spend the time should she awake. I told her to write me a letter, that I would be thinking about her and trying to come up with better advice, that I would be looking forward to hearing from her in the morning each day, if necessary, until this was resolved. She was reassured and calm. "It's amazing how little sleep a person can get along on," she commented. She then informed me that her mother was a "fanatic" about sleep. Mother was always terrified lest she not get enough rest herself and not be able to function well the next day. Yet when Maureen had difficulty sleeping on occasion as a child, her mother would sit her up on the couch with some warm milk and a stack of books, and she herself would go to sleep. I pointed out how abandoned she must have felt, but that now she was a grown-up and could survive the hours after her fiancé had gone to sleep until she could call me in the morning.

The following session resulted in no improvement, but I continued the same tack. She spoke of being measured for her wedding dress. I commented that it was sad that her mother, who lived on the West Coast and was somewhat estranged from her, couldn't be involved. She insisted that her mother wouldn't be interested. I suggested that she might not be quite accurate about that and that perhaps her sleep deprivation was in part a function of her longing for her mother to be with her at this trying time. I suggested that she call her mother and have a conversation with her about having trouble sleeping and also about the wedding, the dress, and all the arrangements. She was skeptical, but the next time I saw her she reported that she had called. The conversation was "nice" and, amazingly, the sleep problem had completely disappeared. "I'm amazed," she said. "You cured me."

In the midst of her panic about her insomnia Maureen asked if she could increase her hours with me from one to two per week. I had resisted this request previously because she had been doing well once a week; a change in the structure of the therapy is significant and something I do not do lightly. Frequency of contact with a patient, I have found, is an important variable and needs to be watched carefully, particularly in the beginning of treatment. People differ in their capacity to deal with the intensity of relatedness that psychotherapy makes possible. Some need a great deal. Some do better with little, at least initially. The factor here is not merely the fear of intimacy a person may have or suspiciousness or whatever, but also the extent to which the person is able to tolerate the change in comfort level, what feels "right."

But the analytic work that Maureen and I were doing around the sleep issue and its relationship to her mother's attitude toward sleep, as well as her mother's perceived abandonment of her when she was unable to sleep as a child, prompted me to agree to the increase in contact. It was as if Maureen were "allowing" more contact. It went very well. But changes in the frequency are always laden with therapeutic traps, and one day she told me that twice a week was too much for her and she would like to return to once a week. Too quickly I agreed, and we decided to return to one session the following week. When she saw me next, after going back to the old schedule, she was silent. Upon prompting she told me that she was convinced that I hated her and that I didn't want to see her at all and that she was a royal pain in the neck to me. She interpreted my acquiescence in the reduction of hours as a rejection and an abandonment. I agreed with her that I was insensitive and told her that I really did want to see her twice a week. She was visibly relieved and the next two weeks were very productive. This was the period in which she contacted her mother and experienced the instantaneous and complete removal of the symptom. Two weeks later she again asked to reduce the frequency of contact. "I don't feel comfortable coming this often." Learning from my previous mistake, I told her that I thought we were doing well at this rate and that I would like to explore with her what was going on inside that prompted her to want to reduce the number of times we met. Just what was it that she was uncomfortable about?

She said that she didn't know, but that we had been doing fine before, that she liked the pace, that this was no longer an emergency. I told her I found it interesting that she would allow herself more contact with me in an "emergency" but not merely to make her life better and possibly get the job done quicker. She was "comfortable" in getting the help she needed if she was in crisis but not comfortable in getting help to thrive! We then had an excellent session in which she reported material to me that she never had in the past. "Is it necessary to 'dwell' on all these painful memories?" she asked. I replied that it was if she were truly to get well and be happy. Besides, she was "dwelling" on them all the time anyway, but when it was chronic pain and not acute suffering she not only could tolerate it but was actually more comfortable. The two things she couldn't abide were excruciating pain *or* feeling better!

In the course of that session Maureen described to me some of the most painful experiences I have ever heard. Her life had been riddled with suffering. This is what she knew. This is what she was "comfortable" with; this is what "felt right" to her. As she began to return to her self, it didn't feel right to her. She was prepared for an accommodation, but not to fly. And this is why change is so hard. Maureen, at least, had put herself in a situation in which she, with my help, could observe herself and her life, the consequence of all the decisions she had made in her life in order to save it. Shouldn't one celebrate oneself for that?

What we have going against us is so enormous that it is tempting to wonder whether change is possible at all. When we consider the world about us and how little we, as a species, have changed from biblical times, for example, it makes one wonder. Today we are fighting wars, just as we have throughout our history. It is our nature, many cry. That is the way it is. Are we "fixed" by genetics and perhaps early infant experiences, perhaps even in the womb? Can we go from "deficient" to "normal"? Can we go from "normal" to "better"? Can we go from "better" to "transcendent"? Can the average person become "enlightened"? Are we "destined" due to biology and previous psychological events? Are all the psychoanalysts and spiritualists deluded? Are all these aspirations mere illusions, just balm to salve another narcissistic wound? Sometimes it looks that way.

Along these lines is the age-old question of whether humankind is essentially good or evil. Right from the beginning we seem to have assumed that human beings are intrinsically evil. In the Christian tradition, we must have a savior in order to be or do good. I think the question itself is an indication of the "spot" we poor humans are in. The concepts of good and evil could only be created by humans because of the uniqueness of our consciousness. The categories of good and evil are man-made ones; evaluations started with us (although we often project them onto God). Animals and all other living things have no such concepts; they just do what they do, what is natural for them to do. When we ask if we are good or evil, this is, in a sense, a trick question. The categories in themselves are artificial, not natural. We created them to exercise our capacity for evaluation.

A better way of posing the question, it seems to me, is to ask to what extent what we do is *natural*, or necessary to maintain survival. This is complicated for us because of consciousness and because of the *awareness* of danger and consequent fear. This fear leads to all sorts of behavior, some of which may be labeled evil. The fear itself is not unnatural, but our consciousness leads us to strategies, many of them incorrect or distorted, and consequently to behavior unnecessarily destructive to others or self. So evil is a possibility, but it is not our nature. Similarly with love. The same consciousness and capacity for evaluation and judgment lead to identification with and empathy for others. There has evolved what appears to be a distinctly human characteristic, love. We can love, and we can be afraid, and finally we can choose. We are, then, neither good nor evil. We are persons with consciousness, and consequently the capacity for fear, error, love, and choice.

One of the reasons change does not seem possible is because of our experience with how hard it is to accomplish. Change is so very hard for two reasons. The first is the depth of fusion. The second is that we have been going about change in the wrong way. When we are in the "grip" of something, there are several layers of psychic events involved. The first layer includes those things we are immediately conscious of. "Below" that are those things that are not immediately conscious but can readily be summoned into consciousness. Third, there are those things that are deeply embedded in our "unconscious" and that are hard to access either because they got there so long ago that they may not be expressible in verbal language or because there are active mechanisms in our mind that serve to keep these "dangerous" ideas and emotions out of awareness. It is in these three layers that we typically work to effect change.

What is not generally realized, both within and outside of my profession, is that there are many other "lines of music," as I like to think of them, deeper than those I just described. Even further below is the life and death struggle that goes on between spirit, trying to get breath and move forward, and the demons that have the self in their grip. This battle is deep and continuous. It involves all the systems of the organism: biological, muscular, emotional, hormonal, vegetative—many nonverbal. The conscious, intellectual, ethical, and moral activities of the higher level are often no match for it. Sometimes the best we can do is simply experience the struggle—do nothing, roll with the punches, sometimes give in. But spirit will always prevail if we persevere. The awareness of this is what people call faith.

A patient's body was compromised throughout her struggle to return to herself. She was struggling with candida during her treatment. She also told me that she had stopped growing at twelve or thirteen. As the therapy progressed she reported that growth returned. Her hips were broadening; her breasts started to grow.

> I'm walking differently, I can sing, my eyes are improving, my nose is clearing. The muscles in my face were all rigid and now they are relaxing. My feet were deformed and now they are improving…as each symptom disappears, I'm remembering when it first started.

I once asked her if she believed the candida was a result of depression or if the depression was the result of her chronic physical problems.

> I've been thinking about that a lot.…I think that very early it was important psychologically. When I was very small I somehow sensed that being totally healthy in my family was just not going to work.…That sounds terrible, I know…*but I could not have grown up healthy in my home.*…It's like Sleeping Beauty…it's connected to the depression…the constant interaction. This stuff began to break down after my mother died.…I'm having a delayed puberty.…The whole way we lived is a function of depression.

How do we fight such influences? Psychoanalysis suggests insight; nondirective therapists suggest unconditional positive regard. All forget we are working against hundreds of psychological years of conditioning and the creation of deeply embedded "core" beliefs. Will one, two, or three hours a week of psychotherapy modify these influences and loose the spirit?

Change has been difficult for us, particularly in Western cultures, because of the failure to appreciate the depth and complexity of the human psyche and spirit. The classical Freudian model of the structure of personality, id, ego, and superego, as far-reaching as it is, still envisions an inner life much more shallow than it truly is. This was because of the scientific *zeitgeist* and the love affair we were having with the human mind and its presumed capabilities. In its "cultural revolution," psychoanalysis willy-nilly cast off the life-and-death struggle between spirit and demons in an attempt to make the complexity of the psyche, as it was emerging through the brilliant technology of free association, manageable for examination and study. We *had* to understand; we *had* to control; we *had* to have a conscious, self-directed technique of eliciting change.

But that is not how we work. We work the way all animals work, the way the trees work, the way all living matter works. We make the understandable mistake of assuming we work differently because our minds are capable of doing some things much better than the animals and the trees. But this is a big mistake. The human mind is as much a trap and a snare as it is a worker of miracles. It is getting this total awareness of mind into focus that is our task.

It is our mind, our consciousness, and the other two factors we have spoken about—a long childhood and flawed caretakers—that have resulted in the deep, primordial, unconscious struggle that each of us is engaged in, that is, between the demons of fusion and the push toward the Transcendent by the spirit. This is where the salient struggle goes on, not on the upper strata of the more superficial characteristics of the person, such as consciousness and conceptualization. The crucial thing is not merely to understand, to master, to effect change, but rather to find ways to help our total person get aligned with that which transcends, not our humanness, but our ego. Intellectual understanding and some of the other techniques or procedures may indeed be helpful, but without an appreciation of where the battle is actually joined and what the proper goal of psychotherapeutic mediation should be, it is as much a danger as a panacea, as much a troublemaker as a healer.

Yes, there is enormous resistance to change. When people approach separating from their chronic selves, when they consider surrendering that which they know and are *familiar* with, there is panic and the tendency to trip oneself up so as to return to the known. I refer to this as the "call back." As soon as we change, we experience a call back into our old ways. This is a crucial moment and one that requires vigilance. Just as a person running a marathon often comes up against a wall of resistance at about the twentieth mile, so too, in an ongoing serious encounter between therapist and patient, there is often a final barrier that seems impossible to surmount. The wall can take the form of physical illness, accident, severe acting out, or frequently, a premature ending of therapy. Sometimes people have to "fall apart" before they can put themselves back together in a better way for themselves. (I prefer to think of this as a breakthrough rather than a breakdown.) Yet the movement into the new is not entirely unknown. There have been happy glimpses of it throughout life; otherwise it probably would be impossible even to aspire to. But the lure of the chronic self is always lurking about.

The therapist too has to hold a steady course at this point. In fact, any time therapists make deep, meaningful observations (mutative interpretations, as Strachey calls them), they must open themselves to their inner demons.

> All of this strongly suggests that the giving of a mutative interpretation is a crucial act for the analyst as well as for the patient, and that he is exposing himself to some great danger in doing so. And this in turn will become intelligible when we reflect that at the moment of interpretation the analyst is in fact deliberately evoking a quantity of the patient's id-energy while it is alive and actual and unambiguous and aimed directly at himself. Such a

moment must above all others put to the test his relations with his own unconscious impulses.[4]

Both therapist and patient have the same problem. Each is assuming that he truly lives in those three strata of mental functioning that I described above. But each is really comprised of more layers of psychic functioning; each is using or not using these many other strata to gain or detriment, with some awareness of this or not. It is similar to the nature of reality itself. We assume that reality is comprised of those layers that we happen to notice. Some of us seem to notice more of reality than others do. But the most aware of us are still noticing only a small part of what reality is. There are infinite layers (see Figure 6–1).

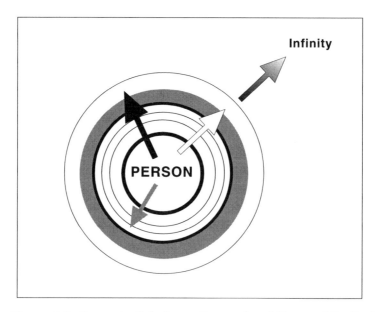

Figure 6–1: Person in Relation to Internal and External Reality.[5]

We operate within the first few concentric circles. We consider those events that we don't understand to be miracles. They are actually events of a further realm of reality we serendipitously bump into. Since our personality is just another instance of infinite reality, we are incapable of understanding, with our flawed and limited consciousness, much of what happens within us. This is disappointing to those who feel they must know everything or see themselves as knowing everything or those who must control everything. The good news is that when we get out of our own way, everything works just fine, as does the universe. The difficulties in our functioning are man-made. Our difficulties in changing are man-made, as well. Change is nothing more than our *stopping* doing those things that keep us from functioning on nature's agenda. When that is done, we get back on track and great things happen.

After a period of experiencing and expressing the despair that underlined her compulsive cheerfulness, a patient began to experience promptings from deep within her. She told me, "There is a woman inside myself that I didn't know was there....She is standing up for herself....She is speaking to people in a way I didn't know was possible." She was excited. Other times she is frightened because this person inside her that is surfacing is threatening to the deep belief system that she has lived with all of her life. She is realizing that she can take care of herself and live life on the promptings of her spirit. She no longer needs to pay keen attention to what others want of her so that she will be loved and will not die.

When change occurs in psychotherapy it is because patient and therapist have touched each other in a place that emanates from deep within each one. Both must change and both must have the courage to let this change happen without fully understanding how it comes about. Change *is* possible. Growing out into our selves is an exciting adventure. But it does not involve force or mechanically shuffling things about. It mostly involves surrender, a yielding of ego and mother-fusion to make room for the life-affirming spirit to arise from the ashes within. Will power has nothing to do with it, save our physically getting ourselves to the places where our spirit has a chance. Will power is directed at behavior, and there is always a much stronger internal and unconscious imperative working against that. Besides, will power is always in the service of ego, and ego, alluring as it is, cannot bring us to our selves. Even in an instance where will power results in change of a behavior, I suspect there is actually something else going on at a much deeper level. Spirit is being tapped, or else the change is accomplished at an enormous price in repression and truncation of spirit.

Change, actually, should be easy, joyous, and gentle, accompanied by sweetness and peace. Change begins with the intention to accept ourselves fully, to realize the enormity of the resistance to our becoming fully ourselves. It involves, in addition, a humble beginning of reliance on a Transcendent, which gently births our shaky, separated self. As far as I can determine, there are no one-to-one interventions that lead directly to change, though sometimes a particular interpretation or intervention may help a person ease over the line into a new way of being. More typically, there are parameters of behavior that set the context in which a person has a better chance of getting on the Wisdom path.

As I mentioned at the beginning of this chapter, I can look over my life and the lives of those I know and those I have worked with, and I can study the theories and techniques developed by those attempting to find remedies for our pain, and the same three general characteristics seem to help change along:

- Intention
- Observation
- Radical self-acceptance

These are the "guts" of all approaches to change. We can employ these concepts immediately and easily to improve our life.

But first I want to speak of spirituality and its relation to change. Psychology was snatched from philosophy, which in turn snatched it from our first attempts to understand our behavior: religion and spirituality. It is time to remedy this artificial breach, one prompted by the hubris of the scientists and made easy to sustain by the tragic faults of some religionists.

Chapter 7

Spirituality and Psychology

℘ℭ

In a therapy group a number of years ago, this conversation occurred:

Patient 1: I find a part of myself that's transcendental; no matter what else my mind or body does, I have a sense of a place inside of me that transcends those things, a very private and secret place that no one knows of but me and no matter how bad things have been for me I never lose awareness of this place.

Therapist: That's your spirit—sometimes we call it self but that doesn't capture the transcendental nature of it. It is the part of you that lives; it needs a body to support its consciousness but it is *you*—an entity beyond your body, though, hopefully, best friends with it....But there is nothing mysterious about it...it's just what we humans are about...our job in evolution.

Patient 2: My anger is my spirit. I haven't found a way to make things better for myself yet but I know I must hang onto my anger right now....It lets me know that a part of me is being abused. I must not lose sight of that.

Therapist: Wow!

Hard as I tried over the past thirty years to be a "good" psychoanalyst and to conform my spiritual bent to the political correctness of the psychoanalytic community, the spirit—mine and others', friends' and lovers' and children's and patients' and students' and literary characters'—continually

105

broke through my scientific stance and increasingly became a force to be reckoned with, indeed, one of the most powerful forces to be reckoned with. Spirituality, once derisively dismissed, gradually insinuated itself into my consciousness and, happily, into the consciousness of other psychotherapists. A lengthy article in the *New York Times* (September 10, 1991), "Therapists See Religion as Aid, Not Illusion," could never have appeared twenty years ago. Daniel Goleman writes: "Growing numbers of psychologists are finding religion, if not in their personal lives, at least in their data. What was once at best an unfashionable topic in psychology has been born again as a respectable focus for scientific research." He cites a review of scientific studies written by Dr. David Wulff, a psychologist at Wheaton College:

> People with the intrinsic orientation (as opposed to an extrinsic, what's-in-it-for-me attitude toward religious beliefs) tended to have a positive view of human nature and to have a greater sense of control over the course of their lives and a strong sense of purpose in life. In addition they showed greater empathy and less narcissism and depression.

Paradoxically, atheists and agnostics also have better mental health than those with the extrinsic orientation, studies have found. The reason seems to be that, although they are nonbelievers, such people "see through the social conformity and superstitious rituals of organized religion, but often have a spirituality of another kind, based on their own quest for truth and meaning," said Dr. Bergin, a psychologist at Brigham Young University.

What to make of all of this? Religion can be helpful to our mental health? Atheists and agnostics can be spiritual? All this is very confusing. And it is made more complicated because we all have deep beliefs on this subject. Every human has a point of view regarding religion and regarding the Transcendent. It is our nature to have to engage the latter. And the former has been, over the centuries, the repository of the ways that men and women have coped with their spirits. Another problem is the confusion between religion and spirituality. Many equate the two, and if they have rejected religion, they automatically reject any concept of spirituality. But spirituality is not religion. Many very spiritual persons have no religious affiliation. Religion is but one of the many ways that a person may choose to express spirituality. But it is not spirituality. As we all know, many folks involved with religion are far from spiritual.

What *is* spirituality? When I was growing up I considered spirituality to have something to do with the sacred. Even as a child there was a part of me that felt whole when I attempted to bring myself in concordance with what I was told was God. Although God was referred to in song from time to time as *magnum mysterium*, there appeared to be no mystery regarding him in the minds of my teachers. They taught me chapter and verse and demanded that I give them back their version of this great mystery. I respected them. I thought they knew. They were adults and they wore special garb, a sure sign to me, this curious youth, that they were specially anointed as guardians of the truth.

Yet, in the midst of all of this I had grave doubts. Hard as I tried I could not miss the inconsistencies, the hypocrisy, the frequent lack of charity both material and interpersonal. I often was tempted to reject the whole enterprise. I was making the mistake of confusing the behavior of religious people with spirituality. At the same time, something in me longed for a meaning that transcended what I observed about life and the dramatic but often "thin soup" of dogma empowered by liturgy. I knew there was a power greater than myself, and I longed to commune in some way with it, yet I was often repelled by those who claimed to be agents of this power. I was tempted by rationality, but that always failed me, too. The matter of ethics confused me still again. I knew that the teachers were often unethical—lost souls as I now would understand them to be—yet they did present explicit guidelines of proper behavior. The scriptures cited were quite specific about this. Behavior was mandated by the decalogue. It was years later that I heard of the beatitudes and emphasizing spiritual development rather than mechanically forcing ourselves to fit into externally prescribed codes of conduct. Yet, at this very time I was having experiences of worship and awe that filled me with loving feelings and prompted me to "do good" and love my neighbor. My personal problems and limitations often rushed in and dashed such moments, but they were real and I believed in them. I just didn't know how to make them more central in my life. Organized religion increasingly failed to help me, but I saw no other alternative.

I had a wonderful experience the first semester of graduate school. I had studied in parochial schools and had just graduated from a fine Catholic liberal arts college with degrees in philosophy and psychology. Theology was mandated throughout. The ins and outs of dogma, scripture, theology, and ethics were debated and obsessed over. It was really quite wonderful.

When I arrived at New York University I experienced major culture shock, even though I had lived in New York all of my life. I was one of two Christians in my class in clinical psychology. I was the only Catholic. I sometimes think this was why I was accepted into the program. Perhaps they needed an Irish Catholic for the sake of balance. It may have been an early instance of "affirmative action"! In any event, I was in the program and there was a course in philosophy of science I was required to take. "Philosopher" that I was, I thought it would be a breeze. It was taught by an experimental psychologist who had published a well-known and widely used textbook in introductory psychology. The class was held in a large hall and there was a large register. Was I in for a big surprise! This hard-nosed scientist turned out to be a poet in the way he spoke of science and the natural order; the world came to be such a work of beauty and purpose. Studying the vast and complex interactions among all living things kept me spellbound the whole semester. It was truly a spiritual experience.

One day the question of science and politics came up. Did the scientist have a responsibility to speak out on the issues of the day? This was the 1960s, and New York University was alive with political activity. Coming from a somewhat conservative background, I remember being a little offended at the use of mimeo machines and the like for partisan political purposes. I rebelled at the uniformity of opinion about everything. Imagine me, offended at regimentation of thought, having come from sixteen years of orthodox Catholic Christianity. This day the professor told a story. He was active in Democratic politics. He lived in Brooklyn and, as a member of a political club, he would campaign on street corners for his candidates. Then he said a most remarkable thing. He told the class that he never mentioned, during his plugs for his candidates, that he was a professor. "I live in a densely Jewish neighborhood where education and scholarship are highly valued. If I told them I was a professor, they might vote for my candidate because I said so and not because I had persuaded them of the correctness of my point of view. That would be unethical." I nearly fell off my chair. In all of my twenty-two years I had never heard a more spiritual or a more ethical statement. And here I was, sitting among all these long-haired, left-wing, avowed atheists and agnostics! I was flabbergasted. What was I to make of this?

It was clearly a spiritual decision that the professor had made. He had made it all by himself, from searching somewhere deep within himself, from his Wisdom place. It was not taught to him from either side of the political spectrum or from any theological body of thought. It involved his own need to express himself, yet it was profoundly conscious of his impact on others. It was service and it was generous and it was kind. I was deeply moved by him. He was clearly a man who had made great progress in psychological separation. Without being aware of it, I was beginning to realize some important things about spirituality and about psychological separation. I was getting my first notions that true spirituality *is* psychological separation.

One need not even think of the Transcendent, as such, to be spiritual. The hallmark of spirituality is the recognition of ego as less than something greater and outside of oneself. Thus my psychology professor was spiritual. He made his own goal—electing an individual who would further the interests that he deemed correct and valuable—subservient to a greater good, a greater principle. He may not have thought of the Transcendent in traditional terms or even as transcendent. Yet his behavior, stemming from humble understanding of his relationship to the universe, was consistent with the greatest of spiritual aspirations. Kindness, tolerance, generosity, fairness, humility, gratitude, tenderness, and sensitivity to himself and others—all these would have been no stranger to him. Although holding himself to high standards, I suspect that he had a profound acceptance of himself as a fallible human being. As a scientist and student of the "handiwork" of the Transcendent, he lived daily with evidence of his limitations.

In this chapter I want to explore this business of spirituality. What is it? Is it necessary? Is it supernatural? What is its relationship to religion? Is religion good or bad? Is prayer helpful or just mystical hocus pocus?

And what is the relationship of all this to psychology? Do psychology and spirituality influence each other? Can't psychology help us all by itself? Can spirituality help us grow in ways that psychotherapy cannot? Can they interact in a positive way? And what about our old nemesis, shame? Psychotherapy seems to have missed the boat when it comes to shame. Can spirituality be of some help here?

Implicit in all of this, of course, lie the old questions. Who are we? How do we function? What is normal and what is not? What is our nature? We must keep our eye on this because all of the confounding questions we have been exploring rest on a clear sense of just who we are and what we are about. Finally, what is the role of spirituality and psychology in helping us psychologically separate to our true selves?

Let's start with religion. When I was a young child there was a woman I would occasionally see when I was at church with my fellow students on Sunday. She would walk up to the altar to receive communion, backward, whip around to take the wafer in her mouth, and walk to the rear of the church, again backward. None of us children ever mentioned this to each other, as I recall. Actually, I was a little afraid. I must have known then, at some level, that if I continued my interest in God and the organization that claimed to represent him, I would, at least on occasion, be in the company of strange folk.

There are a lot of strange folk associated with religion and a lot of strange things have been done in its name. No question about that. But it is heavy-duty stuff it purports to deal with, and when we are dealing with right and wrong and eternity and afterlife and heaven and hell and what you can do sexually, we humans tend to get a little bit flaky. So it is not surprising that so many of us are furious with religion and religionists or effect passionate indifference. There is nothing wrong with this in itself except that in this case the baby that gets ditched with the bath water, at least in the Christian tradition, is the Christ. And the way I understand it, the Christ is that part of the human spirit that can indeed take us to realms of possibility that our "regular" self tends not to bother with.

Another thing is that all the religion-bashing smacks too much of old-fashioned prejudice. If you want to believe that all Jews are cheap and that all Irishmen are drunks, you can certainly find evidence for that position, but having had the ironical good fortune of having had as friends two Irish guys who were the cheapest people imaginable, and two Jewish guys who were the grandest lushes, it is easy for me to see that we are, at the very least, sloppy, and far worse, intolerant, when we judge out of hand.

With all the vices of some of its deacons and with all the faults of any bureaucracy, religion has over the centuries been the vehicle for what I consider to be the deep human need to worship, to receive consolation for shared fear, to show appreciation for life, and, when it is good religion, to receive affirmation that we are good people. There has been no other place for people to have these needs met, and while some consider it anachronistic, we need only go to a good church and see people gathered together reverently to affirm life and draw sustenance from the shared humility and perhaps even a little relief from their shame of not knowing the meaning of it all. In this humility lie the seeds of a certain freedom. With all their "warts," there is a lot of spirituality in many churches, mosques, synagogues, ashrams, and holy places all over this planet, and in the lives of their congregants.

Yet, religion is not spirituality. Some people reject spirituality because they are angry with religion. Some people castigate religion because of their contempt for anything spiritual. Whatever you make of religion, it seems to me that the greatest example of hubris in the twentieth century has been our dismissal of spirituality. Based on a nineteenth-century philosophy of materialism and logical positivism, we asserted that all things would be explained by science in time (a religious belief of the first order), and that human beings are capable of understanding and controlling everything. This philosophical position was harmless enough, but it was often accompanied by an almost semi-totalitarian contempt for those human aspirations that did not fit into this "rational" and "humanistic" mode. Such contempt is based, I believe, on the denial of the reality of our natures and is the newest edition of the narcissism that likes to see us at the center of the universe when all evidence, as we discover it, points to the truth that this is just not so. But our orientation, with its roots in mother-fusion, is deep and yields reluctantly, if at all. *We are still trying to prove to mother just how smart we are.*

Non-religionists run the gamut from the respectful through the indifferent to the antagonistic. The last seems to be comprised of two groups. There are those who have been so hurt or angered by abusive behavior in the name of a particular religion that they have vowed never to have anything to do with it again. Others have the problem of hubris. They will not bow their heads to anything, even life and death. This appears as a heroic stand, but a closer look at the lives of many of these individuals reveals homage to a great many false gods, whether ideologies, people, or addictions. For many, it boils down to ego, a refusal to let go of the source of all "false gods," unresolved fusion with mother. In the struggle between mother and God for these folks, even God loses. Such is the power of mother-fusion.

It helps me, sometimes, to recall that modern science and certainly psychoanalysis are a mere century or so old. It is impossible for humans to have much of a sense of "how it used to be," particularly when how it used to be changes from century to century. This, combined with our tendency toward self-centeredness, gives us a sort of "deepest belief" that our truths, the truths of this moment or this era or this century, are *the* truths. But there was life before psychoanalysis. People figured things out and made good decisions and understood the role of their personal histories and even the unconscious. Read Shakespeare and Augustine. No, go further back. The Bible contains profound truths about human nature and an excellent moral code. We humans had some profound insights about human behavior very early. I sometimes think we have made scant improvement. But go back even further. Buddhist psychology is today one of our most profound, and it was known hundreds of years before Christ. It affirms among other things the reality of the spirit in each of us and the discovery of that spirit in and by the individual. It makes a determined and clear assault on dependency upon others or upon material things. The Tao also provides a cosmology and psychology of self-sufficiency and harmony. In Stephen Mitchell's anthology of sacred literature, the first and earliest entry is from the Upanishads, thought to have been written somewhere between the eighth and fifth century before Christ, roughly paralleling the creation of the Psalms:

> The Golden God, the Self, the immortal Swan
> leaves the small nest of the body, goes where He wants.
> He moves through the realm of dreams; makes numberless
>   forms;
> delights in sex; eats, drinks, laughs with His friends;
> frightens Himself with scenes of heart-chilling terror.
> But he is not attached to anything that He sees;
> And after He has wandered in the realms of dream and
>   awakeness,
> has tasted pleasures and experienced good and evil,
> He returns to the blissful state from which He began.
> As a fish swims forward to one riverbank then the other,
> Self alternates between awakeness and dreaming.
> As an eagle, weary from long flight, folds its wings,
> gliding down to its nest, Self hurries to the realm
> of dreamless sleep, free of desires, fear, pain.
> As a man in sexual union with his beloved
> is unaware of anything outside or inside,
> so a man in union with Self knows nothing, wants nothing,
> has found his heart's fulfillment and is free of sorrow.
> Father disappears, mother disappears, gods
> and scriptures disappear, thief disappears, murderer,
> rich man, beggar disappear, world disappears,
> good and evil disappear; he has passed beyond sorrow.[1]

It has been in religion that the struggle to find meaning and counsel in life was first joined, and for many continues. It is the accumulated wisdom of humankind. Its admonitions to awe and worship and prayer were not merely ways that the current authorities could control the populace, though that was often the perversion of those real human needs. Kindness and tolerance, forgiveness and love, generosity and self-transcendence are, in my judgment, genuine human needs and aspirations. They are our nature, a nature often betrayed by our personal histories, but our nature nonetheless. We are admonished not because it is not our nature to be "good," but rather because we so easily stray from our vocations as humans. Historically, religion has called this to our attention.

In April of 1987 I attended a lecture. The speaker elaborated the special characteristics of a mature person: self-possession, self-communication, self-transcendence. He described such a person as having an ongoing awareness of herself. It was a mark of human dignity that she had freedom of choice. She was aware of her self-determination and took responsibility for her actions, which came inevitably and inexorably out of her sense of self. The speaker further pointed out that every human being has an impulse toward action. "The nature of everything is to communicate itself," he said. To be a person we must communicate ourself to others. He described the person as having a love that is self-diffusing. Finally, he described a sort of vertical self-transcendence, a putting off of self that enables us to be filled with great loving compassion for the world. It is not that we do not love ourselves, but rather that we experience ourselves loving ourselves as part of the whole universe, which is good.

Whose ideas was he teaching? Abraham Maslow's self-actualizing person? Carl Rogers and unconditional positive regard? The speaker was Norris Clarke, S.J., professor emeritus of Fordham University, and he was describing the thought of Thomas Aquinas! Those who sat through innumerable lectures in college on the proofs of the existence of God and the abstract principles of ethics are probably as surprised as I was to find out that St. Thomas was also a sensitive student of personality. And psychological separation as well. The person, he said, is *dominus sui*, master of himself. In an article Fr. Clarke writes:

> In a nutshell, for St. Thomas, to *be* a human person in all the fullness of that term, is to be on a journey. The first two and most central characteristics of personal being, ever in reciprocal interplay with each other, are (1) *self-possession* or self-mastery, through self-awareness and self-determination

and (2) *self-communication* that is at once self-manifestation and self-sharing, the highest form of which is love. The final phase of the journey, if it moves to full completion and does not get stuck in its own finite self-centeredness along the way is (3) *self-transcendence* by which we take on first the good of others, then finally the Great Center of all being as the new center of our own conscious lives of knowing, evaluating and loving. Thus, paradoxically, the last stage of self-transcendence, or self-forgetting, turns out to be the fullest possible degree of self-possession. To be a person, in the fullest sense of the term, is indeed a deep and wondrous mystery. As Heraclitus once said of the soul: "It is so deep that no one can come to the end of it."[2]

From the beginning of time, religion and psychology have been intertwined. One can find this in any tradition. Moses Maimonides was certainly a psychologist, and the tales of Scholom Aleichem are rich with wisdom and psychological insight. From the beginning, all traditions have emphasized the necessity of overcoming narcissism. It has been the great human problem. Clarke mentions a Muslim prayer, "Oh Lord, take away the I that stands between you and me." It seems that from the very beginning we understood in a primary and irreducible way that our tendency toward playing God ourselves would do us in. The consideration of the Transcendent at the same time as we groped to understand how we worked psychologically was not an accident. The fullest understanding of human psychological function involves our attitude toward the Transcendent. It was in the separating of the two that we began to get into trouble, because we wound up playing God ourselves. We are always tempted, we humans, as we advance in knowledge, to yield to the enticement of the Garden of Eden and assume excitedly that we will understand all. But it seems to me that this is beyond us and a dangerous aspiration to boot.

While it is true that we are less efficient, as animal organisms, than are other animals, and capable of more reprehensible acts, which makes us less "godlike" than any other living things, it is also true that we are unique in our ability to reflect on God. I suspect that each of us does this at one time or another, some at great length. This capacity puts us in a peculiar position with respect to God. We *are* God, as the animal and the lily are, but we also must form an opinion about that! Some of us reject the very idea; some effect a jaunting indifference; some religiously insist God does not exist at all; some ignore, some worship, some "work a deal" with God, either to get a good spot in heaven by some behavior here on earth or to try to get some special privilege; some even spend their whole lives paying attention to God to make up for those who seem to ignore God.

My own view is that God is unknowable, not because of any divine characteristic, but because of our inability to think in categories that would make it possible for us to understand something so transcendent. As brilliant as we are, we are stymied here. This seems to be our problem all along the line; we are so brilliant and at the same time so erratic and inconsistent in that brilliance. So we have another one of those painful and challenging human conundrums: We are smart enough to wonder about the Transcendent and yet not smart enough ever to get a satisfactory answer. We often settle for all sorts of superstitions, from the flaky to the scientific.

So here we are. It seems to me that the best we can do under these circumstances is just to notice things—what we are capable of, need to do, our nature, what other living things are doing—and to come to a personal conclusion about the existential issues of whither, whether, and wherefore. For me, there are functions and operations in the universe that are clearly transcendental. I can observe but I cannot fathom. That leaves us with uniquely human things we must deal with, such as the nature of love, psychologically separating and becoming a unique person, compassion, yearning, regret, remorse, revenge, forgiveness, trust, creation, responsibility, good versus evil, social organization, hatred, war and peace, destructiveness, loyalty, beauty, honor, respect, nostalgia, courage, selflessness, resignation, perseverance, masochism, generosity, gratitude, denial, choice, freedom…and so on.

God is our concept of the innate knowledge that identification with the Transcendent is essential to long, healthy, and happy life and survival of the species. *Some form of cooperation with the Transcendent is essential to overcoming narcissism and depends on a highly developed capacity for generosity.*

Many of us are offended by the anthropomorphism with which we speak of God. But what are we to do? We can only speak within our limited capacity to conceptualize and categorize. We must approach that which is essentially unknowable by analogy. There is a real psychological challenge to us here. I believe that one of the evolutionary purposes of religion has been to teach us the necessity of psychological separation and to offer as a solution to this seemingly impossible task the only thing possible, that is, a relationship with the Transcendent.

The scriptures are filled with such a challenge:

For this reason you shall leave mother and father and come follow me.

Hear, O Israel…the Lord thy God is One; thou shalt not have false gods before me.

There is no God but Allah.

It happened that, as Jesus was speaking, a woman in the crowd raised her voice and said, "Blessed the womb that bore you and the breasts that fed you." But Jesus replied, "More blessed still are those who hear the word of God and keep it."

Spiritual writers have used the psychological separation idiom from the very beginning:

> Lord, my mind is not noisy with desires,
>   and my heart has satisfied its longing.
> I do not care about religion
>   or anything that is not you.
> I have soothed and quieted my soul,
>   like a child at its mother's breast.
> My soul is as peaceful as a child
>   sleeping in its mother's arms. (Psalm 131)

Julian of Norwich, a fourteenth-century English mystic, writes:

> A mother's service is
> nearest,
> readiest,
> and surest.
>
> This office
> no one person
> has the ability or knows how to
> or ever will do fully
> but God alone.[3]

Another simple mystic, Brother Lawrence, wrote in the seventeenth century of his search for God:

My most usual method is this simple attentiveness and loving gaze upon God to whom I often feel myself united with greater happiness and satisfaction than that of an infant nursing at his mother's breast; also for the inexpressible sweetness which I taste and experience there. If I dared use this term, I would willingly call this state "the breasts of God." If sometimes by necessity or weakness I am distracted from this thought, I am soon recalled to it by interior emotions so delightful and so entrancing that I am ashamed to speak of them.[4]

How else can we face that final separation from mother? What is powerful enough? Remember, the important thing to keep in mind regarding the human's unique involvement with mother is its intensity, its pervasiveness, its longevity. Scarcely a day goes by that I'm not reminded of it. Gangsters kill to protect mother's honor. Career soldiers cry for mother when trapped or wounded. The elderly call out in the night for her. Hitler carried a picture of his mother in his wallet and would gaze on it lovingly each day. This very morning a friend sent me a clipping from a newspaper in Australia about Nixon and his motivations for both keeping his tapes and then selectively destroying them. After a lengthy discussion of all the political factors involved, the writer concludes:

> It was the missing swear words that caused the fuss. Nixon had directed that every time he or anyone else was recorded swearing, the offending epithet should be replaced by the words, "expletive deleted." The effect was to make hundreds of pages in the Blue Book heavily spotted by this resonant phrase. The public's imagination ran riot. It was universally assumed that the deletions covered up the worst of obscenities.
>
> Even the *New York Times* reflected the national mood of inaccurate sanctimoniousness when it stated in the foreword to its paperback on the tapes, "Shit was the mildest of the deleted expletives." That was untrue. Those who have actually listened to the unexpurgated tapes know that Nixon went in for Sunday-school swearing and precious little else. His deleted expletives overwhelmingly consisted of "goddamn," "hell," "damn," "Christ," "for Chrissake," "what in the name of Christ," "Oh God," and so on. The dirtiest words in the President's vernacular were "crap," "shit," and "asshole." Pornographic swearing by Nixon was nowhere on the tapes. He did not use the familiar locker-room expressions for sexual intercourse, nor any of the four- and six-letter obscenities.
>
> If Nixon's expletives were so mild, why on earth did he remove them from the transcripts? Undeleted they might have caused a negative reaction in the Bible Belt, but that would have been a flea bite in comparison to the mauling he received.
>
> The explanation is that the tapes were censored with Hannah Nixon in mind. The President himself admitted as much to Fred Buzhardt's assistant

Jepp Shepard, who had argued that all those "Gods" and "damns" were innocuous and should be left in. *"If my mother ever heard me use words like that, she would turn over in her grave," Nixon replied.*[5]

The lives and careers of the famous are routinely dashed on the shoals of unseparated fused behavior. What is a match for this?

There are those who contend that loyalty to religion is nothing more than a reinvention of the family and that true believers remain childlike, stuck in their dependency. There are those, on the other hand, who observe miracles of transformation in religious people, changes in behavior that psychotherapy was unable to accomplish. The Twelve Step programs have a strong spiritual (not religious) bent, and anyone familiar with their results cannot help but marvel at the radical transformations in people's lives that no amount of "secular" medicine or psychology was able to come near. And these are not isolated instances. Beneficiaries far outnumber the ranks of patients of more mainstream approaches. Russia has appealed to Alcoholics Anonymous to help stem the tide of its burgeoning addiction problems. The New York City Department of Corrections has pleaded for the formation of such groups in its institutions as the only hope for the rehabilitation of its hard-core offenders. Something is going on.

Sure, there are many "true believers" who use religious tenets and organizations to insulate their spirits from growth and even to manipulate others. Religion, as any bureaucracy, gets corrupt. So do the Boy Scouts, the Democratic Party, Greenpeace, United Way. Bureaucracies provide structure, like governments, which we may dip into, but the responsibility for what we accept, as in all things in life, is ours. It is important to remember—and this is crucial—that organized religion, like all agencies, is there to serve us—not to be served by us. Even the Roman Catholic Church, often vilified, has as a basic tenet the individual's *sole* responsibility for his or her own conscience and his or her obligation to follow that conscience even when it is at odds with the orthodox position. The bureaucracy does not go out of its way to tell us this, but it is true. We must learn this. The problem is not the bureaucracy so much as our *dependence* on the bureaucracy.

This is true of science as well, and certainly of psychoanalysis. Stephen Hawking, in his wonderful meditation on science entitled *A Brief History of Time*, concludes:

Up to now most scientists have been too occupied with the development of new theories that describe *what* the universe is to ask the question *why*. On the other hand, the people whose business it is to ask *why*, the philosophers, have not been able to keep up with the advance of scientific theories. In the eighteenth century, philosophers considered the whole of human knowledge, including science, to be their field and discussed questions such as: Did the universe have a beginning? However, in the nineteenth and twentieth centuries, science became too technical and mathematical for the philosophers, or anyone else except a few specialists. Philosophers reduced the scope of their inquiries so much that Wittgenstein, the most famous philosopher of this century, said, "The sole remaining task for philosophy is the analysis of language." What a comedown from the great tradition of philosophy from Aristotle to Kant!

However, if we do discover a complete theory, it should in time be understandable in broad principle by everyone, not just a few scientists. Then we shall all, philosophers, scientists, and just ordinary people, be able to take part in the discussion of the question of why it is that we and the universe exist. If we find the answer to that, it would be the ultimate triumph of human reason—for then we would know the mind of God.[6]

"*If* we discover a complete theory." If! And how does one *discover* a *theory?* "If we find the answer to that." If, If, If. Science appears to know little more about the ultimate questions we have been reflecting on in this book than it did hundreds of years ago. We are great at developing methods of study and theorizing and promising answers. And the more complex the techniques for explorations, the more the possibility for scientific "true believers" to catch us up in the egoistic delusion, "It would be the ultimate triumph of human reason." What a dogmatic religious assertion!

Then there's psychoanalysis. In a review of Peter Gay's book *A Godless Jew: Freud, Atheism, and the Making of Psychoanalysis*, Michael Beldoch points out:

> Freud's God was reason, and he certainly was as passionate in *this* belief as any devout. Nevertheless, and this is a crucial distinction between believers and *true believers*, he wondered in a letter…if his devotion to reason (which he had once described as like a cancer in himself!), and "the province of the ego, showed a bias against the id…if somehow [he] did indeed carry reason to a fault."

We have here run into a dilemma that psychoanalysis has as yet to confront adequately. We have not yet had a thoroughgoing psychoanalysis of the need to believe, not only as it affects the individual analyst and analysand, but as it affects the role of belief in psychoanalysis as an enterprise, as an "institution," and as a "movement" placed in its proper context in the history of man's ideas, feelings and beliefs about himself....

The issues here are clearly those of the role of reason and belief as they have come to terms with reality, especially unhappy reality. It is crucible enough to bring out the believer even in the scientist. In the section of his book entitled "In Search of Common Ground," which comes after the chapter, "Science Against Religion," Gay refers to Freud's position (in relation to one of his defectors) as "closer to reality." It seems to me that in this casual aside the author grants himself the offhand right to define reality, and thus makes of himself not so much the ever vigilant scientist whom he so admires, as the mere human being, leaning, if ever so slightly, toward the true believer. It is as if, when all is almost said and done, *the best of us*, and Professor Gay surely qualifies without benefit of belief as among the best, *still aspire to the disinterest of science rather more often than we achieve it* [emphasis added].

When he brings his book to an end, Gay turns to a well-known sentence from *The Future of an Illusion*: "No, our science is no illusion. But an illusion it would be to believe that we could get anywhere else what it cannot give us." Freud's brilliant book, with its awesome inquiry into the human condition and its overpowering need to believe, here gives way to precisely what it decries, the need to believe. There is indeed much that psychoanalysis can give, but not so little that can be gotten elsewhere as well. The enduring power of the need to believe will make itself felt, even well-disguised as the very essence of reason.[7]

In *The True Believer* Eric Hoffer writes, "The less justified a man is in claiming excellence for his own self, the more ready is he to claim all excellence for his nation, his religion, his race or his holy cause."[8] True believers are of all stripes: religionists, scientists and science groupies, atheists, communists, classical psychoanalysts, to name a few. All are anti-spiritual, although there may be spiritual members within each of these categories. Some, as in guru groups, actually offer something like spirituality to their followers, but it is growth without psychological separation—a seduction hard to refuse.

In a sense spirituality requires no belief. It requires only observation and, later, intention. Spirituality, in actuality, is just the opposite of belief. *Spirituality is the willingness to have an open mind about the mystery of life.* In a sense, life is the only God we can ever know, and observing life with an open mind, including the life within, is spirituality. Spirituality is following the laws of nature, the Transcendent, in contrast to ego, which is the superstition that comes from fusion and that can surface cannily disguised as one of the groups mentioned above. Spirituality is gazing upon what is. It is the systematic study and appreciation of the handiwork of God. Rationalism is the self-centered, grandiose, superstitious clinging to parental direction that we must know it all. Spirituality is coming to grips with the reality that our existence is a great mystery and humbly accepting that. Spirituality is the transcending of the parental idiom, transcending the very concept of mother and father so that the person, flying on the wings of spirit, can identify with the Transcendent spirit, life itself. Any understanding of this process that invokes our fusion-based parent idiom works against it. But spirituality does not demand faith or belief. *What we term faith is just the emotional assertion that brings our spirit in line with what we already know; it is not belief in the unknown.*

Some consider truth to be that which works. If this is so, then we need only look about us to see what is. We will notice that we are quite limited despite our vast accomplishments and we will not deny this. Nor will we deny the inexorable power of the universe, which has preexisted us and will continue to exist after our consciousness is no longer present, though it is hard for us to imagine this. It is not such a congenial thought, especially to our egos. And we will notice, when we acknowledge these things, that we experience a *natural* increase in awe, humility, love, and power. Science often blinds itself to this truth, and this is nowhere clearer than in the matter of shame.

It has only been in the last decade or so that shame has been a topic of any moment in psychotherapeutic circles. The neglect of shame by the psychotherapeutic community has been a tragedy on several counts. To begin with, the core problem of many individuals has been ignored throughout years of treatment. The situation is turning around now. The Twelve Step recovery movement has surfaced shame because shame has proven the key issue in the lives of countless individuals recovering from addictions.

In addition there have been seminal works in recent years that have focused us on shame. An instance of this is a wonderful article by Robert Karen.[9] In it he dwells extensively on the work of Helen Block Lewis, a psychologist who taught about shame for over two decades, often to deaf ears in her profession:

"The first thing that alerted me that something was missing in our psycho-analytic theory," Helen Lewis said, "was the relatively few but very disturbing cases in which there had been a good analysis, the patients were happy, I was happy, we shook hands, that was it; but a couple of months—sometimes it was a couple of years—later, the patient showed up. The good results had vanished."

In each case a painful life event had intruded. "But one would have thought," Lewis said, "that the person might have been strengthened against the return of neurosis. And what seemed so awful to me, as I listen now to what they were saying, they had an improved vocabulary of self-denigration! Masochistic, narcissistic—I used to shudder at what they were saying about themselves."…

Lewis had been doing research in cognitive styles with the psychologist H. A. Witkin during the forties and fifties. During the sixties they devised a study to determine whether people with certain cognitive styles would be more prone to shame than guilt. In examining the transcripts of the 180 therapy sessions that had been recorded for the study, Lewis found something she had not expected—all sorts of shame-related incidents were going unnoticed, and the patients were developing new troubles as a result ("I could watch symptoms form as I read"). These problems confirmed her suspicions about what had happened to the angry patients who returned to her after supposedly being cured.

So psychotherapy was often ignoring shame, sometimes confusing it with guilt, but other times just plain ignoring it, and sometimes actually inadvertently shaming the patient for having shame! This is the second failing of psychotherapy regarding shame. Not only did we often ignore its presence but perhaps all too frequently actually increased it!

Shame, she [Lewis] decided, was a fundamental aspect of the patient-therapist relationship. "However good your reasons for going into treatment, so long as you are an adult speaking to another adult to whom you are telling the most intimate things, there is an undercurrent of shame in every session." She argued that such shame, if unanalyzed, would remain unconscious and would come back to haunt the treatment.

Lewis began reexamining the published case histories of other analysts, including Freud, and discovered that shame played a more central part than had been understood before. She saw that many analysts not only overlooked their patients' feelings of shame but worsened them with judgmental interpretations, often implicitly shaming them for failing in their adulthood.

Lewis then described a predictable sequence of emotions that followed such moments, in which shame was activated and then ignored in treatment. Hidden rage at the therapist comes first. But how can one be angry at one's therapist, she asked—this person "who has listened to me, who's put up with me, who's said something that really relieved me when I was in a deep state of shame or guilt?"…How evil can you get? Guilt thwarts your rage. In humiliation, your fury points back at your self, and you sink into depression.

Shame, as distinguished from guilt, refers to our experience of self as *essentially* defective. It is not that we feel bad because we have *done* something bad but rather that we *are* something bad. There is a healthy (for want of a better word) shame that informs us of the necessity to monitor our behavior, to be respectful of others and ourselves. Serious breaches of societal or personal standards in this decorum can result in *temporary* feelings of shame. Then there is the shame Ernest Kurtz describes.[10] He refers to the shame inherent in our nature as we become aware of and experience our essential limitedness as humans. "Not being God" is a shameful experience for us and if not confronted and shared can fester inside us or contaminate our lives with seemingly endless strategies of futile reparation. There is also the ordinary shame each of us carries with us due to the natural embarrassments of being a child and being responded to on occasion with little sensitivity. Finally, there is the fearsome shame that many of us have as a result of these ordinary shames being exploded into painful chronic beliefs about ourselves as a result of long years of living in a shaming environment.

Shame is such a central part of our existence. What can we do about it? What can help us? It seems to me that spirituality, both developed alone and in a healing community, is the answer. We can "clean up" psychotherapy a little. I urge students toward a respectful and egalitarian feeling and attitude toward those with whom they are privileged to work. I emphasize the importance of listening and truly identifying with the experience of the other as more important than the "brilliant" interpretation. Without revealing our own life stories, I encourage the therapist to communicate to the patient a clear, if not always verbal, assertion that therapists are *not* models, just fellow strugglers, and that we will help as best we can because that happens to be our role at this particular time. Most of all, I encourage the students and myself never to miss an opportunity to attack vigorously manifestations of self-shaming behavior on the part of the patient. I urge all I teach to read Carl Rogers, who has understood the shame problem without using the word and has advocated the most respectful and attentive attitude toward patients throughout this entire century; he has been ignored by the psychoanalytic community.[11]

We can learn not to shame our patients by a haughty attitude and insensitive interpretations. We can even learn to be more sensitive to the role shame plays in their lives and difficulties (but not without understanding the role it plays in our own as therapists, incidentally). As Kurtz points out, the real healing of shame takes place in caring, not curing. Here, too, we therapists can improve a great deal without crossing over boundaries or breaching objectivity. Much more powerful, in my judgment, is the cure through care that comes when others acknowledge their own shame. This reaching out and creation of a common pool of shame results in the healing of all. You see this in healthy spiritual groups, leaderless groups, Twelve Step groups, wherever the emphasis is on the mutuality of need, the acknowledgment that each human being is incomplete and because of this incompleteness, each needs others.

> Our mutual healing will be not the healing of curing, but the healing of caring. To heal is to make whole. Curing makes whole from the outside: it is good healing, but it cannot touch my deepest need, my deepest hurt— my shame, the dread of myself that I harbor within. Caring makes whole from within: it reconciles me to myself-as-I-am, beast-angel, *human*. Caring enables me to touch the joy of living that is the other side of my shame, of my not-God-ness, of my humanity.... But I can care, can become whole, only if you care enough—need enough—to share your shame with me. Could the same be true for you? [12]

It is the experiencing and sharing of this care that is so powerful a healing and can take us beyond that which psychotherapy can do in itself. Psychotherapy may get us ready for this, as we shall see below, but it is not sufficient unto itself. There is more to go. Participation in a spirit-affirming spiritual group is a great help, a great consolation, a great joy.

Spirituality is the engagement with the Transcendent; each of us must make some accommodation. By the Transcendent I mean the awareness of the power of the universe of which we are a part; the energy that makes all life go forward; the meaning and mystery and origin and destiny of all life and ours, in particular. Vaclav Havel puts it this way:

> Man must in some way come to his senses. He must extricate himself from this terrible involvement in both the obvious and the hidden mechanisms

of totality, from consumption to repression, from advertising to manipulation through television. He must rebel against his role as a helpless cog in the gigantic and enormous machinery hurtling God knows where. He must discover again, within himself, a deeper sense of responsibility toward the world, which means responsibility toward something higher than himself. Modern science has realized this (though not the proprietors of "the scientific world view"), but it cannot find a remedy. The power to awaken this new responsibility is beyond its reach; such a thing can be resolved neither scientifically nor technically. It may seem like a paradox, but one I think will prove true, that only through directing ourselves toward the moral and the spiritual, based on respect for some "extramundane" authority—for the order of nature or the universe, for a moral order and its superpersonal origin, for the absolute—can we arrive at a state in which life on this earth is no longer threatened by some form of "mega-suicide" and becomes bearable, has in other words, a genuinely human dimension. This direction, and this direction alone, can lead to the creation of social structures in which a person can once more be a person, a specific human personality.[13]

This is no easy task. It is vague and mysterious and does not result in clear, unambiguous answers. In addition, for many of us, the whole topic has been soured by organized religion's thrusting dogma down our throats. What should be the vehicle of the expression and celebration of our unique spirits became, perversely, an attempt to squelch our spirits, to abuse and maim, anti-life rather than the very expression of life which spirituality is. Many of us deprive ourselves of something wonderful because of this victimization.

For most, I think, it has been the conflict between spirit and ego, mother-fusion, which has caused the most difficulty in this quest. The only thing I am absolutely sure of when I consider the Transcendent, whatever its nature, is that it is surely *not me*. Once I am clear on that I am free to search for it. When I say it is not me I refer to my ego. Because the Transcendent is everything, myself included. But I am not *it*. Havel speaks further of this search:

> In the first place: As I understand it, spiritual renewal (I once called it an "existential revolution") is not something that one day will drop out of heaven into our laps, or be ushered in by a new messiah. It is a task that confronts us all, every moment of our existence. We all can and must "do something about it," and we can do it here and now. No one else can do it for us, and therefore we can't wait for anyone else.[14]

Once I am clear on that, that I am not it, I am free to engage the mystery, the *magnum mysterium*, in whatever way I can. For me, I constantly have to resist my egoistic deflation at not understanding everything clearly. But when I get free of that and use whatever human skills I have, such as human speech and thought based on my model of human interaction, I am able to reach out to the Transcendent. When I do that, and am able to follow it up with quiet reflection, I have access to the most remarkable information. For deep from within me come notions and feelings that I could summon up in no other way, certainly not by my ego-will unaided by this intention to reach out to the Transcendent. I understand things differently, am prompted toward or away from certain actions, experience certain affects. Changes in my behavior occur "behind my back," often far surpassing those I have been able to accomplish through my will and insight and therapy experience. I am able to access my spirit, the Transcendent, as it lives in me, to free it from its imprisonment by mother-fusion.

What I mean by prayer is precisely the *intention to know*. Acknowledging something greater than ourselves, having the intention to acknowledge it, accepting the necessarily tentative and even groping nature of such contact is all that is necessary. It is said by the "wise" that such behavior is childish, dependent, and self-delusional. All I can say is that when I am able to acknowledge the Transcendent my behavior is *less* childish, more independent, and I see reality more clearly and go about life in a clear and focused manner. I experience a great deal of joy as well.

What is more self-delusional than to insist that the answer to everything in life will come from our unaided egos and will? This insistence, religious in the worst sense, denies the very essential characteristics of human nature, limited and fraught with errors. To protect our egos and mother-fusion, we stumble along in denial about reality and what is possible to us, what really is. Spirituality is finding a way to access the spirit. Prayer is such a way, but it is not the only way. We must find our own way, unique to us. It may involve participation in a group or we may remain on our own. If we are sincere, keep an open mind, and have the intention to know the truth and to do the right thing, we will be all right. The results are the only criteria. Truth is what works!

Dr. Karen concludes his article on shame in a way that betrays the hubris of my profession, the latent egoism responsible for us failing to find shame before our very eyes and a potential flaw in all psychotherapeutic work. He writes:

In medieval Christendom the belief that all people were sinners, that all were unworthy, used this sense of universal defect to bind the community, to maintain a spiritual focus, and, perhaps incidentally, to drain off some shame that might otherwise have become individual and narcissistic. From our distant perspective in a diametrically different world, we can easily imagine how comforting it might have been to know that one was not alone in one's flaws and vulnerabilities, to feel assured of one's place despite everything, to be confident that all were equal in God's eyes.[15]

The only change from then is that now we know we are not sinners, that our pain comes from life and from living. But it is *still* comforting to know that we are not alone in our flaws and vulnerabilities, to feel assured of our place despite everything, to be confident that all are equal in God's eyes. The only thing keeping us from finding that assurance is our ego, our mother-fusion which leads to the insistence that we can do it all on our own.

We must conclude this reflection on spirituality with the other side of the coin. Spirituality can take us to places that psychology cannot. But psychology and psychotherapy are often necessary to free us from the fusion-constraints that keep us from surrendering to the spiritual. There is an inexorable connection between the two. It is our nature to find a Transcendent. Otherwise we get stuck in narcissism; we become dependent on all sorts of things and people and make them our Transcendent. It is when we separate from these false gods that we move from transcendents to Transcendence, and this is spirituality. So while spirituality can take us where psychology cannot, sometimes psychology is necessary before spirituality can do that. Not always. Many people respond to the promptings of the spirit and are able to abandon their residual fusions and mother-surrogates; most of us, however, need help in letting go. In fact, we may use the very exhortations to the spiritual life to berate ourselves. We can suffer under the lash of guilt. We may slip into the quicksand of shame.

Remember, it is a basic principle of growth that we must fully *accept ourselves* in order to mature into the self we truly are. To the extent that we are stuck in fusion, do not accept ourselves, do not *know* ourselves, we will have trouble accessing the spirit.

If a person is angry at his dad and someone tells him it is better not to hate and harbor resentments, "better to forgive than to be forgiven"—and he is able to understand this and release the hate—this is a spiritual advance. However, if he is still mad and "buries" it because of this spiritual admonition, this is *not* a spiritual solution; he will be neither spiritual *nor* sane. If a person hates, he hates, and he cannot be talked out of it. Hate disappears by fully experiencing it, not by denying it or even by expressing it. If we can do that and then forgive, that's wonderful; but if we cannot, the spiritual "solution" will not only not "work" on any level but will actually make us even more angry. And we will feel a failure on top of it: the ingredients of shame and depression.

We are faced here with a paradox. Spirituality keeps us looking to the future, aspiring toward behaviors that are loving and self-actualizing. To this extent it may dissolve psychological conflict, further psychological separation, and even further intra-psychic search and resolution. It should encourage self-acceptance and humility and overcoming of narcissism. Sometimes it does. But sometimes the deep beliefs we have are so powerful they tip the balance in the direction of fusion. Spiritual concepts can even be used in the service of not surfacing these deep beliefs and actually keeping us ensconced in enmeshment.

Bill Wilson, the co-founder of Alcoholics Anonymous, based the recovery program of that fellowship on spiritual principles. It has been dramatically successful. Yet he himself, although he accomplished monumental feats for millions of others and maintained his own growth and sobriety, suffered from recurrent bouts of depression. In a letter to a friend who was himself suffering from depression, Wilson wrote:

> I think that many oldsters who have put our AA "booze cure" to severe but successful tests still find they often lack emotional sobriety. Perhaps they will be the spearhead for the next major development in AA, the development of much more real maturity and balance (which is to say, humility) in our relations with ourselves, with our fellows and with God.
>
> Those adolescent urges that so many of us have for top approval, perfect security, and perfect romance, urges quite appropriate to age 17, proved to be an impossible way of life when we are at age 47 and 57.
>
> Since AA began, I have taken immense wallops in all these areas because of my failure to grow up emotionally and spiritually....
>
> Last autumn, depression, having no really rational cause at all, took me to the cleaners. I began to be scared that I was in for another long chronic spell. Considering the grief I have had with depressions, it was not a bright prospect....
>
> I kept asking myself, "Why can't the Twelve Steps work to release depression?" By the hour, I stared at the St. Francis Prayer.... "It is better to

comfort than to be comforted." Here was the formula, all right, but why didn't it work?

Suddenly, I realized what the matter was. My basic flaw had always been dependence, almost absolute dependence, on people or circumstances to supply me with prestige, security and the like. Failing to get these things according to my perfectionist dreams and specifications, I had fought for them, and when defeat came, so did my depression.

There was not a chance of making the outgoing love of St. Francis a workable and joyous way of life until these fatal and almost absolute dependencies were cut away.

Because I had over the years undergone a little spiritual development, the absolute quality of these frightful dependencies had never before been so starkly revealed. Reinforced by what grace I could secure in prayer, I found I had to exert every ounce of will and action to cut off these faulty emotional dependencies upon people, upon AA, indeed, upon any set of circumstances whatsoever. Then only could I be free to love as Francis did. Emotional and instinctual satisfactions, I saw, were really the extra dividends of having love, offering love and expressing love appropriate to each relation of life.

Plainly, I could not avail myself of God's love until I was able to offer it back to Him by loving others as He would have me. I could not possibly do that so long as I was victimized by false dependencies.

For me dependence meant demand, a demand for the possession and control of the people and the conditions surrounding me.

If we examine every disturbance we have, great or small, we will find at the root of it some unhealthy dependence and its consequent demand.[16]

This masterful statement of an extraordinarily spiritually accomplished man teaches me many things: First, that fusion limits the possibilities of spiritual development; second, that spirituality itself, although leading ideally to self-acceptance and shame reduction, can reach a point where it cannot bring us any further and can even be used by our demons to keep us ensconced in mother-fusion. A cursory glance at the lives of the great mystics surfaces countless examples of this. Perhaps the most important insight Wilson leaves with us in this regard is that it is *dependence* that is at the root of the spiritual blockage. The ego wants something from someone or something outside itself, and it will demand and fight for it. When this frantic attempt at control fails, as it inevitably will, symptoms occur. "If we examine every disturbance we have, great or small, we will find at the root of it some unhealthy dependence and its consequent demand." What a powerful statement!

If I act nice to a neighbor, it may be because I feel loving and it spills out toward her; or it may be because I have the conscious intention of acting that way because that is the way I want to be; or I may be trying unconsciously or consciously to get the approval of my mother, who wanted me to be a "good boy"; or it might be a defense mechanism against rage and contempt, an automatic characterological behavior, part of my character armoring. The latter two motivations are psychological in nature, one a defense mechanism, the other an unseparated, fused pattern of behavior. The first two motivations are in the spiritual realm. A clue to my motivation is the internal state. Am I at peace? Do I expect something from the recipient? I'm daily reminded of my spiritual limitations as I hold the door for someone and experience irritation when that person fails to reward me for my "good deed" with an immediate smile or thank you. Whenever I take the time to reflect on my personal states of disturbance, large or small, I bump into "some unhealthy dependence and its consequent demand."

Availability to the spirit is always the result of psychological readiness. Acting on a spiritual impulse or pursuing spiritual result is to little avail. The self, which does the psychological work, is at the interface between ego (the guardian of mother-fusion) and spirit (the developing, moving forward participation in the life force, the Transcendent). It is at this crossroads that the decision, conscious or unconscious, is made to become available to spirit. Intention is important at this moment and can be "shored up" by spiritual practice, prayer, and meditation. But without the "decision," the surrender, or at least the willingness, the practice itself may be frustrating, the "dark night of the soul." Or these spiritual tools may be employed in a self-centered or avaricious way, a sort of spiritual materialism. Even the awareness of the inability to decide to be available can be an important psychological event pointing toward spirituality.

Sometimes I think that humankind has been on a long spiritual journey toward psychological separation. From the outset we knew that psychological fusion and its inevitable vanity were essential limitations that keep us forever floundering and sabotage our wonderful aspirations and accomplishments. Our first communication to ourselves of this tenuous and frightening reality was in scriptures. In 1983 poet Helen Morrissey Rizzuto wrote the following to me (we had been discussing the symbolic meaning of the Virgin Birth):

The *denotation* of the word, "virgin"—a person who has never had sexual intercourse; untouched in its original state; unused—doesn't seem to be of much help, except in that Eastern way of looking at things. So I asked myself with what do I *associate* the word "virgin," i.e., what are the *connotations*? and I came up with "innocence" ("ignorance," a var.) and "inexperience." If the Gospel writers were trying to teach us a lesson about living, about life on a psychological level, then I think they were going with the connotative sense of the word, meaning although the mother has tremendous power over the child, the mother is really only a child herself. Separation might be seen (made possible even) in this light, that much of what we thought we had with that *special* person we called "mother," we didn't. Much, if not all, of that was *our* creation.

Maybe the Gospel writers were saying, "love her, respect her, but don't get lost in her. Don't die in her—follow Christ and separate from her." The child shouldn't endow her indefinitely with such powers she seems to possess only by virtue of the fact that time determines her role and the child's survival depends on her. The necessarily neurotic bonds (because of her humanness and ours) can be broken by our giving up the dream that she was godlike, all-powerful, i.e., when we recognize that she was, in actuality, a virgin, a child, much like ourselves.

I think in therapy, this is what one does, but one does not start out with the other's innocence/ ignorance, but one's own. Recognition of her humanness (with all its flaws and attachments) is the star we see shining up ahead, at the opening of the cave, a reflection of the light that was within us all the time. [17]

Freud's teachings and the beginning of our deepening understanding of the nature of the mother-child bond and the intra-psychic drama that occurs as we struggle to become our unique self are part of the spiritual unfolding of humankind. There is really no conflict. Both are aspects of the same thing. The movement from fusion to psychological separation is always a dialectic—both personally and culturally. We move forward, and then we dig in. The reaction to Freud's revolutionary and thus spiritual breakthroughs has been the over-intellectualizing bureaucracy of contemporary psychoanalysis. Religion has suffered the same fate over the centuries. But the truth, inevitably struggling to shine through the enmeshments that are our nature, will out. It is as inevitable as the rising of the sun and the movements of the tides.

We live on a planet hurtling through space at forty thousand miles an hour, suspended in the universe, spinning around in a galaxy. The whole thing works perfectly. As I write, somewhere south of here a dog wanders through the woods. As he approaches a particular tree, a tick is motivated by a chemical odor exuded by the dog to release its grip on the bark of an overhanging branch. The tick wafts down to earth as the dog passes by, and it lands on the dog, to continue its life as a parasite to its host. Exquisitely perfect events such as these occur in infinite instances. We cannot presume to understand fully or control them.

If we have been bombarded with criticism about our self-worth and have indoctrinated ourselves with the same nonsense; if we have developed deep beliefs about our self-worth for decades, perhaps hundreds of psychological years, from people we believed truly knew, because our lives depended on that belief, how in the world are we going to correct that? What will save us—gestalt experience, bio-feedback, banging pillows, biological manipulation, rational thinking, medication, affirmations, interpretations, koans?

Psychoanalysis releases the blocks—but it leaves us in a spiritual no-man's land. We can get stuck in two kinds of "religious" conundrum. One can make the psychoanalytic process itself the religion and its spirituality, a sort of dark nihilism, such as Freud apparently experienced; these are the psychological conquistadors, weary and dejected at the end of life, dissatisfied with the reality they have arrived at, hoisted on the petard, I suspect, of an unyielded self-centeredness. Others embrace a pseudo-spiritual solution, one of a former time, a ready-made, fully detailed and packaged spiritual "journey," one they may take mechanically without having to engage the anguish of confronting their personal false gods. In both cases, the spirit is not fully wrested from its "oneness with Mommy."

There is a commonality between the faith of religious dogma and the faith of ultimate scientific explanation. Both are "superstitious" in a sense (fear of the unknown, a false conception of causation). Our ego demands that we know. Our ego demands security. But being "humbled" is essential to true freedom. Being humbled in not knowing everything frees us from the chains of self-centeredness and enables us to begin to have a relationship with the Transcendent. And that is the beginning of the "power and the glory" that can be ours. If all our energy is put into maintaining the myth that we are in control, there is none left for the soaring that is available after surrender to the Transcendent.

Let me summarize:

Spirituality refers to the extent to which the spirit is free to follow its natural course. This is the direct result of psychological separation. To the extent that we wrest our psychic welfare from the dominance and control of our caretakers, we free ourselves from the life plans and attitudes and behaviors dictated by the main idea of our life and the deepest beliefs we developed under the duress of our childhood; to the extent that affect is spontaneously available to us—chronic affect being muted or disappeared—to that extent we will be able to think, feel, and perceive the way the world is through the unique prism of our spirit, not our mother-fusion. What we do then is our spirituality.

We become free not merely from the severe narcissisms described earlier but also from the "normal" self-centeredness of our residual mother-fusion and the deep beliefs about ourselves we formed as a function of the unique characteristics of the human condition: consciousness, an extremely long dependent childhood, the flawed nature of our caretakers. We are free, then, to love, to be generous, to be kind, to be compassionate, to serve, to nurture, to be appreciative, to be in awe.

We will have mastered vanity and as a result will have vast amounts of energy free to live, love, and enjoy life. We will know through the constant focus of radical self-acceptance that we *have* "gotten ours" by our very nature and by being alive. We have nothing more to prove, nothing to protect. While we will have discovered what the Buddhists call "practice" to keep focused on our newfound freedom and ever alert to the "call back" of our old demons—humans seem not able to keep spiritual matters in focus for too long without such "practice," whatever it may be—our natural outgoing love will not be a chore for the most part. Spirituality is the natural result of psychological separation; there is nothing supernatural about it. It, too, is our nature. When we clear the debris of our fusion away, it is our *natural* inclination. Even the prayer of St. Francis, which I have known all my life and believed to be an impossible challenge, an unnatural way of being, is truly natural and a most wonderful description of the psychologically separated life.

> Lord make me an instrument of thy peace.
> Where there is hatred, let me sow love;
> Where there is injury, pardon;
> Where there is doubt, faith;
> Where there is despair, hope;

Where there is darkness, light;
Where there is sadness, joy.
Divine Master, grant
That I may not so much seek
To be consoled as to console,
To be understood as to understand,
To be loved as to love.
For it is in giving that we receive,
It is in pardoning that we are pardoned,
And it is in dying that we are born to eternal life.

Who could do this but the psychologically separating person? It seems to be a fact of nature that the psychologically separating person *wants* to do this and can accomplish it with daily attention to this intention, for it is our nature, and freeing ourselves from the slavery of fusion makes it possible. This is spirituality, the overcoming of vanity in order to love. And it is our nature.

Our attempts, often heroic, to get our instincts in line with these precepts, when in reality they are quite fused and self-centered, is also called spirituality. Spiritual practice can be quite helpful here, because it keeps us focused on the goal of growing out, appreciates the value of the end product, and appeals to the help of the transcendent universe. Sometimes the fusions are so powerful that psychological study of the person is essential for further spiritual growth. Sometimes the spiritual practice itself is a help and motivation in the study of the person and an impetus to psychological separation.

Sadly, there are far too many instances where spirituality and spiritual practices are used in the service of maintaining fusion, connection to parents, and discouragement of spirit. The abuses of this kind are apparent to all. This is probably the single most important reason religion is in bad repute with so many people. Psychologically unseparated people have used spiritual precepts to control others and discourage their growing out into themselves. This is largely because of the narcissism of the leaders, which encourages the dependent fusion of devotees. But this is not the nature of spirituality. It is the exact opposite.

Sometimes spirituality is confused with weakness and excessive dependence. To follow the precepts of the St. Francis prayer is to abandon self, it is argued. It is for wimps, not self-confident folks, not for those with "healthy narcissism." Besides, this is a tough world and we cannot be too kind. Others will take advantage of us.

This is an understandable fear. It, too, stems from early indoctrination, much of which was motivated by the love and protectiveness of our care-takers. In some cases it was motivated by the desire to keep us in a per-petual state of psychological fusion. For the fact is that the psychologically separating person is strong indeed. Freed of the slavery of mother-fusion, the psychologically separating person shares in the strength of the uni-verse. Who in the history of the world has been more powerful than Mar-tin Luther King, Jr., Mahatma Gandhi, Christ, or the Buddha? Nonviolent all, they transformed the universe. No, spirituality is not weakness; rather, it is the infinity of strength that never needs force to accomplish its vision, that naturally prompts love, simply because it is right. The payoff is peace and joy.

A bit about love, incidentally. One word for so many emotions! There is the love between lovers, a very interesting and powerful love. The love between psychologically separating persons has all the wonderful charac-teristics of romantic love *without the fear*. Freud said that we tend to over-value our loved objects, particularly at the beginning. It is almost an emotional illness. I don't know if it is that we overvalue the loved one or just that we allow ourselves to see the true beauty of another human being, and in allowing ourselves to love, we break through our isolation and make contact. We "fall" in love and as we hurdle through new, unfelt space there is the giddiness of absolute novelty. We have taken a chance; we have trusted again. We have put our "healthy narcissism," our self-concept, in the hands of another. We let another tell us, to some extent, about our worth as humans. Such love is freeing and liberating. And it is exciting, because some fusion naturally occurs. At times we become one with the other and experience great relief and joy in that oneness. To do this safely requires psychological separation. A great love is truly a spiritual experience, as we shall see in the next chapter.

Then there is the love for the dependent—the child, the infirm, the disabled. Unlike romantic love, where the excess of generosity comes from the celebration of each other, the love for the dependent is a biological, instinctual impulse, purely natural. As humans we do it easily for our kin, but we also have the altruistic tendency to identify with the beleaguered—particularly if we have accomplished significant psychological separation and are able to love others besides our immediate families. This is an amalgam of our biological instincts and our human "instincts," and as such is perfectly natural for the psychologically separating person.

Finally, there is the love of the Transcendent. It is natural to be in awe of life, existence, the universe, and the force that motivates us. We must form some relationship with this Transcendent. We may abdicate our responsibilities as adults in childish obeisance; we may condemn out of hand because of the errors of the religious person or our own egos. Most of us stumble along, somewhat lost, trying to make sense of it all. We live and love in ambivalence. This, too, is the human condition. It seems to me that it is natural to be in awe, to want to worship, to pray, to express gratitude for life. Psychologically separating persons find their own idiosyncratic way of meeting these needs. When they are on to something right for them, they experience joy and peace and a strong identification with all of life, particularly human life. They have found the truth of the great commandments,

> Thou shalt love thy God with thy whole heart and thy whole
>   mind and thy whole soul
> And thou shalt love thy neighbor as thyself.

In this great invocation lie the mystery and the solution of life. Love—of God, self, and others—is the only thing that counts. And it is all the same thing! This realization in the heart of the psychologically separating person brings great joy and peace. It makes racism and war agonizing and unacceptable. Dietrich Bonhoeffer, hanged by the Nazis at the very moment the Allied troops were fighting their way toward Berlin, taught us that "unless you can cry for the Jews, you are not permitted to sing Gregorian chant."

Yet true spirituality demands nothing. It just is. From the midst of the sixties came this anthem:

> All you need is love…all you need is love…all you need is love, love,…all you ever need is love…all you ever need…all you ever need…[18]

Chapter 8

Intimacy Among Friends and Lovers

෨ᎧᏩ

Wresting our spirits from our caretakers, bringing to a close the most passionate and loving of all relationships, is our sad and daunting task. Joyfully, to the extent we have had some success at this, we become ready to be deeply related to others. Notice I didn't say "have relationships" with others. Rather, I said "become related" to others. Each of us has many relationships. Even the recluse has relationships. Some of our relationships are with people we are tangibly involved with; some are with creatures who live largely in our minds, but they are relationships still. We have been in relationships from the beginning and always will be.

Relatedness is something else. Relatedness has to do with the extent to which we bring our unique selves into contact with another. It involves intimacy and presence. It is actually relatively rare when compared to all the transactions humans have with each other. It is rare, it is hard; it is the best. And it is directly related to psychological separation.

What a complicated job it is to get along with one another. Yet, we are driven to it. And just as all other "natural" things are harder for us humans than for any other living thing, this is, as well, and perhaps even more so.

I read of humankind's concerns for the environment, the population explosion, the debate over global warming. We are not in an age now, however, when we express much concern about the nature of our relationships.

We are still waging wars, abusing our children and spouses and elders, robbing and raping and murdering each other. Arguments and fights and bad will characterize our daily activities and even, perhaps especially, our intimacies. We are certainly putting the cart before the horse if we attempt to solve our global problems and continue to neglect the very basic challenge of just how to get along with one another. The murder and mayhem and global destruction continue, for if we do not separate into our selves we cannot love ourselves and each other, never mind the earth that nourishes us.

Abuse is not caring for the nature of a thing; it results in bruising; in humans, pain. Wherever there is pain there has been abuse. Humans are the only species that can perpetuate bruises. We abuse, are abused, abuse, and pass our abuse on to our progeny and they can abuse again. The earth, surely; but ourselves as well. When we get well enough to notice the abuse, we cry for the earth, for the animals, but we need to get well enough to cry also for ourselves. Ego interferes here again. We hear of the pain a human inflicts upon another and we distance ourselves from it. It is not *us*. It is some sort of aberration. And we close our eyes, forget about it, and take solace in our goodness as we lobby for an endangered species. But it *is* us; it is our nature as long as we are fused.

We are so ill-equipped to relate to one another. Being fused, following a self- (or mother-) justifying agenda, there is little left over to reach out to know, let alone spiritually touch, one another. How are we to really get to know each other? Locked in the prison of ourselves, we remain isolated, strangers sometimes even to ourselves.

Some time ago I noticed in my men's peer group that the suggestions made to a person presenting a problem were, for the most part, knee-jerk reactions, and if I listened carefully I realized that they were the expressions of each person's solutions to his own problems. There was little attempt to understand the other, explore or "mine" for more. How rare it is to listen to the other and not try to fix. The problem with "fixing" is that it serves, primarily, the needs of the fixer. He is the one in need of a "fix." The suggestions often have little to do with the other. They are a compulsive attempt to reassure himself that his solutions for himself are correct. Such "fixing" is a variation of narcissism.

For many years I have been informally observing myself and others in social situations. Some of these situations have been for a single occasion.

But some have continued over years, so my observations cannot be dismissed as merely instances of cocktail party chatter. By and large people "interact" rather than "relate." By interact I mean they "show" themselves and "observe" others. No attempt is made to be intimate and related. Rather, the design is to evaluate others and what they do, say, or are, so as to protect one's own self-concepts and belief systems. Most of all they avoid, at all costs, upsetting their affect control systems; they just do not want to have any emotion. The entire enterprise is self-defensive.

If the other is verbally threatening, they will defend themselves verbally. If the other is "dangerous" (threatening to their self-concept) just by the nature of who he is, or how he presents himself, they will defend themselves by having a "negative belief" about that person, and if the threat is particularly dangerous, when the observer's shaky self-concept feels under siege, the disqualifying belief may have to be expressed outwardly and publicly to the other. The especially narcissistic person has a magical way of balancing his self-esteem by making his negative belief "real" by expressing it in words. Or the person may react with hostility: "Put on a little weight, haven't you…heh, heh?" Most folks are concerned with *self-justification*, not learning, not relating, certainly not caring. Underneath all of this, of course, is a painful dearth of radical self-acceptance. We pass by each other in emotional solitude and isolation, seemingly satisfied if the encounter doesn't worsen our already fragile self-esteem.

We are all locked inside ourselves yet we need each other. We want each other. We often desperately cry out for each other. But we don't know how to *know* the other. It seems terrifying. We are so alone. When we reach out we tend to create the other in the image and likeness of our needs and fears. To the extent we have made progress in psychological separation we have the capability to observe the world around us and see with our own eyes. We have a chance of seeing another for who she is and to get to know her.

To the extent that we remain fused, we have little choice but to make this new person, this new opportunity, a new edition of our old life, our past. We project onto her our inner world. She now becomes a character in our inner drama. She ceases to be herself, who she *really* is. There is no way we can love or be in true relationship with each other. Over the years even our children may become unknown to us, as our parents may be unknown to us in their present realities. We make them up in the fantasy of transference or project onto them roles in the drama of our unseparated lives.

They must be made to fit into the early intrapsychic family that lives in our heads and souls.

But there is hope. Even that tendency of ours can be put to good use if we are on the Wisdom path. If we sincerely desire to know and be known, then even transference is a wonderful opportunity to learn about ourselves and others. It actually is one of the most powerful possibilities of growing out into ourselves that there is. To some extent it is impossible to understand another without what we hear and observe being shaken through the strainer of our own experience. But it has a lot to do with *intention*. If we have a serious intention to understand the other, we will not be unduly distracted by our narcissistic self-justifications. We will keep focused on the desire to know the other rather than to be right. We will no longer need to justify the past. We can be present in that moment when life exists, which is this very second. And we will return to self.

Some time ago I realized that this transference thing, which can be such a stumbling block to our relatedness, is also an exquisitely human opportunity:

> Transference phenomena although discovered in the psychologist's consulting room were not invented there. [Rather] they have always existed, are referred to in literature and folklore. Their pervasive nature attests to their importance as an agent of psychological growth. Transference occurs constantly in our dealings with others. To the extent that each of us has unfinished aspects of personality, to that extent will there be a thrust to relive those conflicts in the re-creation of the present real situation in the form of an older previously experienced one. The capacity for transference is not a limitation, a pathognomic index of a person's functioning, but rather an evolutionary characteristic of the human psyche which enables the correcting of a faulty perception and the resulting cognitive distortions attendant upon them in the context of intimate relatedness. The human being's capacity to perceive a novel situation in an idiosyncratic manner, the capability to weave an intricate mosaic, intertwining the stuff of instinct, past experience, motivation, and intentionality with the hard data of objective matter, is unique and awesome. It is singularly human and represents an evolutionary achievement equal to any other. Each interpersonal perception is a truly creative act.
>
> *The possibility of growth occurs whenever transference phenomena are given full reign and when this takes place in the context of a loving committed relationship such potential is realized.*[1]

The important thing is to have the *intention* to know and understand the other. All human experience can serve that purpose, even our tendencies to obscure and distort. And those very tendencies to distort may provide the opportunity, within a loving committed relationship, to continue the process of growing out into our selves.

Consider the possibilities for human relatedness: lover, spouse, dependent children, peers, peers in need, adult children, parents, adult siblings, friends, acquaintances, fellow humans, fellow living things, life itself, the Transcendent. Each demands a different quality and intensity of "knowing." For the rest of this chapter we will look at knowing and being known and the purposes and joys and resistances that go along with getting out of ourselves enough to really understand another person. We will pay particular attention to intimacy and what happens in a long-term, committed relationship. But we will also consider friendship and its value and the especial importance of friendship with others when one is actually in an exclusive, intimate relationship. When one has found her "reason to live" there is often a subtle abandonment of friends; yet this is precisely the time that our friendships, what I term *companionate affiliations*, are crucial. We shall speak of love and sex and fear and loss and grief. We shall consider how we isolate and keep from each other. We shall consider the nature of communication and contact with each other. We shall consider faulty relationships; we shall consider love.

Let's return to knowing as a jumping-off point. Intimacy involves the revelation of one's self to another as a way of *knowing* the other. One of the greatest pleasures in life is knowing another human being. It is a great joy to know all the nooks and crannies and histories of another as they manifest themselves in the physical expression of a person—his body. Even more pleasurable is the knowledge of a person in his quest for wholeness in his life. It is a timeless, endless task of possibilities, and provides the knower with the great pleasure and personal expression in his new knowledge and understanding. To watch someone struggle with becoming herself in her own unique way is one of the most fascinating of human experiences. It is exciting. It is passionate. Compared to that, transference is old hat. When we are fused, we take a once-in-a-lifetime person and make her into an old character in our repetitive life drama. How boring!

People are fascinating. When I can sneak out of my self-centeredness for a moment and observe a fellow human in her life it is the most interesting thing I know of. But to have the joy of this I must reveal myself some way, as well. There is no real knowing without self-revelation of some sort. Back to our old friend Melanie Klein:

> The infant can only experience complete enjoyment if the capacity for love is sufficiently developed; and it is enjoyment that forms the basis for gratitude. Freud described the infant's bliss in being suckled as the proto- type of sexual gratification. In my view these experiences constitute not only the basis of sexual gratification but of all later happiness, and make possible the feeling of unity with another person. Such unity means being *fully understood* [emphasis added], which is essential for every happy love relation or friendship. At best, such understanding needs no words to express it, which demonstrates its derivation from the earliest closeness with the mother in the preverbal stage. The capacity to enjoy fully the first relation to the breast forms the foundation for experiencing pleasure from various sources.[2]

In an adult relationship *each* needs to be "fully understood." In the truly intimate relationship there is a passion even greater than that between mother and child because *both* parties are giving and taking, knowing and being known, an experience transcending even the mother-child relation- ship which is the model of all later passion. This passion is the stuff of the psychological separation of both parties, for it is in abdicating passion for mother that each makes possible its return with an "outsider." Left behind is the pseudo-passion of furtive (oedipal) sex or the repetition of childish passion in which one or both looks only to be known and loved rather than striving for a true reciprocity.

Having the intention of knowing and being known in a committed reciprocity is the greatest relatedness two people can have. It is the highest of human accomplishments. It is like "knowing" the sunset or the sea or a musical idea that touches the heart. Near the end of therapy a former pa- tient said to me: "I'm learning to love the 'emotional truth' of my hus- band," to which I replied, "This is why we marry: to forge out over time who the other person is rather than to make him or her into new editions of the family; we create the new instead of the old."

Such a relationship involves two dimensions. One is intimacy, the other relatedness. Intimacy is generally thought of as something that transpires between two persons. Actually it refers more to a capacity rather than to an interpersonal transaction. Intimacy refers to those things "most within" us, the mental contents most sacred to the self. There can be disagreement about what those contents are, disagreement both inter- and intraculturally, and they can change from generation to generation. For example, we often think of sexual things as private, almost sacrosanct. In fact, it is common to refer to sexual intercourse as "intimate relations." Nowadays, we know there is no necessary connection between intimacy and sexual relations. If we use as an indication of what is intimate an individual's disinclination to easily reveal something to another, then for many, one's financial situation more readily meets that criterion. Once I inquired of a female patient of mine, whom I had known for several years, and who in the course of treatment had revealed to me the most intimate sexual facts, some details of her financial situation. I remember clearly the look of astonishment that came over her. "That's personal," she declared huffily.

The notion of intimacy, then, refers to psychological contents that initiate in our inner world, the "I within I," if you will. It refers to those ideas and feelings, attitudes and beliefs, fears and hopes, and even the very modes of perception and processing of information—our personal epistemologies—that are "most within us." The issue for us is when, to what extent, why, and under what conditions is that which is intimate transmitted to another. It gets even more complicated because there are different degrees of intimacy. Those varying degrees are represented interpersonally for me by the notion of relatedness. *I consider relatedness to be that dimension of interaction that involves the revelation of intimacies.*

Before elaborating the kinds of relationships that we have and where they fall on this dimension of relatedness, let me be a little more precise about what it is that is the "most within" us. As I have indicated, what is deemed most private and personal may vary from individual to individual, from culture to culture, from generation to generation. Some people may be private about political opinions or religious beliefs because they wish to avoid dispute or fear the poor judgment of others. There are scores of ideas, feelings, attitudes, hopes, and fears that are conscious or preconscious and about which we fear the censure, real or imagined, of others, dead or alive. More basic even than this, and more precious to protect and guard, is our very sense of self. It is our self that we observe being protected when we ride down the elevator with a stranger. Each of us has no real fear that the other will discover a particular opinion or attitude or, perhaps, some untoward sexual impulse or idea. Rather, I think it is our very sense of self that feels jeopardized to some extent in such an instance. Unprotected by a role, can we trust ourselves not to act inappropriately, or to reveal unwittingly by our behavior something of ourselves that we don't want to?

Relatedness means revealing one's innermost self to another. This can be terrifying. We all are so filled with shame. We all fear that to be known will result in rejection, for we all have been taught, to some extent, that to reveal one's innermost self to another is a betrayal of the family. It is very hard for us to do. Yet it is crucial for a loving relationship to be successful. Moreover, no agency of growth is more powerful than a committed, monogamous relationship in which the partners share their intimacies—what is most within—with each other via relatedness. Marriage is no guarantee that growth will occur, but it is a powerful possibility for those with good will and good intention.

Our relationships with others can be placed on a continuum from least to most intimate. Any interaction with another can be characterized by how related the contact is. Relatedness is that quality of relationship that has to do with the degree to which we would be willing, at least potentially, to communicate our innermost contents to another. In addition to these contents, intimacy refers to the revelation of certain characteristics of self that we hold guarded in most situations. In addition to the *what* of our most innermost selves, it is the *way of being* of our most innermost selves that I am referring to here. Let me give some examples: With a person I just met as I walked down the street, I would probably engage in polite conversation, ignoring my reaction to the events occurring all around me. With a male friend of some intimacy I might reveal some sexual thoughts or memories stimulated by a female passing by. With a female friend of some intimacy I probably wouldn't do that, but I might sing softly or run like a madman to get a bus or engage in some other playful behavior, thus revealing myself to her not just by what I say about what is going on inside me, but by how I actually behave with her, how I allow myself to be. In the most intimate of relationships, there is a significant degree of spontaneity, even to the point of revealing the more childish, demanding, unpleasant aspects of ourselves. We sometimes refer to this as "letting our hair down." This latter openness is particularly characteristic of long-term and committed relationships, and such relationships force us to grow.

It is astounding to me how nature conspires to bring us together, accomplishes its goals and provides us, at the same time, an opportunity to achieve our own personal ones. The desire to be intimate with one another is a powerful, inexorable drive that each of us experiences. This overwhelming urge provides us not merely fun and games, but also the opportunity for the completing of unfinished aspects of our personality. The urge for completion fuels the already powerful biological and emotional and sexual imperatives.[3] We come together not merely to love and procreate but to grow! And this is made possible by the evolutionary good fortune that our impulse to mate occurs merely at the time the exquisitely human capacity of re-creating our past, *transference*, becomes full-blown. Both occur when we start, emotionally, to leave home.

When we meet and fall in love and desire to be intimate with each other, when the terrible urges to do this far outweigh our shyness and hiddenness and shame, it is an opportunity for us to examine just where we are stuck as persons, and if we stay with each other for any amount of time we shall, indeed, be confronted with this opportunity. For in the intimate relationship of monogamous devotion, all the distortions and manifestations of our fusion, all our transference potential, will out, sooner or later. It is in the negotiation of theses "regressions" that the relationship will rise or fall and the stretch into new places of psychological separation will be accomplished, or not, for each of the partners.

In this commitment the forces of psychological separation encourage us to reveal our "intimus," that which is truly us, to the other. The forces of fusion on the other hand compel us to stay the same. Something must give, and give it does. A battle ensues. Each regresses, and as unsettling as this is (the honeymoon is over!), what actually occurs is the opportunity to finish the unfinished aspects of our personalities. We psychologically separate and grow out into ourselves. It is not inevitable though that this happens. Many things can happen. The couple may "seal over" emotions and cease to be related in the way in which we are suggesting; they may develop a dysfunctional mode of interacting, a mutual *folie à deux* in which, together, they manage to continue to carry out their respective fused agendas (sometimes these folks look like "perfect couples" to the outsider). Or they may separate, off to further chase the illusion that a good marriage is one in which they will never have to change at all. But a good marriage is precisely one in which we have to change—not because it is the price we have to pay, as many believe—but rather because it is our biological and psychological destiny to do just that. In the good fortune of happening to meet a mate, as eager as you to know and to be known, intimacy will develop that will be the most powerful agency of transformation in your life.

There are plenty of opportunities for misfirings in the long-term committed relationship. All around us we see disturbed relationships. The divorce rates are still growing. Yet I am convinced that the greatest agency for change and growing out into the person each of us is destined to be is a committed relatedness.

Life leads always and inexorably to growth and change. Psychological separation supports this change. Fusion wants to conserve and save, to perpetuate the status quo. Fusion is unnatural, against nature. My urging toward letting go, getting out of the way, is not because we have a real choice. Change is going to occur because this is the way it is. My encouraging each of us to form the intention to psychologically separate is to help us to change for the better, to be happy and fulfill our personal growth process. We can never stop change; it will go on whether we cooperate or not. But if we do cooperate through the intention to psychologically separate, we can have our say about the nature of that growth change as well as having a lot of fun. But fusion is the demonic resistance to such letting go.

Marriage and the family are such a powerful crucible of psychological separation. We must constantly grow to "leave" our parents. We must constantly grow to let our children leave us. Changes occur, constantly and relentlessly, like the water rushing to the sea, unstoppable and enormously powerful. Despite the pain and difficulty and troubles in relationships and families, throughout the world love is fired and formed there. Great feats of heroism occur daily and go unnoticed. There is no more beautiful thing than the lifetime growth of two people in love.

In a loving relationship the joys and consolations of emotional closeness as well as the charge to psychologically separate are equally appreciated by each of the partners. The relationship of each to her own self is valued, worked on, and when necessary fought for. A particularly powerful thing that the long-term committed relationship has going for it is the dimension of time. In this respect marriage has it all over psychotherapy. Time! What happens over time? All sorts of things are possible over time. Some people fuse immediately. Some fight it out but at some point are ultimately taken over. Some are never taken over but run away; some are taken over and physically stay together but never develop intimacy; some give up their selves and become slaves.

But others engage in a wonderful dance of intimacy—between fusion and separation—all their lives. The urge toward fusion and the impulse toward a separated spirit operate in tandem. I like the description of this in Gabriel Garcia Marquez's *Love in the Time of Cholera*:

> She clung to her husband. And it was just at the time when he needed her most, because he suffered the disadvantage of being ten years ahead of her as he stumbled through the mists of old age, with the even greater disadvantage of being a man and weaker than she was. In the end they knew each other so well that by the time they had been married for thirty years they were like a single divided being and they felt uncomfortable at the frequency with which they guessed each other's thoughts without intending to, or the ridiculous accident of one of them anticipating in public what the other was going to say. Together they had overcome the daily incomprehension, the instantaneous hatred, the reciprocal nastiness and fabulous flashes of glory in the conjugal conspiracy. It was the time when they loved each other best, without hurry or excess, when both were most conscious of and grateful for their incredible victories over adversity. Life would still present them with other moral trials, of course, but that no longer mattered: they were on the other shore.[4]

The reader of this novel, which is, above all, about love, is witness to the struggle of the spirits of each of the protagonists to attain such a bonding without damage to their fierce uniqueness.

There is a fierce force in each of us to become who we are. For human beings the long-term committed relationship is nature's way to help each of us finish the unfinished aspects of our personality. On the surface each may look "grown up" and seem to be acting "appropriately" and carrying out life's tasks. Underneath, however, may be the timid, frightened, hopeful child who brings her self, such as it is, to another in an unending quest to cure her herself, to be made whole. It is poignant and touching. This is why each of us stops and looks as a bride descends the steps of the church, even if she is a stranger to us. In a basic, simple way we know what she is about. She is looking for love and solace and wholeness. She is about to place her entire being in the cauldron of intimate relatedness. Terrifying; but avoiding it is more terrifying. And so we persevere.

It is a paradox that while an intimate, committed relationship is one of the most potent circumstances in our attempt at self-articulation, the commitment to psychological separation must precede it. One must have the *intention* to keep on growing out in order to love and to engage in the life-enhancing relatedness of marriage. Without such an intention, particularly if the person is significantly narcissistic, all the benefits are sabotaged.

This is why so many marriages flounder. Each must have the good will to abandon their parents in some basic way in order to forge out a new home and a new being. Without this good will, one or both of the parties will commence to recreate their family of origin, to create a structure in which change is obviated. Marriage is corrupted, although as I said, some such folks make a serious attempt to look like the perfect couple. The essential disorder in this arrangement is often seen in the psychic or physical pain of one of them or, perhaps, in the pain of the children. When such a situation occurs because one of the partners refuses to engage in the intimate dance of regression, expression, and surrender, relatedness ceases to occur. The relationship may remain, but the relatedness, the sharing of intimacies is dead. They, particularly those interested in growth, carve out what Thoreau termed "lives of quiet desperation." Or one gets sick or addicted or in trouble or leaves the relationship. Some stay in such a marriage for personal reasons and continue to grow on their own. This is quite possible, just as it is possible for the person who has left a marriage to continue the growth process. The long-term, committed relationship is not *essential* to psychological separation; it is just a wonderful opportunity which sadly is often missed. The great family therapist Murray Bowen once said, "Differentiating oneself (what I would refer to as psychological separation) from one's family not only required understanding entrenched and complex patterns of family interaction but acquiring the skill, patience and self-control to talk directly with one's most intimate relations without blowing up, giving in, going crazy or running away."[5] What better chance will we have to achieve this than a long-term, committed relationship?

Loving intimacy is both the result of psychological separation and simultaneously the occasion for it. Remember, it is only the psychologically separated person, the one whose spirit is somewhat "articulated," who stands a chance in the thorny business of bringing his incomplete personality into contact with a stranger, who in turn brings hers as they settle down to the business of sorting out their personalities with each other.

Previously, I described psychological separation as being "central-to-self" as opposed to "central-to-other." This notion is sorely tested when one falls in love. We may have left home and made ourselves, in some sense, central-to-self, but often we have been in waiting for the "right" person to come along to again make central-to-ourself. We will then "live happily ever after," each responsible for the other. This is our unfortunate tendency. The collective expression of this is everywhere in our culture, in the marriage ceremony itself. We may no longer be "selfish." We must "love and cherish." In some deep and unspoken place I suspect the unconscious urge to merge with mother again is touched in the congregation. The marriage vow is an encouragement to fuse and it is made with the silent blessing of all in attendance. Perhaps this time it will work. Two will indeed become one and live happily ever after.

Perhaps this time it *will* work, but not because two have become one. They must fight against these injunctions for it to work. Each may become central to the other's *life* but not to their *selves*. As a matter of fact, it *will* "work," if work means a partnership where both grow out into themselves through the honest sharing of intimacies and encouragement of their partner. It will work to the extent that each remains central-to-self, and does not want to become central-to-other, and desires to reach out across the chasm of their separateness to love the other. Rilke put it this way: "Once the realization is accepted that even between the closest human beings, infinite distance continues to exist, a wonderful loving side by side can grow up, if they succeed in loving the distance between them which makes it possible for each to see the other whole against the sky."

It is in the denial of this distance that fusion festers and contaminates. We want to see an "essential" connection between ourselves and the other. I feel this way "because" of you. You "made" me feel this way. But in truth the only essential connection that has ever existed for any of us is that which existed between mother and ourselves in infancy and before. All other impulses in that direction are the deep memory of that bliss which a part of us always seeks to replicate. Another "sad" reality is that any particular feeling a person has is the *sole* responsibility of the person feeling it. No one "makes" us feel anything. We choose to respond to another in one of many ways available to each of us at any time. No particular response is inevitable. Even our love for another is more a decision to love rather than an inevitable response to compelling traits or characteristics the object of our affections happens to have, or we endow him with. If we have the rare good fortune or good sense to select a person to love who is actually "good" for us, and this person reciprocates our love, that is fortuitous indeed.

To love another means to have arrived at a point of being *capable* of loving. We take this quality for granted. We assume everyone has it. Sadly, this is not so. The person who has psychologically separated enough to be able to love does not depend on the quality of the other to be able to love. To need the other to be a certain way is searching, in a sense, for an addiction. To love another actually requires only that you have developed the capacity to love and have freely chosen to exercise it. It is beyond unconditional positive regard, just as radical self-acceptance is. Unconditional positive regard implies "overlooking" a person's limitations. *Love is knowing that there are no limitations*, that the beloved is perfect just the way he is!

To be capable of love, of radical self-acceptance or love of another, you must relinquish your addictions (or at least "intend to," honestly and completely). While passively involved in addictions—substances or people or organizations or gurus—one cannot have radical self-acceptance. Radical self-acceptance means disconnecting from *all* evaluations, first and foremost the family, and secondarily, all addictive elaborations of these evaluations. Anything we become obsessively or compulsively connected to is experienced by us as crucial to our existence. *That fear makes it impossible to love*. Only when we have separated sufficiently from these distractions can we stand truly on our own (radical self-acceptance) and then love another and, in a sense, all others.

Of course, nobody has achieved this entirely, nor is it even possible. The main thing is to be on the road of psychological separation. When one forms the intention, regardless of where one is on that road, she is capable of loving. And loving is just the beginning of it. For when one loves and knows and reveals, shares her intimacy through relatedness, the unfinished aspects of the personalities of each will surface and a lifetime adventure begins.

The psychologically separating person (on the road, remember!) has easy access to his intimus and can readily communicate from it whenever he chooses. He speaks from "I" and, being in touch with his feelings, can easily communicate them to you, but only if this is what he desires. He is not interested in winning, being right, or controlling your reaction to him, so he tends to be spontaneous and has energy available to experience who the other is as well. He communicates himself to the other and then waits for the other to respond. He does not react to this response until he is sure the other is finished with his thought. He then takes a few breaths to let the import of the other's communication sink in and he, himself, has access to his own inner experience, affect, and thought. He then may react. His communications are characterized by patience, "allowing" each to know himself or herself and each other and communicate with clarity. Sounds like your last conversations, right? There is actually great resistance to such directness.

Those in resistance to intimacy are of two broad types and each has a language, a fusion "lingua" as I like to call it which, while different from each other, actually serve the same purpose. That purpose is to find out what one needs to know without revealing one's own intimus. This can take the form of being extremely guarded and hidden, asking loads of questions designed to elicit information without letting the other know where he is coming from (communicating from "behind a tree" as I like to think of it), or the opposite, being so involved in the intimus of the other so as to be impervious to one's own. Figure 8–1 on page 152 describes these two types, and then the psychologically separated one.

Recall that fusion is characterized by one's feelings and thought processes being intertwined with another's. The first general category (Type 1 in Figure 8–1) is dramatically illustrative of that. As an example, there was a woman in treatment with a therapist whom I supervised some ten years ago. The patient, a well-functioning, accomplished individual, was especially vulnerable to her mother's preoccupation with her. She recalled walking down the street one day as a child of 12 or 13 holding hands with her mother. A boy she knew was approaching. The girl pulled her hand from her mother's. The mother responded, "I know what you did…you care more about that boy than you do about me. You care more about what he will think of you than you do about how I will feel." The girl was devastated. Rather than helping her daughter in her natural movement toward autonomy, this mother worked against it. Twenty years later, the patient reported the following. After a phone conversation with her mother, she was running in the park with a girlfriend. As she ran she was preoccupied that her mother seemed depressed when she told her she was going for a

Type 1: Codependent, depressive, encapsulating communication	Type 2: Schizoid, narcissistic, paranoid communication	Psychologically separated: Intimacy
The other's intimus becomes more important than one's own. Memory is totally of other's intimus, not one's own. When there is trouble, will work to change or "improve" the other, but deep down feels to blame. Often finds it impossible to leave.	*Type 2A:* The person does not reveal own intimus. Will not participate in "shared intimus." Memory is only of narcissistic reference or paranoid protectiveness. *Type 2B:* The person reveals himself or herself but has no interest in the other. No ambience is created. There is no memory; the person does not take in intimus of other. Little capacity for compromise. Quick to leave.	Related communication. Person shares intimus while retaining his or her own. Memory for shared intimus. Concern for each other. Celebration of each other's victories. No envy. Little competition. Love. Free to leave when there is trouble but will face it first and attempt to resolve it; grows as a result in either case. No need to change anyone.
"I'm nothing without you. I would die if you ever left me."	"I don't remember that you told me that. Are you sure?"	"I'm so happy for you! I knew you could do it."

Figure 8–1: Two types who resist intimacy and the psychologically separated person.

jog. Her mother's "upsetment" upset the woman. My supervisee suggested to her patient that perhaps her mother disapproved of her having fun, that is, running. This was an accurate and helpful observation. But in addition, I believe, the mother was upset at the daughter having an affective state that was *different* from hers, unfused, separated; and this was what the patient had to come to understand: separation is a two-way street. People with particular separation problems typically have parents who have worked against it because of their own anxiety about being alone. They "bind" their children to them by discouraging independent feeling and thinking.

In this instance the mother and daughter were in a pact: As a child, she believed that her mother was all powerful and if she did it mother's way (the right way!), she would live forever and be safe in her mother's protection. She also believed that her *commitment* to mother *made her mother immortal*, and if she separates (understood as abandoning mother), mother will become mortal and die as well. The bind is twofold; to separate means you will die, but it also means mother will die. What we are dealing with here is experienced in the unconscious as homicide and suicide!

This patient would say to my supervisee: "So, fine, how do I separate?" What she was really saying was: "I'm not going to. Show me the way and I will deny it," and "You are asking me to kill and die!…Do you know what you are doing?" Ironically, in the middle of this work my supervisee reported an incident in her own life in which she was confronted with the same problem. She was skiing in Vermont and got a call that her own mother might be dying (she didn't). My supervisee stayed up all night with the magic belief that if she stayed awake, her mother wouldn't, couldn't die.

I tell you these stories to remind you that the motivation behind psychological fusion is very deep. We are not bad because we have these profound forces working within us. It is our nature, given the fact of our consciousness, our long childhoods, our having parents who suffered the same problems. All humans suffer with this one way or another, this woman, her therapist, her supervisor, you and me. It's not my purpose here to elaborate all the ways this plays out. Suffice it to say that when our preoccupation with the feelings and behaviors and thinking of the other is more than with ourselves, we are not then in a position to know and communicate our own personal intimus, which is a *sine qua non* for an intimate relationship. The tragedy is that such preoccupation precludes the very thing we want so desperately.

The other style of being-in-the-world that interferes with intimacy (Type 2 in Figure 8–1) involves ways that we stay out of the intimus of the other and do not reveal our own. Here the fear of losing one's individuality is so great that entering into the *ambience* (which is the term I use to refer to the mutual sharing of intimacies) is avoided at all costs. Sometimes the person stays to himself or is painfully shy. Sometimes the person is interactive but one cannot "feel" him as being present. Sometimes the person will share his own intimus but remain impervious to the response of the other. You might phone such a person a few days after an interaction and inquire about what he has communicated to you, and he will be surprised that you bring it up, if he remembers telling it to you at all. He has not really shared; he has "dumped." He has no interest in your participation in his intimus. He was really engaged in a solitary exercise; you just happened to be there.

Sometimes the person is so paranoid that his fearfulness enables him to see only potentially dangerous aspects of the communications. Such a person often misses the forest for the trees. Everything must be made to fit into his elaborate structure of deep beliefs. There is no room for experiencing the intimus of the other. This is also true of the narcissist. What passes for communication is the constant checking out of the dangers to his intra-psychic set-up. You will often feel misunderstood with such a person because his reaction to your intimus will not be an understanding of your shared intimacy, but rather a jumping-off place to reassure himself that his belief system is correct and he is safe. He may tell you what to do or tell you what he thinks you should be feeling or thinking that is consistent with his belief system. He may get testy if you disagree with him. He is actually quite anxious when there is any challenge to his life view, which he believes to be essential to his and perhaps his mother's existence. Again, as I have emphasized before, the narcissist has a stake in making this "public." Words are magic to such a person. To say it makes it real.

All of these variations have at their core a terror of psychological separation and illustrate the particular style of staying fused with mother that the individual has created from the stuff of his unique experience. Even those whose conscious expressions reveal hate of a parent are, in reality, fused and preoccupied to the point of not being free to love.

Clues to an enmeshed interpersonal orientation can often be seen in the "fusion lingua." "You are my reason to live; I'd do anything for you; I can't live if living is without you; you made me love you; you made me feel (whatever)"; "I'm sorry I made you feel (whatever)"; "you are always on my mind; I 'meant' to do it, or I intended to give you a birthday party" (as if the intention is the same as the deed). "If you need me I'll drop everything and come running; you are so wonderful." It is not always easy to distinguish heartfelt expressions of love and appreciation and value from enmeshed communication. Psychologically separating communication generally starts with "I." "I love you and feel wonderful when you do (whatever)." Enmeshed communication generally starts with "you," referring to the other rather than to one's own state of internal experience.

Type 2 communicators also do not come from "I." They will also tell you "you are (whatever)" and rarely, if ever, speak of their own inner experience. They are great questioners. They want to "find out" rather than reveal their intimus to you. In fact, that is the last thing they want to do. The result is all "pseudo-communication." If a Type 2 communicator has an admiring feeling toward you, his communication might go something like this: "Is it expensive living in New York?...And you have to keep up a good appearance, too, don't you?...Even a haircut must cost a lot...You can't just go to the barber like in the old days (heh, heh)...(At this point you haven't the slightest idea of what he is driving at but you don't know what to say)...I wonder sometimes where people get their money...Do you go to a salon?..." (After some more questions you might inquire nervously, "Do you like my hairdo?") He would answer half-heartedly but ingenuously, "Oh yeah...it's very nice...but it must cost a fortune." What he really means is "Your hair is dynamite; I'm flabbergasted by how beautiful you look; I would like to have dinner with you (though I hope you'll split the bill)[6] because if all goes well I'd love to go to bed with you." Unlike the codependent, whose communication almost always carries an enmeshed overtone, with the narcissist and paranoid it is extremely hidden.

Contrast this with the communication of two people intent on growing out and eager to share their intimus with each other and to know the other. Such individuals generally start with "I" because they are comfortable with their feelings, and know they have a right to them and a right to express and communicate them. They are not fearful lest something bad will happen to them if they reveal themselves. At the same time, they are fully available to understand and value the communication of the other in a non-defensive way. If they have a negative emotional reaction to the transaction they communicate this, again coming from "I" ("I feel angry when you criticize my occupation" rather than "You're really hostile, do you know that?"). If the communication goes well there is a shared intimus (see Figure 8–1) in which each now shares something of the other's. That shared aspect of each becomes as important to the other as to himself. But this is true only of the shared intimus! There is still a major portion of self that is retained. The psychologically separated person is comfortable with this balance and as the relationship grows in relatedness, the shared intimus increases as well. Each always is the final arbiter of just what that balance is, and each respects the other's right to decide this, although they may not speak of it in those terms.

The crucial thing is the extent to which a person is able and willing to reveal who he actually is (intimacy) to another whom he is interested in knowing (relatedness). Unrelated people rarely use "I." They use the pronoun "you" even when referring to their own inner experience, thus implying that it is a "generic" rather than a personal experience. They use the plural "they" to refer to an individual, thus lessening the personal, more intimate and related quality of their contact. "I met this person the other night and 'they' worked for IBM." I remember hearing a psychiatrist in rounds at a hospital referring to his patient as "they" and wondered just how related he could possibly be to him. All these misuses of pronoun, person, plural instead of singular, are hints of the conflict a person has in actually expressing, in an unguarded way, his inner experience.

When intimate relatedness has occurred there is memory for the event. When the communication has genuinely become part of the shared intimus, each remembers the other's intimus as if it were her own. Reference is made to it, not for the defensive purposes of the paranoid/narcissist, but out of genuine concern. The central-to-self person responds to the intimus of the other and the memory of it, and the other responds to that; each experiences being known and cared for. The Type 1 person is totally enmeshed in the communication of the other and ceases being central-to-self. Consequently, no real intimacy is possible. The narcissistic "pseudo-communicator" has no response to your remembering his communication. That is not what he is interested in *now*, and he reacts to your concern as if it were an intrusion.

Truly intimate relatedness is characterized by *presence*. Each of the parties "shows up" for the other for the most part, and each does it while continuing to be central-to-self. As opposed to over-involved, smothering intrusiveness or self-centered information gathering, each of the truly intimate manifests care. *Care* is the *freely* given human concern regarding the welfare of another. In such a relationship there is little fear of betrayal. Betrayal is generally charged by those who depend on someone to do something or be a certain way. But dependency, itself, is a betrayal of intimacy. Dependency is getting someone to do something for you instead of being present to that person. Love and loyalty and relatedness are *presence* in intimacy in a relationship, revealing your intimus to another. *Fidelity is the commitment to one's own psychological separation, to the capacity to be happily alone, and to the intention to be present to others, particularly the beloved.* True fidelity is not so much a question of refraining from doing what you want when you are not with the other, but rather being present when you are with her. It means also letting the other be alone with himself when he chooses to be. This, of course, means being faithful primarily to yourself. Fidelity to another means fidelity to yourself, first and foremost. And then care is born.

Presence, then, is the state of readiness to relate. This quality does not depend on intelligence, education, or socialization. It is not sophisticated. It was characteristic of the young mildly retarded couple on the bus that I spoke of above. It certainly was true of the "half-witted" man from the almshouse that Thoreau found so engaging. Presence consists of a willingness to come in touch with one's own inner experience (intimus) and make that available to the inner experience of the other. The "making available" is presence; the actual sharing of the "most within" of each other in contact, or just as a way of getting to know the other, is relatedness. Being aware of my own inner experience is a crucial epistemological tool. When I am in touch with myself, for example, I am able to "hear" the other at a different level and I can get a truer meaning of his communication. This is presence. If the other is doing the same, the give-and-take is relatedness, even if the content is something frivolous, such as the experience of a football game. Even then I am experiencing my friend experiencing the football game as I make it possible for her to experience me experiencing the game.

Isolation is the withdrawing of presence (intimacy and relatedness) in favor of fusion with mother. It is not necessarily correlated with being alone, away from people. When one is alone and *present to self*, this is not isolation; on the other hand when one is with others and *in transference*, rather than present, this is an instance of isolation. Isolation is not being alone. Isolation, rather, is *not being with self or others in presence*. The antidote to isolation is emotional communication, and the characteristics of such communication are:

1. Speaking from "I"; not asking unrelated questions.
2. Feelings: experiencing and communicating them.

3. Experiencing the other; not responding until the other has completed the thought. Not formulating the answer, but rather listening to one's spirit prior to responding.
4. Patience.

Emotional communication leads to the overcoming of transference in relatedness. It results in seeing the other just as he is. And love depends on overcoming transference, as does psychological separation. Wisdom is seeing with one's own eyes, and the apotheosis of wisdom is seeing what is as it is. Philip Roth wrote, "Oh, my god, I thought—now you. You being you! and me! This me who is me being one and none other!"[7] But the wondrousness of this knowing is purchased at a price. In order to see the other clearly, we have to make our way through the fog of our fused distortions and the unfinished aspects of our personality. Fortunately, when we are committed to a partner, we have a long time to do this. We may gradually begin to distinguish who he actually is from how we seem compulsed to see him.

So love is the overcoming of transference—both in the capacity to love and in the ability to receive another's care and concern. *To love another adult is to surrender the extraordinariness of the parent-child relationship.* When we truly love another deeply, it is not transference but rather the redirection of the tremendous capacity for love which we experienced with mother. This is why, incidentally, it is so important to show appreciation to one another, letting the other know how much the other's love means to you. In loving we have overcome narcissism, or chronic fusion with mother (ego); we concern ourselves with a person outside the family. He is seen, understood, appreciated, and admired. We need to encourage each other in this. It is not easy.

Fusion is the re-creation of the source of narcissism, oneness with mother, in another and becoming one with that newly created mother surrogate. The other is not known, understood, appreciated, and admired in her own right. Rather she is constructed in the image and likeness of mother and the psychic characteristics of that early relationship are experienced in the present. Compare true love, where the self is enhanced, exhilarated, self-confident, and enriched in its interaction with the world and all the activities of the spirit, to fusion, where the self is depleted, anxious, possessive, and withdrawn from the world.

In love, the lovers are drawn toward union, the connection of two separate selves in blissful relatedness, the culmination of this being sexual union.

In fusion, on the other hand, the persons are drawn toward oneness with each other, the surrender of self in the service of security and safety. It is an anxious connection, sometimes feeling safe, but always at the expense of self. Sex is often interfered with because true sexual relatedness expects two separate selves reaching out in selfless communion. The anxiety one feels at the prospect of true love and joyful sexuality is because one senses that psychological separation is a prerequisite for this love. To truly love another, a piece of narcissistic self-love, a way we remain connected with mother, must be relinquished. As in all separation steps, it is accompanied by sadness, mourning, and fear. But as it is accomplished, these feelings yield to joy and the pleasant exhilaration of becoming more of oneself.

Even sex has its root in the infantile passion of the child and mother, which continues in some form throughout childhood. The passion of that early sexuality must be brought into the loving relatedness of the couple. Sometimes the passion is inhibited as a way of not fully leaving mother. Sometimes the sexuality of one or both of the persons remains furtive, secret, a silent oedipal loyalty, often expressed symbolically outside the intimate relatedness. To become fully sexual is to be exquisitely psychologically separated. Is it so surprising that parents resist their child's sexuality or that so many adults avoid it or make it illicit? To bring the full passion of mother-child into the loving relatedness of two adults is a characteristic of true loving.

There is no reason why a man and a woman who are on the separation path cannot like, love, grow, and revel in the deepening knowledge of each other, though there often seems to be. For both, the obstacles reside in the difficulties in separating from mother, although this operating dynamic may be quite obscured. Men and women have the same capacity for intimacy, relatedness, and caring, but each has them interfered with in different ways. For both boys and girls, the approval of mother is the most important thing in life, for it made us feel loved, which meant security and safety. For the male this often means being the "hero"; for the female, it means becoming like mother.

As a result there are profound differences between the sexes which include even the very modes of cognition.[8] The separation task is somewhat different, but each must transcend the compulsivity of gender roles in order to love and relate. For example, men must be like father, and in this identification a boy is helped to move away somewhat from his fusion with mother. But the girl must identify *with* her mother. She has it both easier and more difficult. She does not have to face the shocking terror of separation the way the male does; she is able to "hold onto" the mother in ways the male cannot. But this identification with mother makes it more difficult to separate and give full rein to her spirit. For a woman, the greatest obstacle in achieving full psychological independence and freedom has to do with this subtly difficult developmental task, how to be "like" mother and, simultaneously, grow out into her own unique spirit. The enemy of women's liberation is not men (men will let women do whatever they want, just as they will not do whatever women forbid) but rather the failure of some women to separate sufficiently from the natural tendency to emulate mother so as to put her unique stamp on her life and sexuality. The ways a woman learns to seduce a man keep her secure in her connection with mother, which, in a fused person, may be more important than the man, himself.

Both men and women have the same overall task of wresting themselves from the undue influences of their early caretakers, to become whom each really is. This task transcends gender. In relationship to the other, each must relinquish sex-role stereotypes that interfere with intimacy. This keeping each other enmeshed, each in their own way, with mother. This gets us to the question of power.

There is no war between the sexes, only people who *live in fusion* and are not free to *let someone else into their lives in intimacy*.[9] Those who are not present to the relationship either by emotional absence or the extremes of dependence are not free. These ways—and there are others—are attempts to master the relationship by their own life strategies. They believe they must be "one up," in control, have power over the other. If, in the struggle between the two that ensues when one is involved in power over the other, the power seeker does not yield this character defect, the other must leave. If the other doesn't, then he, too, is interested in power. In any dysfunctional relationship, both parties are playing out their own strategies, their own long-learned ways of staying fused with each other despite how it appears to the casual observer. Even in the dramatically sado-masochistic relationship this is so. A few years ago, Joel Steinberg was convicted of abusing and causing the death of Lisa, a young girl entrusted to his care. Harvard child psychiatrist Robert Coles examined the role of his partner, Hedda Nussbaum, in their horribly destructive parental arrangement. As I mentioned earlier, Coles pointed out that the masochist is not merely a victim but that, in studying this case, one can begin to see "the masochist as a sly, insistent, clinging aggressor feeding off and provoking constantly a tormentor's rage." It is easy to take sides in such situations, but in any dysfunctional relationship both parties are scrambling for power, each over the other. The "codependent" person needs to be indispensable and the exclusive source of essential gratification to another in order to feel safe. The addict needs to be "sick" in order to be loved. Both are based on an infantile longing for mother and both result in controlling, enabling, acting out, victimization, blame, and even death.

But there are those on the separation path, intent on being central-to-self and looking for another who is not interested in fusion but in the fresh loving of two independent people. Such persons, incidentally, generally have other friends because they enjoy love of all types and know the intimate, monogamous relationship is but an instance, albeit special, of friendship in general. "Ordinary" friendships have many distinct qualities. They are not as intense as that of lovers. They typically do not involve the regressions I have been speaking of, yet they are wonderful in themselves. Friendships flourish when two people trust each other enough and enjoy each other enough to seriously discuss their lives with each other and not use that openness, in any way, to control the other. It is good, too, that committed lovers have other friends because in the most psychologically separated among us there is a powerful pull toward enmeshment once sexual intimacy is initiated. Other friendships can serve as a check on that tendency and help preserve us as central-to-self.

We come to the end of this reflection on intimacy. It has all been so logical, so reasonable, so "linear." But of course, our lives are anything but linear. I extract from the whirling vortex of our lives a strand, a theme, and focus on it and its qualities and its vicissitudes for the sake of clarity, to make a point. But the clarity obscures the reality, for we are all in this spinning complexity which we know to be our lives.

Animals seem to have it so easy. They just "do it" and while there are uniquenesses among them, among all life down to the most basic and primitive, these are slight when compared to us, children of the long childhood, the consciousness, the faulted parents.

We live in an infinite array of feelings and senses, and when it comes to relationships with each other, the possibilities are endless as well. We have such complicated and even encumbered pieces of life with each other. Relatedness is the most fascinating aspect of ourselves. So unique, so human, so ultimately unfathomable. For the most simple needs our contacts with each other are so rich and so vulnerable. Man and woman seek each other out, huddle together for comfort and security and even eke out some pleasure and gratification, yes, even some satisfaction and joy. Within the geometric expansion of the infinite possibilities for each, in the midst of all these transactions, spirit keeps us moving forward, growing out unto ourselves, if we surrender.

Any discussion of love must also address loss. Grief comes to lovers. All who would love will know grief, and even those who protect themselves from it knew it once. "Let your hearts be broken," Stephen Levine, student and teacher of grief and loss, always says. To be truly human is to let your heart wrap around *all* feeling. Everything we have ever loved or will ever love we will lose. Have compassion. Have mercy on yourself. And yet life is short; now is the time to love.

We have all known the loss of a beloved. When this happens a torrent of grief is unleashed. We mourn not just for the loss of this person but of all our prior loves, all those whose lives have been intertwined with ours, all those to whom we have given a piece of our souls, and cradled a piece of theirs in ours, and of course, mother. When I have had this experience, it is as if everything I knew or could count on became unglued. First I fight vigorously to avoid my inundation by pain and anguish. I deny, I bargain, I fight with the beloved, hoping to spare myself by trading hate for love. But it is to no avail. If I have loved and lost, there is the price to pay and I must pay it. I find myself despairing. The world looks different to me. There is no hope. I will never love again. This has been my last chance. My demons, like vultures circling a dying animal, pounce upon me in my weakened condition. If I am smart I receive solace from those who love me. I may even find the strength to pray, to appeal to something larger than myself to help me through the abandonment of yet another false god. Yet, in all likelihood it is not all addiction. I am able to love and I, indeed, loved a fellow human being. In every love relationship we give a piece of our soul to another and, in turn, receive a piece of the other's. It is a nonrefundable gift because if either withdraws from the relationship, that piece of soul is destroyed; it is not returned. When a human being withdraws her love from me, a piece of myself, that which I have given to her, is killed. When I withdraw my love from her, I kill a piece of her. We are thus traumatized and guilt stricken, abandoned and reminded of our other losses, desperately saddened and weakened, vulnerable to the assault of our own demons. We are messes.

We experience many losses as we live life. Some are necessary losses, though perhaps not all. Nevertheless, the grief is always the same.

Growing out into yourself involves emotionally leaving the family you came from, and even any family you may have created. It means being able and willing to experience being totally alone—one with yourself in the world—and simultaneously being emotionally merged with all living things that are, ever were, and ever will be.

Does this mean we cannot have loving relations with our parents and siblings and children and lovers and friends and acquaintances? Just the opposite. In the inner atmosphere of the truly psychologically separating spirit, it is for the first time actually *possible* to have *genuine* relatedness. We acknowledge that we are all fellow strugglers and we can love, support, and celebrate each other. Because each relationship has its unique characteristics, each is like a fingerprint. And those we have blood with, those we have years with, those we have special physical, psychological, and spiritual relatedness with, etch our souls. They actually help us separate—define our selfness. We need each other to become ourselves.

But it is love with a stranger that first provides the possibilities to confront the unfinished aspects of our personalities and to yield the old ways to make way for a return to who we are. An exclusive, long-term committed relationship demands this of us, and as such it is a gift. Our other friendships are powerful supports and do the same, but to a lesser degree. Intimacy and relatedness clear the way for us to open our hearts in love.

It is sad to give up our old fused ways, but it is also exhilarating, because to be a live, psychologically separating human is thrilling. We give up our childishness, our avaricious needs to have people re-create old roles. We accept our life, our existence. We appreciate the absolutely unspeakable gift of being alive, and our payment for that gift is to be alive and to pass it on.

We love, we lose our lovers, we pick ourselves up, dust ourselves off, vow we'll never love again, and then we do, if we are lucky. For we are lovers, we humans, and the most poignant thing about us is that, in spite of it all, we try again; we reach out across the chasm of our essential aloneness to bridge it with our love, and we often do. With all our limitations, human love and human friendship are the greatest things about us. And when we have found it, if only for a moment, it is the best there is.

Chapter 9

How Change Occurs

℘℃

We know that nobody really wants to change, despite our constant haranguing of ourselves and each other. Nobody *can* change either, at least in the way we are told we should. Isn't it a joyous reality that we don't have to?

What we call change is return—return to the natural growing out of self with which we entered life and which always operates, no matter how stuck we may be at the moment. The Spirit keeps moving us along, although sometimes there are weighty obstacles. Releasing the Spirit is what we're after, finding a way to return to our true selves, permitting the growing out into ourselves to happen in a fuller and more free way.

In this chapter we will discuss the three ingredients essential to all growing out and to all successful methods that people have employed to help each other. They need no techniques, no equipment, no medicine, no therapist even, although sometimes a therapist or spiritual advisor can be very helpful in the process. With or without another, the deep understanding and appreciation of these ingredients help us release ourselves from the grip of our earliest caretakers and to see the world with our own eye, to learn to love ourselves.

Intention

Change is not simple. We may not really want to change but may be yielding to the wishes of someone else. Or perhaps we are responding to the wishes of someone from our past, someone we have made part of us. We may have accepted standards of behavior that are actually at odds with our spirit. So, on the conscious, expressed level or deeper there may be conflict in even our intention to change.

I think most of us deeply accept ourselves in the sense that we know ourselves and understand, at some level, that we are what we are largely because we chose to be or felt we had to be. But we generally *don't* accept ourselves in the sense that we accept that acceptance of ourselves. We deeply believe that we must be the way we are, yet we judge, condemn, and generally make ourselves miserable. That whole process may, in itself, be part of what we believe we are and must be. We may feel we have to be miserable, and we can use the discrepancy between what we feel ourselves to be and what we believe we should be to torture ourselves.

So when we want to change something we have a dilemma. We often go to a "helper" to define what needs to be changed, while at the same time we have a deep belief that no change is possible, or we get into a delusion that this helper is magically going to accomplish something. The therapy situation, to use this as an example of a "helper," is fraught with impossibilities from the outset. It has implicit in it the seeds of failure and increased feelings of worthlessness. Why should we ask ourselves to change, particularly if we believe, perhaps in some deep recess of our soul, that what we are at any particular moment in time is our best judgment of how to be?

The immediate problem that must be dealt with by the helper is why the person believes he must change and the profound lack of self-acceptance that this implies. If the person indeed wants to change something about his behavior, then why does this discrepancy between the expressed intention of the person and his actual behavior exist? Flavoring this inquiry will be the pervasive self-condemnation that most of us carry with us at all times. With a little luck and massive good will there may arise a relationship between the two parties that will enable the study of the individual in a loving and accepting context. This, in turn, may result in *his* juggling around some of the variables inside himself that have prompted his behavior. All this may result in new decisions and new behavior we call change. This may come from a place so deep in the person that the activating variable may never be consciously known to either party, and both must accept this with humility.

The helper, for her part, must have as her intention not placing her values on the person consulting her. This is where Carl Rogers was so brilliant. He focused *entirely* on the inner experience of the client. Even interpretation was avoided. Although interpretation was the chief agent of change for Freud, he, too, in his "abstinence" was careful not to impose his opinions on the patient. Even the interpretation, if done correctly, should just bring the patient that little bit of awareness that he himself had gotten to by dint of painstaking examination and analysis of resistance.

One of the difficulties in goal setting is the implication that achieving the goal will provide happiness. Even when the goal is achieved, happiness is not necessarily the by-product. Sometimes just the opposite occurs. I knew a man who ardently believed that once he became a millionaire all his problems would be over and he would be happy. When he achieved his goal, he did not become happy; he worried even more about the preservation of his newfound wealth and then became more depressed because he discovered that what he had worked so hard for all his life did not make him happy.

Happiness is a function of our relationship with ourselves, as Quentin Crisp is fond of saying.[1] When Christ said it was harder for a rich man to be saved than for a camel to get through the eye of a needle, perhaps he was referring to how few millionaires seem happy. In fact, when happiness is seen as depending on *anything* outside our relationship to our self (and our Transcendent), the project is doomed to failure. Similarly in psychotherapy. We need to make sure why a person wants to change and examine first the implicit self-condemnation in these aspirations; make clear that the change in itself may not result in happiness; be ever mindful of the changing nature of intentions and the ever-present danger of their use in the service of demonic self-hatred, for if there is anything that will absolutely prevent growth and expansion of the self, it is self-condemnation.

One day I was pointing out to a 36-year-old art director that our behavior at any moment is the end-product of the best information and meaning we have available to us at any particular time. If this is at odds with our conscious intention, it is because we are not fully aware of that part of us that is influencing the decisions. Rather than criticize, it is time for loving observation. Criticism comes from the demons, who do not want us to grow out into the fullness of our being.

Walter: I just realized that the critical voice is my father's.

Me: Can you live without your father on your back?

Walter: I don't know.

Me: It means separating from your father.

Walter: I always believed that if I silenced it, its power would show itself in other ways....I'd fuck up without a word, in even worse ways.

Me: If left to your own devices.

Walter: I don't know....I never even considered living my own life.

Me: That's what seems to be at stake here.

The trouble with bio-energetics, rational emotive therapy, and certain self-help approaches like neuro-linguistic programming and inspirational offshoots is that they assume that to "know" something about how the mind and human behavior work enables us to "do" something, based on that knowledge, to "improve" ourselves, "accomplish" something, or "control" our feelings. Control is the key concept here. So we throw ourselves at our problems, and we often fail because we have not dealt with intention. And when we fail, our self-esteem actually gets worse. Even when we think we know what we are aiming at we may be mistaken. If a conscious, logical, rational goal is not accomplished, it may be for many reasons, some of them better than the conscious "owned" one.

Nature has its own plan for us. Sometimes a psychological conflict or inhibition may be a protection against a physical, life-threatening illness that the individual is not aware of. Alcoholism, for example, is, on some rare occasions, a defense against a more malignant psychotic process that blooms when the alcohol is withdrawn. Schizophrenics have been shown to have a lesser incidence of malignant cancer than the general population. These are extreme cases, but I mention them to remind us that we must develop humility in developing goals. If we do not have this perspective, the process of attempting to change may unwittingly become the very agency of torture that the attempt to change was designed to correct.

Let us return to the man who was fearful of women. By forming an intention to understand his relationship to women with no specific goals in mind other than that, and by observing his behavior and, of course, by radical self-acceptance, he noticed he was attracted to ungiving women. He would become involved with such a woman, and even when he realized he wasn't getting much nurturance, he found himself unable to separate from her. He then began a repetitive pattern of attempted resolution. First, he tried to change her by relinquishing his own needs and being so "good" he believed that she would have to be nice to him. When that failed to get the desired results (as it inevitably did), he changed strategies. He rapidly ran through the sequence of becoming more demanding, then angry, and finally depressed. Or he would explode and the woman in question would get rid of him. Over time we discovered his penchant for self-centered and narcissistic women and his *compulsion* to remain in an unsatisfying relationship. In compulsively replicating his relationship with his mother, *an ungiving, narcissistic woman, whom he indeed could not leave*, he maintained his familiar psychic experience. Over time, as he more deeply experienced the "grip" he was in and shed the nagging self-criticism that generally accompanied this realization, the compulsion began to weaken its hold on him. He began to experience deeply his new understanding of what was going on inside him. He gradually and gently let go of the deep beliefs and chronic affects and was able, for the first time in his life, to be available to a more giving woman. He was separating psychologically.

If our intention is to understand who we are in our relatedness to the world, each bit of discovery can be received with a tender and delicate respect. We need not be too quick to improve. Improvement, after all, is only a hypothesis. We do not know what purpose a symptom may serve. We must be humble. Then we may step up to pain, shame, our deepest beliefs, and learn to dance with them. We can do this alone, but a therapist can be helpful. Fully experiencing the trap we are in begins the process of dissolution. The invocation to change is, in a sense, an aggressive thing; growing out into oneself is better considered as a gentle matter, suffused with love and acceptance and softness, like the birthing of a baby, messy but joyful.

In therapy we may notice the changing nature of intention. What we came to treatment for is rarely what we wind up understanding as the most significant issue. After a while, the charge to change, the demand to change, even the wish to change evaporates. We become totally absorbed in being and knowing who we are and loving that.

Observation

At the end of an initial interview with new patients I suggest this. I urge them to put aside their desire to change for the time being and focus rather on observing themselves and their life. In the time until the next appointment I encourage them to become "watch persons" of their lives; to notice what they do and how they feel, how it is between them and others, and what actually happens. I tell them to try not to judge themselves but to observe that too, if that is what they do. Inevitably the next session is miraculous. For most, it is the first time they have paid attention to who they are and what they do, at least for a very long time.

We begin the journey of fascination with our own processes. Most of us have never been encouraged to do this and, perhaps, have actually been discouraged from it. Try it. Just for a week. It will be a wondrous experience.

Stephen Levine wrote:

> It is in letting go of old models, opening into "don't know," that we discover life. It means getting out of our own way in the same manner that a healer gets out of his own way and lets the extraordinary nature of the universe manifest through him. He is not doing anything. As a matter of fact, for a moment his self-oriented doing has ceased so that he may become a conduit for the energy of wholeness. So, too, in the openness of "don't know" we watch the healing come about. We experience the melting away of old knowings and expectations. We begin to experience the joy of simply being, in love with all that is.
>
> When we no longer cling to our knowing, but simply open to the truth of each moment as it is, life goes beyond heaven and hell, beyond the mind's constant angling for satisfaction.[2]

It is another one of our limitations as humans that there is interference in this natural, essential tendency to notice and explore our world. Observe the infant. She is totally absorbed with the world, in looking, making judgments, reveling in her new discoveries. In our misguided love and ambition for her we often interfere. We tell her the names of things, we tell her what to look at and what not to, we solve the problem for her when a little patience would enable her to do it herself. We teach her to evaluate right from the beginning; this is "good" and that is "bad." Thus the process of exploring the world is immediately contaminated.

Most animals explore while their mothers protect. Being human often interferes with the natural exploring tendencies that facilitate independent perception and lead to wisdom. As a result, most of us remain in a child relationship to someone or something throughout life. It becomes extremely difficult for us to trust our own perceptions. We *must* have the validity of another person.

The tendency to rely on the perceptions of others seems always at the ready despite our best intentions, hard work, and even accomplishments toward independence. I was struck by this last winter when I was visiting a friend in Mexico. I have done a fair amount of traveling by myself and although I am a little anxious at the beginning, and have to fight deep beliefs that I will never be able to manage on my own, learn the currency, communicate and what not, I do, and I have done it quite adequately. But this time I met my friend at his home and for the next several days we were together, walking on the beach, talking, traveling around on public transportation and in cabs. My friend took care of all the money transactions, and I straightened it out with him later. One night we went to town to have dinner with some of his friends. After dinner, when we were calculating our respective parts of the bill, I asked my friend how many dollars I owed. One of the others looked at me and said, "You're in Mexico, you know."

I realized by that remark how dependent I had allowed myself to become while traveling with my friend. If I had been alone I would have learned the currency and enough Spanish by this time to flirt with the waitresses. But with him I became a dependent child counting on a "parent" to take care of business. He was polite enough to do it, but it could not have been fun for him either. I was astounded at how quickly I was willing to drop my own perception of the world for his. I suggested we spend the next day apart, and I went to town by myself, negotiating the written and unwritten rules of riding public transportation and just getting along in this quaint Mexican town. By dinner that night I had caught up and was holding my own. I was able to separate again from my self-created mother-surrogate and reconnect with the Transcendent both within and without.

Psychotherapy can be divided into broad categories with respect to the locus of the intrapsychic initiator of change. One set of orientations emphasizes the conscious, goal-directed, "willful" behavior of the person. This approach actually includes some strange bedfellows. Psychoanalysis, for example, teaches that "insight," the proper understanding of the relationship between cause and effect as a result of the "return" of the repressed, will "lead" a person to change his or her behavior. This implies that there is no psychic event in between the insight and the behavior. Ironically, behavior therapy, cognitive therapy, and even certain inspirational approaches share with psychoanalysis the outlook that once something happens, whether it is insight, conditioning, "correct" reasoning, or motivation, behavior "changes." But it often doesn't.

The other broad category includes those approaches that believe implicitly or explicitly that the person changes by "releasing" certain ways of "holding," whether that holding is to people, events, behavior, perceptions, ways of thought, beliefs, or chronic affects. The release is not a conscious, goal-directed thing, but rather occurs from a part of the person not ordinarily addressed by the above approaches. My point of view is that it is the spirit rather than ego that is appealed to. That appeal is made largely through the encouragement *to be aware*.

To observe, to focus clearly on exactly what is happening, is a psychologically separating act in itself. The minute we do that we are in charge of our life. Even if we experience pain, it is *our* pain we are experiencing. Although suffering, we have ourselves. Noticing our behavior and inner processes interferes with the free reign we permit the demons when we operate automatically and unthinkingly. Just by noticing the randomness of our thought processes, the inconsistencies, the irrationalities, the confusion, the pain, the grief, we are reclaiming our lives. That awareness in itself activates spirit. We begin ever so subtly to move in the direction of self-regard. Changes begin immediately just by the determination to notice our lives. It is amazing. We begin to discover that we have unwittingly turned our lives and destinies over to the forces of fusion and have been, for the most part, unaware of it! We may abuse ourselves even for this, but by now, if we are lucky, we have sown the seeds of compassion.

If a person were to spend a year doing nothing save observing himself—his behavior and feelings and thought processes; his relations with loved ones, peers, authorities, those who rely on him—he would grow out into himself enormously. But there are ways of going about it that may intensify and broaden his opportunities to observe.

Meditation is one such way. We commit to spending a certain self-prescribed amount of time each day relaxing and noticing what goes through our mind. Our intention here is to think of nothing. We may use a mantra to help quiet and empty the mind, or we may merely attend to our breathing. We attempt to accomplish nothing but to observe. It is the ultimate example, in a way, of being a "watchman" of our life. The results are always startling, particularly at the beginning. In contrast to the ordinary observation that I have suggested, simple "stepping outside of ourselves" to notice our life, meditation is much more focused. There is no refuge in duties to be attended to or even goal-directed thought processes. In fact, the whole idea of the exercise is to empty ourselves of our thought processes. Immediately we realize that such emptying is virtually impossible! An incessant flow of chatter, some of it seemingly focused, some of it more akin to a dream or the random thinking just prior to sleep, occupies our minds. To meditate consistently enables us to face the reality that most of our waking consciousness we are out of touch with significant dimensions of our being. It is a wonderful, although occasionally upsetting, confrontation with our self. And it is enormously healing both on a physiological as well as psychological level. Just this intense awareness, by itself, helps us get on the right track. This constant awareness of where we are "off the beam" very often sets in action the correcting mechanism of spirit, and healing occurs.

Another type of structured experience that results in focused observation is psychoanalysis or psychotherapy informed by psychoanalysis. Psychoanalysis by its structure and intentions enables a person to observe dimensions of his experience that no other approach has been able to achieve. In the first place, it is the study of the relationship between therapist and patient. It is a chance to observe par excellence and to talk about it and understand it as well. The very process of talking about it and understanding can, itself, come under scrutiny and observation. Psychoanalysis is a virtual laboratory of life. Just about all that is possible between humans happens in this laboratory. Joyce McDougall once said,

> The psychoanalytic adventure, like a love affair, requires two people. It is not an experience in which one person "analyses" another; it is the analysis of the relationship between two persons. The analyst's participation, forged from his own psychic strengths and weaknesses, enables him to feel and understand something of what his patients are experiencing; at times, he identifies with them—the child as well as the adult, and the man as well as the woman in them—while at other moments he finds himself experiencing the thoughts and feelings of those figures of the past who have left an indelible mark on the analysand's psychic world. His most precious guide in this difficult voyage without maps is his intimate if fragmentary acquaintance with his own psychic reality. Thus the analyst shares with his analysand an experience that is in certain ways more private, at times more intense, than his relationships with those near and dear to him.[3]

When we were speaking of the mother-child relationship in chapter 4, particularly its unspeakable intensity, I used as an illustration some of the ideas of the child analyst Melanie Klein. We spoke of the infant "introjecting" the mother's breast and, psychically, the mother herself. Very deep distortions in the perceptions of the young person develop around this time and are reinforced and modified through the continuation of the introjection-projection process throughout development.

This is very technical stuff and difficult to understand. Suffice it to say that there is a constant interplay between the feelings of the child and the real or imagined feelings of the mother. The child may be angry at some real or imagined deprivations (and life itself dishes those out to us no matter how loving mother is) and may project that anger onto the mother. But this is, in itself, very frightening to the child, because of her love of and need for her mother. So she introjects it back into herself and it becomes even stronger than it was before. Her new perceptions of mother, and later on of the world in general, are tainted by this internalized negative feeling. She projects again, introjects again; the process continues right into adulthood and shapes our relationships with all the parental surrogates we tend to create. No wonder we have such difficulty in getting along with each other!

Good psychoanalysis makes it possible to observe this process. The patient makes the analyst into a sort of "auxiliary" conscience, which frees the patient from his ordinary self-imposed restraints. He is able, then, to know and communicate his "untoward" impulses in the sessions. It is sort of like "checking the superego" at the door or using the analyst as a psychological heart/lung machine, by which the analyst takes over for the moment a psychological function to give breathing room for the rest of the psychology of the person to function more freely. When this happens, the direction of all the internal process moves toward the analyst. It is in the negotiating of the direction of these impulses that the person gets to take a look for the first time at his distortions in perception. The unique circumstances of the psychoanalytic situation plus the skill of the analyst make this possible (on a good day!), and the patient gets to understand these distortions by seeing the discrepancy between his feelings and beliefs toward the analyst and how the analyst actually is and behaves.

Classical analysis attributes this change, in the main, to the "interpretation." I tend to think that the same deep, inner process of spirit that we have described above is the actual mutative principle. But in any case, psychoanalysis provides a profound opportunity to observe just who we are and how we function and to learn of the ways we have developed to survive that have resulted in the abdication of self. It can be one of the most beautiful and uniquely healing of all human relationships. Even "interpretation," *the* agency of change in the psychoanalytic technique of psychotherapy, can be understood as observation and experience of ourselves found nowhere else in life.

There are many ways that we may take a good look at ourselves, from the most casual to the most structured. It is a fascinating adventure. As we do, we will notice the omnipresent human plague, the scourge of all of us: unrelenting self-criticism and abuse. And so the third and final and most important leg of the triumvirate of growing out into ourselves, that which completes intention and observation, is radical self-acceptance.

Radical Self-Acceptance

Try this: Wake up tomorrow and from your first awareness witness carefully your evaluation of yourself. Make this your most important activity for this one day. Be sensitive to the smallest detail. Notice the slightest emotion. Notice what you tell yourself about that. Notice what emotion you have about that emotion. Notice what you do next. Notice the thoughts that run through your mind. Make the entire day a meditation, even as you attend to all your other activities. Have it out with yourself this day. Get a bead on yourself. Whom do you think you are? How "good" are you? Do you like yourself? Are you happy with yourself? Do you love yourself? How much? Is there abuse going on? Do you maintain a fog about yourself? go about your tasks without much self-consciousness? Maybe you are in the grip of an obsession, something that won't leave you alone, your mind racing out of control.

Be careful that you don't let this little reflection become yet another occasion for an assault on yourself. As you experimented with observation you probably saw the malignant self-criticism most of us live with; we berate ourselves for even berating ourselves. Be patient with yourself about this. It is human nature. Have compassion.

What we are discussing right now may be the most important factor in our very existence. Life is about this—just how much we love ourselves. If we love and enjoy ourselves, we are free and are living life to its fullest; if we don't love ourselves, we are being deprived of the most important thing in the history of the universe, our life.

Being out of touch with just how wonderful we are is double trouble. It keeps us from truth, and it keeps us from joy. Yet, there is an agency in us that works full time to do just that. We don't need to join that demon! We may not be able to stop its operation just yet, but we can make a decision this very moment to have mercy on ourselves. We can make the decision to know that this self-criticism is delusion, not our fault, and we can form the intention this very moment to begin to let it go.

One of the reasons that radical self-acceptance is so crucial is that *no change can occur without it!* We begin to grow out into ourselves to the extent that we begin to love ourselves better. Change never occurs when we lack respect for ourselves. Remember, in the Alexander technique, the position of the head was the "primary factor" in the body's realignment. In human growth or return to spirit, radical self-acceptance is the primary agent. In fact, radical self-acceptance is the primary autonomous act, the most profound psychological separation step of all. It implies two irreducible psychic events: "I am enough in myself" and "I take the power of evaluation of myself to myself."

No change can occur without acceptance, at least not in the way I understand the word *acceptance*. The psychological and spiritual literature is filled with references to acceptance, self-regard, good self-concept, healthy narcissism, healthy self-love. I use the term *radical* when I refer to self-acceptance because I mean an attitude that surpasses or transcends the ordinary uses of the term. It is beyond evaluation.

First, acceptance means "to receive willingly," to accept completely any particular characteristic or behavior. It is a receiving of ourselves, a witnessing completely without judgment. We may be curious or charmed or shocked but never critical. We let our *opinion* of ourselves alone. We may modify our behavior because of the demands of reality. But our basic nature we accept as a given. We are neutral. Second, we love ourselves *as a decision*, much as we might love another. Loving is really more a function of our capacity to love than of the attractiveness of the beloved. This is true of ourselves as well. We love ourselves because we choose to, not because we are any particular way. Loving ourselves radically and unconditionally has nothing to do with our worth—as if there were such a thing as worth. We are worthy, as a rose is worthy, because it is life and as such it is beautiful. Radical self-acceptance is the total love of self that transcends even unconditional positive regard or a "wonderful" evaluation of ourselves. It is totally without evaluation. It accepts what is and knows that it is good. It is an aspect of worship; it is a hurrah, a salute to life. In loving ourselves with no strings attached, fully and without reservations, we need not be anything in particular except *capable* of full, complete, unencumbered love. And as we love, we deepen our relationship with ourselves. When we beat ourselves up, we are in relationship to a negative parental image, not to ourselves. We are fused. To *radically* love ourselves, then, is to separate, to be free. This is why it scares us so.

Radical self-acceptance and "change" may seem on first blush to be mutually exclusive. If I accept myself completely and without reservation, why would I want to change anything? This may be true about the fierce admonitions to change that we generally direct at ourselves. Radical self-acceptance and fierceness do not coexist. But there is a gentle urge to change that does not come from a sense of something being wrong with self but rather from a spirit message that tells us that there is more for us to be, more for us to enjoy. It is not so much a desire to change as an intention to be more of who we are. Actually, only truly radical self-accepting persons will refuse to tolerate hurtful behavior in themselves. Self-criticism and judgmental evaluation actually are likely to prompt hurtful behavior, while radical self-acceptance, eschewing fierce change, paradoxically generates growth more than anything else. No behavior is tolerated that leads to discomfort. And no intended change will occur deeply without radical self-acceptance. It is often the most troubling behavior when deeply accepted by us, when all aspiration to change it has been abandoned, that changes "behind our backs" perhaps because of the profound love implicit in that degree of radical self-acceptance.

As in all intentions, we must be humble in our aspirations. We may not really know what is good for us. And sometimes what we consciously wish to change may be behaviors that have served us well. Sometimes we grow beyond a person who has been our friend and we must move on. We do this, hopefully, with consideration and tenderness, mindful of the sensibilities of the other. So, too, with aspects of ourselves that we want changed. It may take a long time. We need to be patient and avoid grandiose expectations, for they stem from fusion with mother. We are what we are, and at any moment that is a function of the conflict between spirit and demons.

Self-acceptance is the full realization that we are not God—the ultimate psychological separation, the spiritual act of knowing we are all right just the way we are.

———————

Receive yourself willingly. This is who I am and it is absolutely OK. Quietly, and breathing gently, try thinking this: "From this moment on I am going to forgive, accept, and receive myself in my entirety without exception."

———————

The intention to free ourselves from the negative influence of our early caretakers does involve commitment, constant examination of our intentions, vigilant observation, and, of course, unrelenting radical self-acceptance. We must be ever mindful of ways to countermand the propagandizing with which we daily must contend, both from inside and out. We need to find nurturing rather than toxic relationships and foster them. We need to find structures in our lives—groups, societies, churches, synagogues—that provide encouragement, acceptance, and nurture. To stay alone is to stay with mother. We need to affirm ourselves each day in ways that make sense to us and that work. *We must tell ourselves each day that we love ourselves.* We must say no to old behaviors that have consistently hurt us. True courage is not jumping out of a foxhole and attacking the machine-gun nest. True courage is saying no to a piece of cake when we are trying to lose weight. True courage is any step—and it is generally the small ones that are the most important—that goes against deeply ingrained parental imperatives and injunctions. It is the daily turning down of the invitations to the dysfunctional dance. And it is the immediate forgiveness of ourselves when we miss the mark, for sometimes we *will* miss the mark.

Change or growth or development in personality comes not so much from doing the hard things but rather in determining to do that which is doable. As the wonderful old philosopher Mae West put it, "I never yield to temptation unless I have to." The trick is in courageously resisting temptation *when we can.* Sometimes attempting to do the impossible is actually engaging in the battle of wills, assaulting the demons with ego. But we can never win, because ego is part of the demons! This is not the way of spirit. The way of spirit is to surrender ego to spirit and acknowledge our powerlessness in dealing with the demons. That surrender and acknowledgment of powerlessness neutralizes the demons and strengthens the spirit and gradually over time the task becomes easier. When the task is easier, it is the time for it to be done. And this requires humility and patience and cooperation.

Like everyone, I have been struggling with these matters since I was a boy, and I am still struggling. On a practical, human level I forgive myself for not knowing and accept that fact as part of my nature. Yet I make a decision to try to understand in a humble way, mindful lest my narcissism interfere with my joy. I have decided to forgive God the divine mystery and my finiteness and to have fun, to be happy. I have decided to intend to have an "easy life," which is to have "hovering attention," right intention, and absolute acceptance, and then to do that which needs to be done (not always so easy to do), trying to keep well below my perfectionism and just a notch above my sloth. But there *is* work to do. Wresting the spirit back and chancing the new in the midst of an eternity of influences is my task.

Before bringing the chapter to a close, let me summarize the main points I hope you will bear in mind:

1. Change happens by itself when the right conditions are created. Don't try to force it.

2. The beginning (and constant companion) of all change is radical self-acceptance.

3. Most change occurs in the context of intention, observation, and radical self-acceptance.

4. Intentions are crucial, must be made clear, but must always be tentative. We don't always know what is good for us, at least on the conscious level, and have to monitor this carefully. Accepting where we are at the present and observing are often the most efficient approaches.

5. Observation is crucial because we are encrusted with psychic habits developed over what is experienced as centuries of psychological struggle. Observation and other powerful methods such as meditation and psychoanalysis help us to see just how we work.

6. We are working against centuries of "propagandizing," and we must develop powerful tools of self-propaganda to combat these influences on a daily basis. We must take responsibility for loving ourselves and seeking out in our environment people and situations that are nurturing. This is a daily obligation.

7. Step up to pain, shame, dependent beliefs, and learn to dance with them. Fully experiencing painful affects evaporates them. We need

not be afraid; no one has died of a feeling. They are ours. Make friends of them.

8. As we patiently and lovingly approach our struggles in life following these principles, we will notice change occurring "behind our back." If we can gratefully surrender our egos at this point, we will return to ourselves little by little—and sometimes lots by lots.

Part Three

The Practice of Radical Self-Acceptance

Chapter 10

Breaking the Shame Habit

ℰꝏℭꝶ

Shame tells us that what we do is not human. And yet shame itself is the most human of characteristics. Who has not experienced shame?

From time to time there is an outcry that what we humans need is *more* shame. When shock at the outrages of certain people prompts some to condemn them, to shame them, we actually worsen the problem. For shame breeds shame. Shame itself can lead to shameful behavior. Perhaps guilt may help to lessen bad behavior. Certainly the reaction of reality will do that—but not shame. Shame leads to even more shame. Both those who accuse others of shameful deeds and those who are accused feel shame and pass it on. "Shame flows downhill," and *healing* is the only remedy for it and whatever elicited it and whatever it leads to. It can have a value, as I have said, but only between you and you, never between you and anyone else or between anyone else and you. We'll get to that in a moment.

Once I was staying in Sedona prior to attending a conference in Phoenix. I live in a big city with excellent transportation and ordinarily have no need for an automobile. When I travel I rent one, which is a lot of fun—that is, until I need to use any gadgets, because every car I rent has different ones, and I have to learn about them each time. I generally discover this when I go for gas. I fumble around desperately, looking for the tank lid release lever, which can be anywhere from right next to the driver's seat to a spot buried deep in the inner recesses of the glove compartment, as I and a crowd of interested onlookers discovered together one sunny morning, a few years back, in South Egremont, Massachusetts.

I am also not so good at pumping gas myself. I often get flustered and have to ask questions of the attendant. This day in Sedona, the young woman who had to direct me was also serving a line of customers in the grocery store and was very impatient with me. I returned to the car feeling humiliated. I managed to get some gas in the tank, and all the while I was preparing my speech to her about how she had been unkind to me and so forth. Fortunately, it took me so long to fill my tank that I had a chance to realize that she had shamed me, and that I was about to return the favor. She could then go on and shame someone else, and I would drive away feeling shamed because of what I had done to her. Therefore I determined not to shame her, and I went back inside to pay the bill. She was less flustered—I noticed that she was also minding a young child—and she flashed me the most wonderful smile. "Everything go OK?" she asked. I assured her everything had, smiled back, and both of us parted in a friendly mood. The shame habit had been broken for that moment. Ever so many times in the past I had failed to break it; ever so many times I had passed shame on. But in Sedona that day I had not passed it on. There was a little more healing in the world.

I told that story at the beginning of my presentation the next day in Phoenix and what happened was remarkable. The entire audience got excitedly involved, and we had a wonderful hour together. I hardly took notice of the voluminous notes I had prepared. Everyone was fascinated with shame.

We were all psychologists, and yet shame is new to us. Once when I was a patient in psychotherapy my therapist exclaimed, "You have so much guilt!" She didn't realize, nor did I, that what she was referring to was *shame*, not guilt. I had guilt, too, but what I had "so much" of was shame. Shame and guilt are not the same. Guilt is a bad feeling accompanying a deed which violates our own standards of what is right and wrong. It refers to something we have done. Its remedy is to correct the mistake we have made, to acknowledge it to ourselves and the other who is involved, and to make some kind of restitution. Optimally, that should be that. I am suspicious of a guilt that lasts more than twenty-four hours after it has been taken care of. If you have acknowledged your mistake to yourself and the other, and done the best you could to make up for it, you are emotionally and spiritually in the clear. If you are still suffering, something else is going on. It generally has to do with shame.

There is guilt that has to do with feedback to ourselves when we have blinded ourselves to what is good for the universe. In that blindness our moral evaluative mechanism is temporarily disconnected, generally motivated by self-centered willing of some sort. When it comes back on, we are confronted with the discrepancy between our carefully honed sense of what is right and our actions. The "fever" that alerts us to this discrepancy is the painful affect called guilt. And as with fever, it is an important indicator of disease, spiritual dis-ease. Such guilt is our friend. It says nothing about our value as persons. It tells us that we have made a mistake; that we need to do something to remedy the situation. Hopefully, the evaluative mechanism, our conscience, is well tuned: it does not let us off the hook too easily but it does not torture us either. If we are lucky, we have a well functioning conscience, influenced by our interactions with our parents and the world, but ultimately accepted by ourselves as making sense, now that we have had a chance to look around and observe a little of how the world works.

But there are kinds of guilt that are not so friendly. The first actually appears to be a lack of guilt. Here our evaluation of ourselves is so shaky—the narcissism I have hinted at—that it is virtually impossible ever to acknowledge a mistake. To make any mistake is devastating. So we don't let guilt in, or we deny it to ourselves and others. These are the folks who find it impossible to apologize.

The other side of the coin is the person who is riddled with guilt over past mistakes. No amount of forgiveness or reparation will do. The self-flagellation and suffering are relentless. In both instances the root of the suffering lies in fusion with mother. The basic issue is the inability to psychologically separate to the point of making even your conscience your own.

This latter difficulty with guilt is related to shame, for *shame is the anguish at the belief that you are basically, essentially, and irredeemably limited, that you are "not enough."* It is the conviction that you are flawed, faulted, *not fully human*, and, what is worse, there is nothing you can do about it!

Guilt has to do with doing. Shame has to do with "being." Guilt tells us that we have done something bad. Shame tells us that we have *not* done something, that we *cannot* do something, and because of that we are "worse than" bad. The same behavior can elicit shame as well as guilt if we believe that there is something *wrong* with us for even having made a mistake. Shame tells us that we are *not enough* and that *we have not done enough*.

Shame can be a friend, too. Shame can remind us that we are not living up to our vocation, that we are not fulfilling our calling, that we are not co-creating with the Transcendent One in the unique way that we can. The poet who does not write, the lover who does not select a partner, the person whose self-will keeps him separate from forming his will to something greater than himself—all these folks may feel shame. Shame can be a reminder that we are selling ourselves short, that we are not fulfilling our destiny. It is a good reminder. It is good for us to become who we truly are, and shame can be the fever of the soul that draws our attention to our selling ourselves and the universe short. It often has a tinge of sadness with it. Pay attention to this shame. It is healthy guidance. But don't persecute yourself even for this.

Unfortunately, most shame is not good for you. To review: There are two types. One type stems from your having been abused in some form, a psychological shame. The other rises simply from the observation and experience that it is a part of our very nature to be limited, an existential shame. Both types of shame lie to us. They tell us that we are not enough and cause us anguish. The psychological type is the result of having been told in some fashion that whatever we do is not enough. This sets us out on a lifetime quest of trying to become enough by doing more and more in a futile attempt to remedy this deep belief. But there is no "enough" that one can achieve. We are enough just because we are alive!

We may have been the victims of abuse in a physical or sexual or emotional way. Children tend to take responsibility for this abuse as a way of protecting themselves and their mothers. The result can be a lifetime of fusion and shame. This is profoundly difficult to overcome.

Still others, paradoxically, have experienced shame at their *accomplishments*. Whatever sets us apart from others may threaten us with abandonment, somewhere deep inside us, and unless we are supported and encouraged by parents we may feel shame. These are the folks who are afraid of accomplishment or who "snatch failure out of the jaws of success." It is not commonly understood, but this is a form of shame, too.

These types of shame may be considered "neurotic" in that they stem directly from interactions with our early caretakers and are sustained by our fear of separating from them, both psychologically and emotionally.

The other type of shame that haunts us, the "existential," is because of the very nature of being human and our personal experience and awareness of limitation. This is the type of shame that got us into trouble in the Garden of Eden because of our *refusal to accept* that there were some things that we just could not do—our refusal to accept that we were not God! Many of us suffer all through life at not being able to accomplish tasks that our egos tell us we should be able to accomplish, and these overweening egos have much to do with our fusion with mother. If we are "one with mother," there should be nothing that we cannot accomplish! We have chronic shame at our "lacks." We "should" be able to do everything. We should be able to make mother happy. We should be able even to overcome death. Our difficulties in accomplishing these impossible tasks result in shame.

It is in the struggle with this shame that our true freedom lies. As we make progress in surrendering the fused notions that are so offended by the reality of our limitations, we will begin to see ourselves as part of something much larger, and at the same time we will be free to pursue our uniqueness. A suggestion of peace and even joy will begin to insinuate itself.

We are all riddled with shame. It is part of the human condition to feel shame, both the "neurotic" kind and the "existential" kind. And as was true in my experience in Sedona, we tend to pass it on. If we are inundated with shame—and shame itself makes us feel ashamed—we are often prompted to engage in "shameless" behavior. Much of the behavior we are unhappy with in ourselves is prompted by the experience of the hopeless grip of shame. So shame creates shameful behavior which prompts shaming behavior in others, which leaves both the "shamer" and the "shamee" shamed. One of the most common manifestations of this is *contempt*. We are self-contemptuous due to our perceived "lacks," and we tend to be contemptuous of others as well, seeing *them* as lacking. This is a makeshift way of relieving our own shame, understandable but never really successful, because it gets us into trouble with others and eventually with ourselves. We feel guilty or mean-spirited. We don't like ourselves very much when we are this way.

It is essential that you understand that *there is no way to remove all shame from your life*. It is like a bacterial infection. It will happen; it is human nature. It cannot be avoided. It is one of the limitations of being human, and while this awareness prompts some folks to have even more shame, it can also be the beginning of letting yourself off the hook, of accepting yourself. It is our nature; no one can avoid it. Why feel bad about it?

Recently I participated in a weekend workshop for singers. At the end of the first day each of us had to stand before the others and sing a song we had just learned together. That night we had to prepare a song of our own choosing to perform the following day. If ever there was an activity designed to surface shame, it is singing before others. Standing up there, emotionally naked and unprotected by our strategies of communication, we had to contact the audience from a place inside us over which we had little control. How dare we do this? Who do we think we are? People will see the truth about us. We do not sing well enough. We *are* not good enough. We are awful! Without exception the members of the workshop were overcome with emotion, and flooded with shame. Shame is like a cold that never goes away. Some days it is mild; other days it is debilitating. It is chronic, and certain circumstances may always elicit it.

When it is at its most severe it tells us that we are worthless. It makes us feel that we are subhuman. Not only do we not do enough, *we are not enough.* Not only do we make mistakes, *we are mistakes.* We don't belong on this planet. We are worthless pieces of garbage. But this belief is illusion. *Your joy or your misery in life hinges on getting this one straight.* You are not a mistake. You are innocent!

So: there's the shame that's personal, that challenges us to be all that we can be. This shame can actually be a help. And then there's the shame of our situation in the world, existential shame, the awareness of our essential limitations as human beings. Those limitations are the truth. That's the way it is. When we stop fighting this we can grow out into ourselves, return to who we truly are. Finally, there's the interpersonal shame, the "building into us" of convictions of worthlessness resulting from the abusive ways in which persons have treated us. I consider as abuse, incidentally, situations where children are allowed to develop the deep belief that they are responsible for the welfare of a caretaker.

Once shame has taken deep hold and becomes part of us, situations can reinforce or trigger it. *Reinforcement* is those situations or persons who continually abuse us even though they weren't the originators of our basic shame. They constantly stir it up and reinforce it. *Triggers* of shame are any persons or situations, some quite innocent, such as my singing workshop, that elicit the shame that is already lying dormant within us. Reinforcers or triggers do not *cause* the shame—it is there already—but constantly stir it up.

It is an unfortunate human tendency that we tend to pass shame on, as if we will get relief from our shame by eliciting the shame of others. When this characteristic becomes chronic we act like perpetual "victims" whose only relief for pain is to launch an attack on others. Someone in the present must be held accountable in order for our shame to disappear. This never works; it just perpetuates the problem. It creates self-shaming, and very often keeps us from the real issue. For those who shame us today are rarely the causes of our shame, and focusing on them paradoxically "protects" the original source. Sometimes we even have the original source wrong. Chronic unrelieved rage is a symptom of chronic fusion with mother. Constant longing and railing only keeps one firmly ensconced with her. Whether it takes the form of feeling helpless and depressed, or of being the angry victim, or of vengefully passing it on by shaming and contempt, *our shame is ours*, and the beginning of its healing is the full acceptance of that. It is our only hope. Otherwise, our entire life will be about shame.

It is crucial that we help ourselves with this. *There can be no consistent joy without breaking the shame habit.* We suffer, and we continue to pass it on in our contempt, judgment, and criticism. When enough of us get together in our shame, we pick another group to have contempt for and attack them. And if a whole country or ethnic group organizes their shame in this fashion we have war, for the sake of the "motherland" or the "fatherland." War and prejudice are the institutionalization of shame. And although this is not our fault, the remedy must start with us.

And what is the remedy? Let's go back to our principles of change. First, we must *intend* to break the shame habit, to *consider the possibility* of life with minimal shame, to not be at its mercy. Second, we must *observe, observe, observe*. Don't fight it. Immerse yourself in shame. Feel it, observe it, witness it. *Accept it.* Notice the conditions under which it is elicited, notice who prompts it, notice what we say to ourselves at the time, notice our impulse to attack ourselves or to lash back. Notice the tendency to shame ourselves even for feeling shame. Watch it all. Observe, observe, observe. And breathe. *Don't try to change anything.* Employ slow deep breaths.

Accept yourself for having shame. Make it your own. Remind yourself that it is the human condition to feel this. There is no escaping it. Regardless of what anyone says to you or has ever said to you about this, it is perfectly natural to feel shame and to feel it frequently. It is delusion, but it occurs—all the time. The common cold is a form of illness, but it is natural. It happens all the time. Tell yourself that it is OK. Tell yourself that you love yourself. Tell yourself that you are innocent. Accept yourself as a person with shame. It is the human condition. It is the human disability. There is nothing wrong with *you.*

We don't have to let it get the best of us. Take care lest you criticize yourself, alone or in front of others. Sometimes we tend to do this, or we ingratiate ourselves, to ward off the anticipated attacks of others. Just accept the experience when others shame you. And when they begin to treat you well, don't hold their past criticisms of you against them. Remember, they were shamed, too; otherwise they wouldn't do it to you. Let the cycle end with you! And healing will occur "behind your back."

Let your felt shame be the occasion of a rededication to radical self-acceptance. Form the intention to love yourself completely, unequivocally, fully, *unconditionally*, without reservation. When shame is triggered—and the trigger may be a success as well as a "failure" or criticism—it has a life of its own. It is like adrenaline pouring into your bloodstream, or a cold which must follow its course regardless of our interventions. Don't take it on directly. Realize that you are powerless over it. The bad feelings, the crazy ideas that will not go away despite every attempt, will just have to exhaust themselves. When you stop fighting, they disappear much quicker. Nature takes care of it. But realize that the bad feelings and critical ideas are the things that are nuts, not you. What is crazy is the content of the shaming thoughts and the fact that the shame attack is happening at all.

Would that *good* feelings would run through me with such abandon! I woke up feeling wonderful this morning, but there is a good chance that something will happen today that will dash that feeling and summon up my shame. One event in the past can be the occasion of a lifetime of suffering, but good feelings take daily attention. Be aware of this and develop self-loving practices. Be aware that compulsive ideas of shame are delusions about which you can do little directly once they have started. Remind yourself that there is *nothing wrong with you.*

Good feelings are fragile. Enjoy them, but be prepared for shame attacks on them. Don't be discouraged. Be active in the creation of good feelings. Study what makes you feel good and what makes you suffer. Make a "pat yourself on the back" list of the good things you have done, and constantly remind yourself of the loving appreciation of you that your friends have shown. Do it daily. Write it down. It is not our nature to remember these things as it is to remember what is "wrong" with us. We need all the ammunition we can muster to fight shame and its crazy-making ideas and its debilitating emotions. And in the midst of the vicious accusation that shame makes upon you, tell yourself over and over again, "I am innocent." And breathe—slow deep breaths. Notice where the feelings are in your body; accept them. Love yourself.

If you do these things consistently over time and relief comes too slowly, consider the possibility of getting help in the observation of where you are stuck. Find a good psychotherapist, one who is not afraid of the unconscious, who is committed to his own psychological separation, who really listens, who is kind, and who is not afraid of God either. Some folks find medications helpful. We know little about the biological causes of psychological or spiritual suffering despite what some doctors say. It is tempting to seek magic in a bottle or capsule. But there are side-effects, as well as the possibility that you may be trying to avoid delving deeply into your emotions as I have urged you to do. But keep an open mind about it. First, try speaking to a live person. And never medicate yourself. Go on or off medications only under careful medical supervision.

Shame is isolating. When we are shamed we tend to look down and away. We believe that we are not fit for the company of others. But this is exactly when it is most helpful for us to be with others. A powerful remedy for shame is communication, being with and sharing with others, both formally and informally. Attendance at church, group therapy, membership in clubs (particularly those with a service orientation), athletic events, self-help groups, even concerts—all these remind us of our shared humanity. We are all suffering. Let us be with each other in our suffering whether we speak of it directly or not.

When we suffer, our human tendency is to scramble around for ways of fixing ourselves. We feel shame for having the difficulty and shame for not being able to fix it. Our next step generally is to seek out other humans, such as doctors. This is good. We can do much to help ourselves, particularly if we are open to surrendering to the universe, and to listening for the instructions of our spirits. Friends, lovers, priests, doctors—all can help us enormously by their wisdom, devotion, and compassion. Don't deprive yourself of any of these helps. But the most profound remedy is spiritual. When we suffer we are painfully aware that we do not possess the power to help ourselves, to make things better. We need to consider having a relationship with a higher power, one which may provide us with the best hope for banishing shame.

Chapter 11

Loving Yourself Madly

ஐௐ

In Old Saint Paul's Church in Baltimore, there is an inscription dated 1692 which succinctly suggests a beautiful philosophy of life. You may have seen it. It is called "Desiderata," that which is to be desired. One line reads, "Therefore be at peace with God, whatever you conceive Him to be."

I do not presume to suggest anything to you about your conception of God, but I am convinced that each of us has one. Only the peculiarities of mother-fusion, a subtlety of self-centeredness, would prompt us to fight this reality. Clearly there is a power greater than ourselves that runs this universe, however mysterious. Go to that beach by yourself for a time and watch. No man-made computer can match what you will experience deeply if you allow yourself.

It is ironic that there is such resistance to the acceptance of this reality, an obstinacy which blindly believes that science knows all or is closing in on all there is to know about the workings of the universe. Some even maintain that it is "childish" to acknowledge such a power. "Mature adults" know that such a belief is not consistent with being independent "realists." Yet none of the great scientists, deeply aware of the profundity and majesty and mystery of the working of the world, denies the notion of a power greater than ourselves. They stand in awe of it. What needs to be understood is not the reality of a higher power but rather those things that interfere with people having some grasp of that reality and coming to grips with it in their own lives.

What stands in the way is fusion with mother.

A higher power is something larger and more powerful than ourselves, the existence of which reminds us that *we* are not all-powerful, and the participation in which provides us with *power*, particularly to do things which we may have not been able to accomplish on our own. So who do you think was our first notion of Higher Power? Mother, of course. Some of us have great difficulty throughout our lives in relinquishing, on the deepest of levels, that first belief.

What often is posed as the "adult" position about the higher power is actually a disguised expression of the grandiosity of mother-fusion. For, in reality, the conscious pursuit of a "relationship" with a spiritual transcendent is the only way we can truly, both emotionally and psychologically, separate from mother and fully become who we are destined to be: ourselves. It is the most powerful remedy for shame, as well.

There certainly have been abuses committed by people claiming to speak for this "higher power." Human organizations are fallible, and all material things are corruptible. It is sadly true that much shame has been generated. This is particularly tragic, for the truth is that the intention to formulate your will in accordance with that of the power of the universe will lessen your shame. It will free you to love yourself, unencumbered by the opinion of others, regardless of whom they claim to speak for. You will need to please no one. You will just need to be open to the Spirit of the universe as it lives and co-creates in you as the unique, once-in-the-history-of-the-universe-person that you are.

What a spot we are in. We are flawed by our self-centeredness. An appeal to a power greater than ourselves can help us move beyond this self-centeredness. However, this very self-centeredness keeps us from making such an appeal. And even when we consciously seek it, the ways we remain fused with mother often interfere with the *development* of our spirituality. What are we to do?

There is actually a lot we can do. If you are forming the intention to separate out into yourself and have been observing, as I suggested, and have been receiving the emotions and thoughts, sometimes crazy or crazy-making, that come up for you, without distracting yourself from them by self-defeating behaviors, then you have been doing a lot. If you add to that the determination to radically accept yourself, warts and all, then you have been doing a lot. If you have been doing psychological work, perhaps even observing yourself via psychotherapy, then you have been doing a lot. If you have been loving others, perhaps consciously following a spiritual path, then you have been doing a lot.

Psychoanalytic psychology is a step on the long evolutionary journey of humankind to overcome our narcissism. It teaches us something about how this self-centeredness works within us and where it comes from. It has even suggested remedies for loosening its grip on us. Yes, psychoanalytic psychology is a great moment in our spiritual history. It has taught us about psychological fusion, and it has been brave for doing so, for there is great resistance to knowing this. We have been talking to each other about it in our scriptures from the beginning. We have been urging each other to overcome it. But we have made little progress over the centuries. We have been stuck.

We must be in the process of psychologically separating in order to be spiritual. We must clear away the blockages of narcissism, the vestiges of childlike connection to mother, to have a grown-up relationship with a higher power. And in the process of doing that, overcoming mother-fusion, that very spirituality will reinforce psychological separation. For no human power alone could loosen the grip on us of our first higher power, she in whose hands our very lives and self and well-being rested for those hundreds of psychological years, and whom we adored.

But our self-centeredness, an expression of the secret pact with mother, may keep us from searching for the Transcendent. And many of us who want to have such a relationship may have it limited by residual mother-fusion. We may sincerely want to be spiritual but we may be stuck and we may suffer, because to be spiritual the spirit must be free, and the only way it gets free is through psychological separation. Without this we are stuck with a child's conception of God, or one that is similar to the one we were taught by mother or "authorities." In fact we may use such a conception of God as a way of staying fused. God the *Father* and Holy *Mother* Church become symbols for our enmeshment in our own family. True spirituality demands psychological separation, growing out into ourselves, and enduring the suffering that such growing out sometimes entails. The anguish of the mystics speaks eloquently of this. *One has to leave mother to be spiritual.* In this sense, spirituality is psychological separation.

If I am nice to someone, it may be because I feel loving and it spills out toward him, or it may be because I have the conscious intention of acting that way since that is the way I want to be, or I may be trying unconsciously or consciously to get the approval of my mother who wanted me to be a "good boy," or it might be a defense mechanism against rage and contempt, an automatic behavior, part of my character armoring. The latter two motivations are psychological, one a defense mechanism, the other an unseparated, fused pattern of behavior. The first two motivations are in the spiritual realm; the first is spiritual in itself, the other might be considered "spiritual practice." There is no way to know this by simply observing the behavior. It is the motivation that is crucial, and a clue to that motivation is the internal state of the actor. Is he at peace? Is he resentful? Does he feel superior, or even nothing at all? Does he expect something from the recipient? I'm daily reminded of my spiritual limitations as I hold the door for someone and experience irritation when that person fails to graciously reward me for my "good deed" with an immediate smile or "thank you." Whenever I take the time to reflect on my personal states of disturbance, I will bump into some sort of dependency which insists on a particular response from another. This is my fusion.

The availability to the Spirit is always the result of psychological readiness. Acting on a spiritual "impulse" or pursuing a spiritual end product is of little avail. The access to spirituality is psychological. The self (which does the psychological work) is at the interface between our ego (the guardian of mother-fusion) and spirit (the developing, moving forward participation in the life force, the transcendent). It is at this crossroads that the decision, conscious or unconscious, is made to become available to spirit. Intention is crucial at this moment and can be "shored up" by spiritual practice, prayer, and meditation. In fact prayer is the most powerful form of "intention." But without the "decision" or at least good-hearted willingness, the practice itself may be frustrating, the "dark night of the soul." Or these spiritual tools may be used in a self-centered or avaricious way, a sort of spiritual materialism.

I remember a session with a young man named Warren. After some time in therapy, he began to notice what he referred to as "amazing" changes in himself. He was more interested in the world; he felt better about himself; he was happier. We spoke of these changes and his apparent desire to do things differently, to see the world as it really is rather than through the tunnel vision of the past. It seemed as if he were letting go of something. Warren had been obsessed with hatred of his father, and I suggested that perhaps this is what he was letting go. He considered this.

Later in that session he told me he wanted to visit a person in his firm who had been given notice of termination and who, as a result, was being shunned by his fellow employees. Warren wanted to show support for this man. "Why are people shunned?" he asked. "Why are you *not* shunning him?" I replied. In this regard I mentioned those who helped the Jews in captivity and those who didn't, and the files of the Stasi, the former East German secret police, which revealed how widespread betrayal is even among loved ones. Warren's increasing psychological separation was prompting him to see the world differently. He spontaneously wanted to do the right thing.

Spirituality refers to the extent the spirit is free to follow its natural course, and it spontaneously expands as consciousness does. Before one is free to be spiritual he must diminish the blockages to contacting God, however you conceive him to be. *Psychological fusion must be overcome before spirituality can prevail.*

The great commandment is: "Thou shalt love thy God with thy whole heart and thy whole soul and thy whole mind, and thou shalt love thy neighbor as thyself." In order to love God with your whole heart and soul and mind, you have to let go of mother. You must relinquish her as your higher power. Only then are you free to truly love your neighbor, and, just as important, to *love yourself.*

But there is another side to all of this. Although psychology is a great help, indeed a necessity, it suffers from its own narcissism. Human psychology is stuck in the belief that we can figure out *all* things for ourselves, and can solve *all* problems by ourselves. This is its tragic fault. Psychoanalytic psychology is a crucial step along the road to freedom, but by itself the searching person can never take the final step beyond his narcissism and shame and envy. As far as he may have bravely come, he winds up stuck in a dark nihilism when his "independence" ultimately fails to provide him with serenity.

So just as psychological growth is a necessity for spiritual growth to go as far as it can, so, too, spiritual growth is a necessity for psychological growth to go as far as it can. This is not as ironic as it may seem, for the psychological and the spiritual have been intertwined from the beginning. The first psychological texts are the scriptures. Psychology has been a part of spirituality all along, even before philosophy, and later science, snatched it up.

The spiritual imperative is to *surrender*—to surrender to the mystery and surrender to the sacred. Paradoxically, this surrender is the opening to new and more profound realms of reality. If we reject this basic human task, part of us dries up and atrophies. When we have transcended mother, we are on the threshold of transcending reality as we have previously known it. But the narcissism of psychology resists this; it tells us that we can know it all by ourselves, by our wills, and that all there is consists of that which our human vision can provide for us. It denies our essential limitation. It places us directly back in the quandary of the Garden of Eden.

But when we make the conscious intention to surrender our wills to a higher power, we stumble upon a new reality, a transcendent reality, an infinitely unfolding reality. It seems like hocus pocus when such folks try to explain the events that they are now free to be aware of, and their capacity to accomplish things that have been absolutely impossible before. It is actually no more than their entry into an ever widening sphere of what is real and natural, one that has been clogged by the narrowness of our fusion-vision. When we both psychologically separate *and* surrender to the *magnum mysterium*, the great mystery, we are inundated with aspects of reality to which our self-centeredness blinded us. There is nothing superstitious about this. It is just *more reality* than we are used to! Relationship with the Transcendent takes us far beyond what we have previously known and experienced. It is the tragi-comedy of our hubris that we would prefer a more limited vision of reality, but one that we could understand and control, over the magnificence of infinity and its possibility, one which would provide so much more for us, but over which we would not reign!

Various personal approaches to the Transcendent, and religious institutions with all their limitations, represent humankind's desire to live in the sacred and make whatever contact we can with the great mystery. And from the very beginning it was experienced that things could be accomplished in one's life by such contact, even though the explanation of these events could only be made in the language and reality of the age, which may look simple and even dumb to us now (I wonder what they'll think of us a few centuries down the road). But it was also in the gatherings of these seekers that compassion for others was encouraged and preached, the compassion so desperately needed to offset the violence of our unseparated emotions, the self-protectiveness of tribalism with its roots in mother-fusion, which horrify us even to this day. Love and compassion were taught as the antidote to self-centeredness and envy. Generosity would replace avariciousness. Shame was banished in the realization and acknowledgment of the inevitability of our essential limitations. We accepted that *we* were not God.

Psychology teaches us that we are not responsible for the reactions of others. But spirituality teaches us that we need be mindful of the *sensibilities* of others. It teaches us to see our neighbors as fellow sufferers, not as aggressors or opportunities, but with compassion. Psychologically separated from the caretakers of our childhood, we can see our oneness with all our brothers and sisters, including our parents. Whatever our beliefs or our assertions, the truth of our spirituality is in the love of our neighbor.

What good news it is that our spirituality, made possible by the readiness of our psychological separation, winds up being the cure for both shame and narcissism, each a side of the coin of fusion with mother—and for envy, too, as we deeply realize that we are enough in who we are. We can dare to "let go"—and to let God be God.

Bill Wilson, the co-founder of A.A., wrote in the final pages of his essays on the Twelve Steps:[1] "*True* ambition is the *deep* desire to live *usefully* and walk *humbly* under the grace of God" (emphasis mine). In this statement he discovers again the deepest, laser-sharp clarity of spiritual wisdom, as did St. Francis when he taught that "it is in giving that we receive."

Spirituality is marked by generosity and a dedication to usefulness to others. Giving, generosity, service and usefulness alone can stand up to the two eternal human *bête noires*: self-centeredness and shame. *Generosity* is both the hallmark of psychological separation *and* the very spiritual quality that cures us of the final bite of fusion.

These spiritual urges, freed by psychological separation, are the muscle and gristle of *love*. In each conscious encounter with the demons of self-centeredness and shame, these spiritual clarities are always victorious.

Finally, as the great commandment reminds us, you are free to love yourself. No longer imprisoned by shame and self-centeredness, you can experience yourself as God does, you can love yourself without reservation. As we leave oneness with mother, we move toward oneness with God and ourselves. We replace mother with a higher power. We can then replace the need for approval by mother and mother surrogates with love of ourselves. We will have radical self-acceptance, and not the grandiosity of the "mother-elect" with its constant vulnerability to shame and its constant seeking of justification by fellow human beings. We will approach total freedom from the evaluations of others. For radical self-acceptance *is* spirituality. And wisdom is seeing the world through your *own* eyes, your unique vision, and co-creating with the Transcendent.

You have forgotten how wonderful you are. Picture an eighteen-month-old toddler dancing happily, surrounded by beaming adults. You were that child at one time, unencumbered by memory, with no history of yourself either for yourself or for others. You were sheer joy at that moment, and when that joy would be dissolved, it would be by an event of the present, not by a message to yourself. You were wonderful that day; everyone knew you were wonderful. Even you knew that you were wonderful. And you are just as wonderful now. You have just forgotten, that's all. Things have happened; opinions have been formed; philosophies have been forged; deep beliefs have arisen. But underneath all of that, you are as wonderful as you were that day.

You are the perfect you the way you are. Even if you are suffering beyond belief this very moment, it is not because you are not the perfect you. There is nothing wrong with *you*. You may wish to get relief from your suffering. You may form the intention to do so; you may observe yourself and life and your own life, by yourself or with a helper; you may strive toward radical self-acceptance. By doing these you will lighten the pain. It will take some time to loosen the blockages to the spirit, but it will happen, and when it does you will not be any more perfect than you are now; you will just suffer less.

Psychological separation, growing out into yourself, is *separating*, not arriving at any clearly describable place. It is a process, a dedication. The most humble of us who takes a tiny step toward self may be more courageous and accomplished than the very gifted person who does great things without much effort. There is no measuring these things. The only arbiter is you, your honest encounter with yourself. All that is needed to be on the Wisdom path is *intention, observation, and radical self-acceptance*. The result will be a life beyond your wildest dreams but not one that we can envision or strive for ahead of time. We must leave that to the transcendent nature of things. But this is not a reality that pleases our ego. Many of us would prefer growing less and suffering more so long as our ego can take the credit. Merely to form the intention, observe and radically accept ourselves, and receive graciously what the universe provides as a result, is ego deflating, even if what we get is far beyond what our limited selves could have accomplished by our egos and wills alone.

I attended a reunion of my men's peer group recently. I have not been a member for four years, but I knew all of the eight men who showed up. Four were still active members. At one point I suggested that we share what we have learned about life since the last time we were all together. A lively discussion ensued. When it came my turn, I told them that I had discovered that radical self-acceptance is my most important task for the rest of my life, and that I was determined to go about it with vigor and determination. I had many plans, many projects I wanted to accomplish, many people I wanted to love more and better, but first and foremost was my determination to search relentlessly for ways of re-experiencing the truth of my innocence, to feel the joy that is the human equivalent of looking like a beautiful flower or a sunset. Like my friends in the group and like you, I have suffered a great deal in this lifetime and I wanted to reduce my suffering. I wanted to remove, as much as possible, that part of my suffering which came from old fused notions and habits.

Two of the members started an abstract conversation about "why" people did not accept themselves. Then a third said that he did not think it a good idea to accept oneself so readily. "Ten years ago I was a mean and selfish person. If I had accepted myself then, I wouldn't have changed and the people who are in my life now might not be. You have to be careful about accepting yourself. How would you change for the better?" Most of the others seemed to agree. They began speaking of the "monsters" of the world—Hitler, Stalin, the person who blew up the federal building in Oklahoma City. "Should these persons radically accept themselves?" "It's OK if the good people do, but what about the bad ones?"

"Do you really think the mayhem and murder and cruelty going on all around us in this city this very moment is being done by people who *love* themselves too much, who *accept* themselves too much?" I replied heatedly. Everyone ignored me. The discussion continued about just who should accept themselves and who shouldn't. There was considerable passion. Finally I interrupted: "You're all afraid that if you completely accepted yourself you would have to look at where you don't love yourself, and if you did that there would be the danger of leaving your mother!" No one seemed to hear this either as the discussion about making sure the bad guys didn't love themselves continued. Why are we so afraid of loving ourselves?

In between "insight" (of psychoanalysis) and "self-determination" (of cognitive or will therapies) lies the "I," the self, *which must be nurtured by acceptance* in order to take responsibility for itself. We tend to avoid this responsibility by endless intellectual insight or repetitive and constantly failing determination, because to realize *the responsibility of the "I"* is to elicit the terror of our underlying fusion-based fear: I will not be able to take care of myself and I will die. Radical self-acceptance is the primary autonomous act. It is a profound separation step. It implies that we are *enough* by ourselves. We no longer are little boys and girls trying hard to become "better" in order to please Mom.

Radical self-acceptance is receiving oneself willingly and completely. It means that we completely accept as ourselves *any* particular characteristic or behavior or feeling. Does this mean that we never wish to change something? Not necessarily. However, the desire to change is not prompted by self-hate, self-criticism, self-loathing, guilt, or shame. We may have a sense that we are not yet fully who we truly are, and we may wish to move toward that fulfillment. But we are humble in that ambition, realizing the difficulty of relinquishing old ways, understanding that, in some sense, these behaviors have been friends. We also acknowledge that our notion of what would be best for us at a particular moment may be incorrect, or at least limited.

Radical self-acceptance is accepting yourself exactly as you are: receiving yourself with no strings attached. *This is who I am.* You bring no evaluation or judgment to yourself, either positive or negative; you needn't do anything except to take yourself in and enjoy your experience of being alive—just noticing, observing, and, in as neutral a way as possible, *receiving* yourself exactly as you are in this moment with no caveats or conditions. "Learn from the way the wild flowers grow. They do not work or spin. But I tell you that not even Solomon in all his splendor was clothed like one of them" (Matthew 28:29).

Is this not freedom? Relief? This is *release* from all our demons and *is more important than change itself.* Radical self-acceptance is *ceasing to aspire toward anything*; we move in the direction of joy. *To give up self-evaluation is psychological separation.* We are what we are; what is of necessity is, and that is to be one with the transcendent. Love of self and others is the celebration of *what is* with *no desire to change it.* As soon as you want to change it, it is less love. Love is *knowing* without trying to change, knowing the other *just as is,* not a mixture of "as is" and "as I want you to be." Self-acceptance is the same. And lo and behold, just as we lose interest in change, it often occurs "behind our backs."

In group therapy one night we batted about this question: Is it possible to have nothing about us—present behavior, memories of the past, thoughts of the future—elicit suffering and shame? Everybody became disoriented.

It is hard even to think of these things. It is hard because such a state of existence implies psychological separation. When we have separated from mother, we are free to accept and approve of ourselves, free to approve *just because we decide to*, not because we meet any standard. We no longer need parental approval. We no longer need the approval of anyone. We are free. We can then release ourselves from the agendas of the past and choose the new in our lives as we come upon it.

The reason that we experience joy in spiritual events, or in a new love, or the birth of a baby, is that these release us, for the moment, from the chronic sense of unworthiness that each of us carries within. This release seems possible for us with a guru, or fellow seekers, or in the presence of new life, or a beloved. But to release unworthiness *by oneself*, alone—that is the challenge. This is more than *replacing* a fierce and critical parental image with a more loving and nurturing one. This is psychological separation, *a decision to know your worth simply as an alive person, a co-creator with the Transcendent.* You overcome your resistance to wisdom, see freely what you can see, and, in your own "God-sense," look at yourself and others and joyfully say, "It is good." You give up the compulsive need to have control over yourself and others. Not only are you not more self-centered and selfish, you are actually *more* loving, tolerant and generous to all living things.

Loving yourself madly is not selfishness. Selfishness is parsimonious; love is expansive. Selfishness is when you think there is not enough and you must hoard everything for yourself. Radical self-acceptance is knowing that you *are* enough, and that there *is* enough. When you love yourself madly you want to give, you want to share. There is no room for selfishness, avariciousness, greed. You love yourself and it spills over onto others. You are generous and giving because you are safe in your self-caring. Selfishness comes from fear. Radical self-acceptance transcends fear. It is joyous, it is expansive, and it is sweetly humble.

The charge of "selfishness" toward someone truly striving to love himself comes from the demons within which do not want to see anyone truly psychologically separated. It threatens their secret pact with Mom with its hidden grandiosity and its willful ambition to control, its hubris. The deep acceptance of any limitation, our essential humanness, is very hard for us. There is in each of us a grandiose belief that we should have no limitations or parameters at all. We may disguise this by self-criticism, masochism, or whatever, but it is there, an underground standard by which we measure and torture ourselves. We cannot accept ourselves because we refuse to give up this grandiose image. Once again, it is ego, and fusion with mother fuels this delusion. Making peace with life demands continual surrender to reality, acknowledging that we are limited, that we will die, that we are not in perfect control. This last surrender is the hardest—that we are not in perfect control, even over our destinies. It is a dramatic blow to our narcissism.

Actually, we are flawed only when compared to our grandiose expectations of ourselves. We are what we are—merely human. It is when mother-ego distorts what we are that we have trouble, whether you call it psychopathology, hindrances, evil, or sin. The very notion of perfection only comes from our perception of the demands of mother, real or imagined, and the need for her acceptance. Self-acceptance is the ultimate psychological separation, the spiritual act of knowing that you are not God, but that you are just fine in your humanness and "imperfection."

Radical self-acceptance is so torturously difficult for us! To accept ourselves as perfectly OK with all our limitations, relinquishing ego and grandiosity, means leaving mother. And leaving mother means accepting graciously the omnipotence of our transcendent, and even surrendering to death as none of our business. The payoff for all this is a life of joy, pleasure and love, experiencing a fullness and power we did not know was possible. By our gift of surrender to the universe, by our generosity, by our goodwill, we get all life has to offer.

Have as your intention a complete and total acceptance of yourself and everything about you. *Stop trying to change yourself.* Accept yourself as a given. Notice "mistakes" but don't "try" to change them, and *never* make your mistake an excuse for self-abuse. It is human to make mistakes. You are what you are. If you surrender to that, and *sincerely intend to be* what you are supposed to be in the transcendent (as opposed to egoistic) scheme of things, then that is what you will become. Whatever that is, humbly accept it. Remember: self-acceptance *precedes* any change. If change is to occur it must start with loving yourself radically! It is such an irony that we fear that we will not change if we totally accept ourselves. When we love ourselves madly we will not tolerate any behavior in ourselves that will interfere with that love. *For this reason, radical self-acceptance is the most powerful agent of change there is!* No real and long lasting change is possible without it.

When I am disturbed, the essence of my disturbance is what I call "short-ness of radical self-acceptance." Like shortness of breath, I don't have enough life-sustaining self-love. When anything about life disturbs me, it is short-ness of radical self-acceptance. When I demand too much of others be-cause of my dependencies, the disturbance is shortness of radical self-acceptance and the need to get it from outside myself. When I criticize others, it is shortness of radical self-acceptance. When I am contemptu-ous, it is shortness of radical self-acceptance. Shortness of radical self-ac-ceptance often comes from shame, and we know that shame often prompts us to humiliate others, whereas radical self-acceptance expands and tends to envelop others in loving affirmation. Whenever I behave badly, for any reason, or about anything, or with any provocation, it is shortness of radi-cal self-acceptance. I am not loving myself sufficiently that day.

Just as is true in our struggle with shame, we need to develop strategies to help us love ourselves. Strange as it is, loving ourselves does not seem a natural thing for us humans. Self-centeredness, with its connection to mother-fusion, seems more "natural." The spontaneous love of the toddler appears awkward for us as adults. Each day I am engaged in the struggle between my Transcendent-born spirit which wants me to love myself madly and my mother-fusion which wants to keep me dissatisfied with myself, wallowing in an unseparated swamp of trying to better myself to win Mommy's approval. If I keep on trying to improve she will be proud of me and I will be safe with her in the familiar feelings of malaise, and I will live forever. Or I rebel only to come sheepishly back in search of her approval, real or symbolic.

I need all the help I can get to love myself. I start each day reminding myself that I am not God and asking for help in doing what is right for me to do that day. I sign up with the universe. And I form the intention to love myself. Sometimes, I say, "I love you, Jim." Try that yourself. Tell yourself that you love you, and use your name. How did it feel? Sometimes I have great resistance to saying it to myself, to telling myself, in a personal way, that I love myself. Other times it is easier, though it's generally a little awkward. I have no trouble telling my children or my friends that I love them, but it's a little awkward telling myself. Strange, isn't it? But I do it, like a shy teenager.

Most important, I *form the intention* to love myself that day. I get myself on track. I do all the things I suggested to you when we spoke of "growing out" and "breaking the shame habit." Sometimes I'll discuss my self-accusations with myself when they arrive—and they generally arrive at some time or other—and try to reason with myself. This rarely works. If I am inclined to blame others I pray for them, wishing that they receive all the good things I want for myself. Sometimes I join the self-attacks and make them deliberately worse. I help myself "bottom out," and sometimes I actually feel better because I have stopped fighting. Mostly I *enter deeply* into the feeling, whatever it is, trying not to pay too much attention to the racket in my head, just as I might try to ignore the overly loud bass on my neighbor's stereo. I go about my business. I can always do that no matter what is going on within. And I try not to act out. I try to avoid doing something that my demons desperately want me to do, something that I can regret later, something that will fuel the fire of my self-contempt. I go about my life. I take care of business.

I've arranged my life so that I have wonderful friends, membership in organizations, and hobbies that give me great joy. I'm blessed with a loving and psychologically separating family. I try to be of service where I can, and I make some effort to keep in shape physically. I work on my spiritual life, particularly mindful of the shortness of my life, and how happy I am to be alive. And over time I feel better about myself. As a result I am more and more happy and eager to pass on what I have learned, as so many others have done for me.

Loving oneself madly, radical self-acceptance, does not so much mean that we always are feeling good, but rather *that we have taken a stand about ourselves.* We become determined to love and accept ourselves *as we are,* and we will receive whatever comes to us about ourselves from that vantage point. To be self-critical, as the Buddhists teach us, is *delusion.* We can be aware of the delusion, stand apart from it somewhat, take a position about it. We need not prove our value to anyone. We need not fight with anyone. But we shall never join our demons by public self-deprecation. We will respect all living things, especially ourselves. Our philosophy will be to feel deeply what we feel, affirm our self-love, and do the dishes when they need doing.

Bad feelings and crazy, self-critical thoughts will pass like a river running to the sea, and our basic love will seep through from under the hatred just as sure as the sun will rise and the tide will come in and there is a wisdom guiding the universe. Our deluded self-centeredness can fool us for just so long. Joy awaits.

Loving yourself is not self-centered, not uncaring, not indifferent to the plight of others. Loving yourself madly, radical self-acceptance, total, unremitting, profoundly deep self-respect, is the purpose of life. It only takes two things: the deep intention to do it, and all the courage you can muster.

Chapter 12

Joy

ॐ

Just as shame is what we experience when we believe we are not enough, joy is the emotion we experience when we know we *are* enough, when everything about us is acceptable to us, when we truly know deep down that we are perfect the way we are, although there may be things about us that we or others think need changing.

The naysayers of joy say we shouldn't expect it, or at least extremely rarely. Some feel they can only go after it with drugs or addictions, and they suffer a terrible price. Suffering, sadness, misery, pain and loss is the human condition, others say. Work, work, work to improve yourself, and you are never done. There is no time for joy.

Joy is our birthright. As with the toddler and its mother and father, joy is the celebration of life. We have the right and the obligation to pursue it full-time. We deserve to clearly know the truth that we are wonderful. We are gifts to our parents and to the universe, just as our children are to us. We are God's partners. Let us rejoice and be glad. Re—JOY!—ce.

We all live in a massive distortion which obscures the reality that each of us deserves the highest of awards *just because we do life*. Remember: We don't know where we come from, we don't know where we are going, we don't know what our life means. We love, starting with mother, and we have to separate from her and from all our subsequent loves. We know there is a higher power and we reach out in our fog, but we really don't know how to get to him or her—even the sex of this *magnum mysterium* is a human approximation. We know somewhere that we must forge a relationship with ourselves, and if we are lucky we do, though it is very hard. And then we die, and it seems we lose that relationship, too. No matter what we involve ourselves with or how we distract ourselves, these realities linger somewhere inside us. Yet we survive, we endure, we persevere, we pass it on, and, for the most part, we make the best of it. *We are good sports, we humans.* The notion that we should beat up on ourselves *for anything* is preposterous.

Distressingly often when I say these things to people, there is a groundswell of opposition. "If all I do is have fun, how is the world going to function?" "If I don't try to change all my bad habits, I will not be a good person!" The list is endless. And it is the *ferocity* of the rejection of joy that is the amazing thing. True, we must think of our duty; true, we need to spruce ourselves up here and there. But shouldn't the idea of having more joy in our lives cheer us up a *little*? It has that effect on me, though God knows I eke it out by daily combat with my demons. I have come to understand that at the bottom of our joy phobia is the fear of losing mother. For joy is eminently separate. It is the most personal of decisions. To be truly joyous you must be able to stand alone, perhaps propped up sometimes by those on either side of you, but alone in your wisdom, seeing the world with your own eyes in your uniqueness and oneness with the Transcendent.

And this uniqueness, this personal vision, is purchased by the commitment to psychologically separate, to form the clear and resolute intention to wrest your life, your emotions, your thinking, your acts, to wrest who you truly are, back from your earliest caretakers. We will never feel the frequency of joy of the toddler. Too much has happened to us; we are no longer the *tabula rasa*, blank screens with no memory to haunt us. It is too late for that. But for this much it is not too late: to make the conscious decision to lead our own lives, to search for our vocations as persons. *We can unequivocally commit to being on our own side.*

No matter what madness rushes through our heads and no matter what compulsivities may have us in their grip, no matter how bashed we may be by shame and guilt, no matter how discouraged we may become at our self-centeredness, we can always tell ourselves that we love ourselves. For our suffering is not because of us. It is the human condition, and it is a strange condition, full of mystery. Embrace that truth and forgive yourself. Live each moment, and disregard whatever negative thoughts anyone has about you—*and show yourself.* You owe it to the universe to contribute your specialness. Do not be afraid. We will never be toddlers again, but we *can* have a great time here on earth as grown-ups. We are called to love and receive ourselves fully and have joy as a result.

It is a sad truth that mother cannot save us from death (though most of us still desperately hold onto that notion, generally way below conscious awareness). No one can. Don't throw away your life in the belief that homage to her, or to a surrogate through fused thinking, emotions or behaviors, will save you. Refusing to forgive yourself, tenaciously holding on to guilt, wallowing in shame or any kind of suffering will get you nowhere. It is a waste of time and of your life except where it gives you information about the world. But loving yourself fully and completely *with absolutely no exceptions*, and deeply desiring to make your life part of the higher wisdom of the universe, will often result in joy, and it will even make possible a happy relationship with your mother, in person or in your mind!

One day when I was meditating, experiencing grief over the loss of a romantic, exclusive relationship with a dear friend, a remarkable thing happened. I was allowing myself to feel this grief—to accept it fully and to accept myself fully feeling it—when I got the inspiration not only to accept it but to welcome it. It was not an unfamiliar feeling, this grief, albeit an excruciatingly painful one, one known to just about all of us. I had a sense that I had in this moment an opportunity to be transformed in some way by this feeling, that if I welcomed it rather than analyzed it or suffered it begrudgingly or acted out upon it, I would possibly surrender something I had held onto fiercely since early childhood. To put words on the feeling, it was something like this: You have not been able to cure Mommy or make her happy; you are bad and undeserving; this pain may save you from extinction but it might not as well; you just might not survive this at all.

When I welcomed this feeling, immersed myself in it, I discovered myself weeping quietly and a feeling of sadness for myself, which had been lingering in the shadows of all this loss and fear, came into the forefront. I began to weep more fully, and I realized that the loss I was dreading was actually the loss of myself. It was a reminiscent feeling, but one I had shoved away whenever it came into consciousness. I was going to die, and I was very sad about it.

There was nothing I could do. It was a fact. I was powerless over this reality, my death. Why should I do anything when it wouldn't make any difference in what really mattered, my eventual lack of existence? Why should I even take good care of myself, to extend my life, since I couldn't save it ultimately? Why should I do anything? Why should I love my neighbor? Why should I engage myself with the Transcendent? A cruel joke has been played on me. I was allowed to taste consciousness, and it was to be taken from me! Why should I love when that love inevitably would be taken from me one way or another?

I wasn't angry at this, only sad. At the same time, relief came over me, the calm that comes with the direct experience of truth, the resolution of some torturous conflict that had exhausted me and never got anywhere. I noticed also that the grief was gone. The problem was not really the loss of the other person! Rather, it was the loss of the denial of the reality of my mortality that I had created through this relationship. I had reexperienced that sense of safety that I had had as a child with my mother. Nothing terrible could happen to me. She wouldn't let it. I often was terrified when my own children were young, fearing that I would not be able to save them, for example, if a plane we were traveling on were to crash. What would I tell them? I knew that their belief in my omnipotence was a myth, yet I identified with them because I hadn't accepted as myth my own parents' omnipotence, even though both were dead. This myth, this primitive belief, is so powerful that it persists in the unconscious despite every possible indication to the contrary. I could not live without this woman, because I could not live without my mother. Who would save me from extinction if not my mother-lover?

The answer that day was that no one would save me from extinction—not my lover, not my mother, no one. In this sadness, in this calm, I realized I had a choice to make. What would I do about my realization that I would not live forever and that no one could save me, that I was alone? In the midst of all of this came the haunting awareness that in a secret, central sense, we are each alone, locked inside ourselves, never to be fully known or fully to know another.

Having it out with ourselves honestly and determining for ourselves how to live in the face of the inevitability of death are among the most courageous things a person can do. The composer Shostakovich said:

Fear of death may be the most intense emotion of all. I sometimes think that there is no deeper feeling. The irony lies in the fact that under the influence of that fear people create poetry, prose, and music; that is, they try to strengthen their ties with the living and increase their influence on them.[1]

They also tend to fuse. Psychological separation is a step toward death, which is one of the reasons people resist it. We hold onto fusion, a sort of death with consciousness, resisting separating out into our uniqueness, our mysterious vocation to express while we are here, and then to release into oneness with the Transcendent. Each of our egos is fused with mother to some extent, and fearfully we hold onto it and resist letting go of her hand, psychologically separating.

I intend to be kind, but it shocks me just a little bit less these days when I get caught up in the concupiscence of meanness. I believe myself to be on the Wisdom path, but each day catches me selfish, gluttonous, lustful— you might as well lay out the whole deadly seven, first among which is pride. I have them all. Sometimes I revel in them rebelliously; sometimes I reject them in a merciless morality.

But this much is different. Today I am likely to catch myself up in such an act. When I feel the guilt I can say, in some fashion, "Big surprise!" I am a human being, and I am *this* human being. This is part of me. Who do I think I am not to be so? This is certainly not all of me, but it is me, but it *is* me. No denying it. I can let go of it. And then my meanness and all the other vices seem to lessen just because of my radical self-acceptance. Amazing, isn't it?

If I outgrow the lash of narcissism, I can be a free agent in my life, accepting what has been, responding to the promptings of reality and becoming, in full throttle and joyously, who I am. I know finally and inexorably what my patient Patrick discovered some years earlier—that I was not the problem.

When we enter the separated place, the Wisdom place, our inner atmosphere is transformed. It is a pure and clean place. It deals with the moment. There is no mother there, no God even. There just is. This is the place the mystics try by all manner of exercises to get to. But no magic is necessary. It is arrived at by relentless psychological separation. There is nothing and no one now between us and death. That realization makes us hesitate, but is also our liberation. It is heaven. We transcend even the Transcendent.

It is beyond acceptance, as well. The separated self sees and knows and understands what is. It has no judgments or opinions. It is devoid of evaluations, which are unseparated. It is one with everything and it is the capacity not merely to love but *to be love*. It *is* the Transcendent.

We come to conscious life for a brief while to celebrate. It is given to us to know the nature of life; to love, suffer, rejoice, mourn, fight, be born and die; to know it in a conscious way, to muse on it, and to give voice to God's words, "It is good." And so we trudge along, loving, losing our beloveds, continuing to separate into our best and unique selves until we lose that as well; and we do it lovingly and laughingly, with the courage to feel all that needs to be felt as we move along, and to keep on loving and doing what needs to be done. We make mistakes, acknowledge them, and pick ourselves up and keep moving toward life. This is the human expression of the Transcendent.

It is coming to the time, dear friends, when I must say goodbye to you, and I have one more thing to tell. Now that I have suggested all you might do to psychologically separate, be yourself, find God, love and be happy, I must tell you that we all miss by a mile. I jokingly tell folks that it is definitely possible to do it all, but that it takes a minimum of one hundred years of living until the job is completed. So develop a lot of patience and tolerance for yourself and others along the way.

We will feel all there is to feel, and then we won't; we will intend to separate out and to observe and to radically accept ourselves, and then we won't. We will experience shame and steadfastly refuse to pass it on, and then we'll forget. We will be open and honest with others and our lovers, and then we won't. We will be glad for the happiness and good that comes our way, and then we will lose it to envy and jealousy. We will form the intention to participate in the plans of a higher power, and the next moment we'll drop the whole program and rush willy-nilly into headstrong and selfish and self-defeating behavior.

Most of us miss by a mile, all the time. And we'll probably continue to do so. But this much we can always do. We can pick ourselves up, dust ourselves off, affirm that we love ourselves even when we are not inclined to, and resume where we left off. And know we are not alone, nor are we weird. It is our nature.

Perseverance is our strength: chipping away; keeping at it gently but persistently; accepting the accommodations we make in our relationships yet patiently trying to be more giving; most importantly, building daily our devotion to loving and accepting ourselves *just as we are at this moment*. No one or no thing can truly prepare us for all that life will demand of us. It seems that as soon as we have one thing pretty well figured out, we are faced with an entirely new stage of life, for which we have no preparation at all. Take it easy on yourself. Have compassion. Oh, and don't forget your sense of humor! I can't claim to know much about the essential characteristics of my higher power, but I am absolutely certain of one thing: he has a joyous and robust sense of humor. I'm sure he's holding his sides in laughter most of the day, and that he wants us to do so too. Better than the wisest counsel from theologians and philosophers and psychologists is a good belly laugh. Go for it! The "laughing Buddha" is my man.

A few final thoughts about Mom. A patient told me that he feels so unfused with his mother these days that he is able to attend to her needs—she is in her eighties—with no resentment. When we disentangle our fusion with mother, it does not mean we reject her. Often, we are able to relate lovingly and generously for the first time. When you cease being enmeshed either in hatred or in over-estimation, you are free to see Mom as a separate person, and you, as a separate person, can truly love her and forgive her and appreciate her and even be grateful—or at least be just, and at peace about her. When you "let her go," you can relate to her, you can love her. She is your friend, not your higher power. When fear has abated through psychological separation and spiritual growth, the poignancy of our enmeshment with mother can be surrendered to the deep love of special friends. You no longer believe that it is *essential to her welfare* for you to be a certain way or to do certain things. You no longer need to live your life desperate for her love. You will be free.

You know, since Columbus discovered America, there have been 65,552 persons or so who have contributed biologically to your existence. You have had 65,552 "grandparents" since then. And all but four of these you share with your parents. Your mother is just the last in the long line of ancestors, and she shares most of them in common with you! She is just a fellow human being, though perhaps with a very special place in our heart.

Before Columbus arrived, and to this day, there is a tribe of Indians living in Colombia, the Kogi. By the good fortune of geography, civilization has made few inroads into the life and ways of the Kogi, and they appreciate this, constructing elaborate obstacles against intrusions. Some "moderns" have gotten through and have been taught a lovely philosophy of life which describes our relationship to earth and nature and the universe. The word they have for God is "Mother." They constantly refer to Mother. Mother wants us to be kind to one another; Mother wants us to rotate the crops. When pushed for a definition they say that Mother is "the mind inside nature." The Kogi recognize that what we hold on to so frantically in our biological mothers is really the purview of the Higher Power. They even give that Power its proper name. We are all, our mother and ourselves, children of this Mother, the mind inside nature.

That Mother cooperates with us. She is mysterious, but she lets our spirits, unique person that each of us is, continue to be born of the mire of our past experience. She lets our spirits emerge. When we live in this Wisdom place, the world simply works better. The help that appears for us seemingly out of nowhere seems miraculous. It is just that we become open to more of the infinite reality, both within and without. No longer deafened and blinded by fusion, we hear what our spirits are trying to tell us. We see more of the universe, as it is.

Thank you for staying with me. It's time to say goodbye. We will probably never meet, but I know that you are struggling to become yourself as I am and as countless others are, all over the world. We are all in this together, and I send my love and encouragement and congratulations to each of you, wherever you are. May Mother, the mind inside nature, embrace all of her daughters and sons in love and peace and joy, and may we love her back.

Be well.

Appendix:
The Person on the Wisdom Path

෫෮

Psychologically separating, being on the Wisdom path, wresting back our selves from our caretakers, growing out into who we truly are—these are lifetime tasks. And it is the process, the dedication, not the goal, that is essential, that will provide us with a joyous life. Who wants the *end* of the rainbow? The rainbow is quite enough. As we persevere on this path our life will get better and richer not because there was anything wrong with us before but rather because we are now about the business of releasing our spirit, becoming the unique person in the history of the universe we truly are.

If we make the *spiritual* act of *intention* to become our unique selves, and follow this with observation and radical self-acceptance, we will have crossed over onto the Wisdom path and will spend the rest of our life at whatever rate is best for us, growing out into ourselves. We will continue to become who we are.

Should we form this "intention" and seriously observe our life, by ourselves or with the aid of an analyst or spiritual friend, we will notice certain changes occurring "behind our back." We will notice an increase in the productivity of our thinking; we will feel more feelings and accept them as our own; our interactions with the world will be characterized by productivity and creativity rather than achievement and accomplishment; we will be much more "present" in our engagements with others; we will see an increase in independence. We will need no guru but will find ourselves the final arbiter of our actions; we will be able to be alone; we will be related, capable of sharing intimately with others; we may or may not have a special monogamous relationship, but we will not be promiscuous; celibacy will be a possibility; we will celebrate our life but will be humble. There will be little denial—we will see what we will see; we will accept ourselves and others. We will be tolerant, empathic, and compassionate; we will be grateful to and for life, and generous. We will tend to be pacifists, seeing that war is futile and that nationalism and over-identification with our particular group is a reflection of fusion and leads to death and destruction. We will accept our impulses to form a relationship with the Transcendent. And all of the movement in all of these dimensions comes by itself, not as the result of conscious goals.

So what happens to us when we get on the Wisdom path? What do we look like; how do we function? It cannot be said too often that being on the Wisdom path has nothing to do with any particular accomplishment. It has to do with process.

In a sense, it is quite ordinary. Left to our own devices we do the right thing, move onto the Wisdom path. What is extraordinary are the ways we derail ourselves due to the sometimes overwhelmingly difficult situations we find ourselves in. No, the Wisdom path is quite ordinary, although, perhaps, not chosen often enough.

I remember the summer between my junior and senior years in college. I was in the Army Reserve Officers Training Corps (ROTC) and had to spend six weeks training. I was sent to Fort Bragg, North Carolina. It was hot, very hot. In my barracks were young men from all over the eastern seaboard. It was basic training, with all the discomfort and misery that that entails. We were generally up at the crack of dawn for company formation; then we ran from one activity to another until just about bedtime, when we had to prepare our gear for the next day. At night, as we shined our boots and cleaned our rifles, we shot the breeze and managed to have some laughs.

I remember a fellow, I think his name was Joey, with whom I was quite taken. He had a tremendous sense of humor, was always kidding around, always cheerful. He also had a girlfriend, whom he had left to come to camp, and he would get frequent letters from her. This was the late 1950s and sex, at least in my circles, was pretty furtive and incomplete. Naturally, we were all obsessed with it. Joey, on the other hand, was having a full-fledged, fully sexual relationship with his girlfriend, and he had the letters from her to prove it. They had given names to their genitals and referred to them that way in their letters. "Mary misses John soooo bad," his girlfriend would write, and those who bunked next to him and were privy to this sentiment would be beside themselves. Consciously, I wanted to dismiss Joey as something of a buffoon and certainly "immoral" (good 1950s Catholic boy that I was), but deep down I knew he was onto something that was right. There was something natural and healthy about this young man, much as I didn't want to admit it.

One night we were coming home by truck from a particularly long and difficult day. We had been learning to fire mortars and bazookas, and the firing range for these weapons was far away. It must have been after midnight, we knew we had to be up in just a few hours, and we were absolutely exhausted. Covered with dust and with the smell of the canvas tops of the trucks and ourselves in our nostrils, we staggered out of the trucks into the barracks building.

Now, three or four of the platoon had been assigned the transport and safety of these large weapons. When we arrived back at the base they had to be disassembled, cleaned, and stored. This meant more work. The four who had been babysitting the weapons all day got stuck with the duty as the rest of us disembarked the truck and made tracks for our beds.

I remember it clearly. I was in bed under the sheets. The lights were out. All of a sudden the lights went on and standing in the middle of the floor, still in his filthy fatigues, was Joey. He was furious. "What the hell is the matter with you guys," he shouted. "Don't you think those guys are tired, too? How the hell can you go to bed and leave all that extra work to those men? Get your asses out of bed and help them." There was a mad scramble out of bed and down to the truck; by working together the weapons got taken care of and all of us were able to go to bed. This was never mentioned again. Joey returned to his cheerful, joking-around self. But the incident has stayed with me for thirty years.

What I had experienced with Joey, although I was decades away from getting some glimpse into what it was all about, was a person on the Wisdom path. He was natural, earthy, kind, and generous. Even more important, he thought and felt for himself. Like those who helped the Jews in Europe in the 1940s, he knew what was right and what was wrong and he had no difficulty in acting upon those principles. He felt deeply and without apology. He thought for himself. He saw the world through his own eyes. Barely a man, he had separated psychologically to the point where he was on the Wisdom path.

Yet there was nothing dramatic about Joey. He was an ordinary guy. But he was himself and has been a model for me for years. (If by some miracle you read this, "Joey," thank you for the example you set for me that summer.)

Joey was a very spiritual young man, although I would not have thought so in those days. His sexuality would have precluded my thinking of him in that way. But lusty, loving sexuality, expressed or not, is the epitome of spirituality and psychological separation. In fact, spirituality is the very process of psychological separation. And this process has little to do with goals and accomplishments. The affect that accompanies psychological separation is the same for a baby learning to crawl as for the most accomplished person. *It is the experience of the separation process that is crucial: that is separation.* Separation is separating; it is a process of the spirit although it can be aided by psychological analysis and other conditions which we will mention in a moment. *It can never be identified by the nature of the achievement in itself.*

The spirit and the demons live side by side, and each of us without exception must engage in the struggle. The mentally limited person who heroically struggles each day to get dressed and negotiate the transit system to get to a sheltered workplace, where she will put all her energies into relating, loving, and producing—what will I ever do to match this? The schizophrenic who stands apart from her hallucination and does her work anyway; the choreographer who faces a new challenge amidst the terrifying demonic belief that he no longer knows how to create—all of us are creatures of the spirit and are the same, regardless of the aesthetic evaluation of the product.

Getting on the Wisdom path takes nothing more than forming the intention, conscious or unconscious, to see the world through our own eyes and to interact with it in a competent way. Without realizing it, we move into the realm of the Transcendent, because understanding the world deeply is probing the mysteries of life, and the affect that accompanies this is enthusiasm (which means, incidentally, "with God"). Look at the baby steps of the infant. They are accompanied by hilarity and extreme joyousness and are repeated despite the hard knocks. Infants and young children are very spiritual in that sense, which is one of the reasons we love them so. We love their unbounded energy, their joy in risking separating, their perseverance despite pain and setbacks. They are engaged in a holy task.

The major characteristic of the psychologically separating person is being central-to-self. It is, as we have seen, to be in the service of our own life. Growing out is the increasing unfolding of the reality that we are responsible for our own life and equally important, that we are capable of meeting that responsibility to ourselves. When we realize no one can do it for us, no one can live our life, no one can save us from death, then reality *must* be understood. Denial is rejected, dependency is abandoned, and the grip of our fusion is confronted. There is a deep understanding of who, exactly, our parents were and the realization that the basic interference in our life is our deep-seated fear of our parents' disapproval. What will they think of me? When this deep, deep fear is acknowledged and the supposed safety that that belief presumably provides is abandoned, we are really free to do what we want: free to love and to work, as Freud put it, free to know the world outside the family; free to live our own life, our one and only life.

Oh, what we go through to deny this reality that we can take care of ourselves. What pain and anger and panic and sickness, physically and emotionally, we put ourselves through, unwitting though we may be. And when we get on the Wisdom path, life is not so easy either. It takes courage. There is no role model for our unique self. We must create it from inside, and this demands a peculiar courage. I call this the courage to be nowhere. Each movement forward is disorienting and involves a dramatic internal restructuring—"growing pains." Some form of the stages of mourning must be gone through. Yet the prize is worth it, for we no longer have to live in the confusion of a self-centered life and look to the false gods of transference. We are free to venture out and to explore the ultimate Mother, the mind of nature. We can see reality; we can see what we can see. And the sky is the limit!

Overall, there are three general ways that psychological separation takes place:

1. In relationship with ourselves: for example, radical self-acceptance, observation.
2. In relationship with others: for example, love, psychoanalysis, companionate affiliations.
3. In relationship with the Transcendent: for example, intention, prayer and meditation, worship, awe.

We separate out into ourselves in relationship, and it is in the framework of these three types of relationship that we can see the offspring of our commitment to the Wisdom path. Just what is it that happens to us in the process of psychological separation?

In each of these three modes of relationships we can look at the changes that occur in us from the point of view of (1) *structure of our personalities*: our relationships with ourselves, our capacity to think clearly, have emotions, our deep beliefs; (2) our *values*: what we believe and cherish as we are released from the tyranny of our fusion-serving deep beliefs; and finally (3) our *behavior*: we begin to change from mere acting or doing to behaviors that are actual *expressions* of our separated selves; we attend to the psychological and spiritual "hygiene" that supports us on the Wisdom path. I will describe below the changes that occur over time in each of these categories—self, interpersonal, and Transcendent—in terms of structure of personality, values, and behavior.

This is my view of what characterizes us as we travel on the Wisdom path. There will be considerable overlap in each of these categories, for each has an impact on all aspects of our lives. Some will be mentioned lightly if we have gone into the matter at some length before. Others will be elaborated to round out our treatment.

Relationship with Self

Structure of Personality

The psychologically separating person will experience *internal* changes in the following areas.

A. Thinking. We have spoken a lot about this. To begin with we notice that we are actually *permitted* to think! We have confidence in our capacity to think things through and to grapple with complicated issues. We do not automatically "know," and most of all we do not automatically accept the teachings and conclusions of authorities. We deny little of what is about us. We allow a deep understanding of just who our parents are, and while not condemning them, we do not delude ourselves regarding their strengths and weaknesses. Ultimately we forgive them, but first and foremost we understand who they are. Because of this freedom of knowledge we are able to know the world in a much deeper fashion than most people. Once we allow ourselves to know the truth about our parents, we can know the truth about anything. We have a deep grasp of the nature of reality. But in this process we have humility. We know our limitations, and we know our strengths as well. We see things as they are, not necessarily as we wish them to be. Our thinking is largely organized by reality and a desire to know the truth rather than by egocentricity.

B. Perception and absorption. Our perceptions, made up of the unique intermingling of our perceptual capacities and the objective nature of a thing, result in creative and powerfully true understandings of reality. Generally accompanying this exceptional accuracy of perception is the capacity to become actively absorbed in something or somebody. This is distinguished from fusion in that we don't "become" that thing but are capable of "entering" it deeply and thoroughly while still keeping our identity intact. This capacity, *absorption*, enables us to understand deeply and to co-create reality with the Transcendent.

All reality is all around us at all times. We see what we can see, what we personally are able to see, despite the consensually validated pressure *not* to see that comes from family, internal structures, mate, and society. As we become central-to-self, more reality is available. What we need to see is there for us. Memory directs us without our being aware. We may be directed to books or people from the past. We may put ourselves in situations where answers we need appear. Everything we have ever experienced is available to us; everything that *is* is available to us. The main thing is getting *ourselves* available, and that comes from psychologically separating and getting on the Wisdom path. The main difficulty in doing this, once again, is ego. Humility is necessary to abandon egocentricity. Humility involves seeing what is. Egocentricity involves seeing what we want to see there or think should be there or even feel more comfortable with being there.

C. Affect/Emotions. As in the case of productive thinking, psychologically separating persons are able to feel everything. We accept our feelings,[1] "own" them, and can experience their full range. This is truly remarkable because there is such prejudice against emotions in our world. This has several roots. Emotions, as we have seen above, are powerful epistemological tools, and thus they are discouraged in our upbringing. We are not supposed to know too much. In addition, emotions often frighten our caretakers, who themselves have been enjoined from feeling their own emotions. It is no surprise, then, that there is little education about emotions. It is usual, as I work with a new patient, to discover these inhibitions, especially about anger. Otherwise intelligent and sophisticated persons may be terrified of their anger because they do not know the difference between annoyance and homicidal rage. They have no confidence in their ability to control themselves or temper emotional expression. Also, they believe that if they experience their feelings they *must* express them. As a result, they shut down completely. It is amazing to them that there are many shades of anger and that we can learn to express our angry feelings appropriately if we feel they must be expressed at all.

In fact, many, if not most of us, are shut down when it comes to our emotions. Psychologically separating persons, on the other hand, are not afraid of emotions. They welcome them both for what they teach about the world and because they are important and valid expressions of their selves. They are the color of life. We see this in children. Before they are "socialized," they express their emotions fully and with gusto. They are free in this respect. Psychologically separating individuals are comfortable with and capable of expressing all the "life-oriented" emotions ranging from joy through sadness to anger. And they are free, should they choose, to experience them fully *without any expression of them at all*. They know that this full experience of them will dissolve them; they needn't express them to "get rid" of them. They only express emotions when they decide it is helpful to do so.

Remember: There is no such thing as a *bad* emotion or a *bad* thought. Emotions and thoughts are not behaviors, and only behaviors can be "bad." We can revel in our "bad" thoughts and feelings. They will do no harm, although their denial might. "Bad" thoughts and feelings are a natural response to life. We can accept them and accept ourselves having them.

Psychologically separating folks rarely experience for long "death-oriented" affects such as anxiety, depression, guilt, and shame. These are the pseudo-affects associated with the chronic affect-states of fusion. Of course, as humans, psychologically separating persons experience these too, but such affect-states are not really acceptable to them and they work to discard them. They work toward releasing all suffering and grief, both theirs and that of others, for they have a stake in the world being a happy one. Their lives are characterized, for the most part, by joy and mirth. They work toward creating an intrapsychically joyous environment.

D. Power to choose. We know by now that most of our growing out into ourselves is not the direct result of conscious effort. There are all sorts of things we must do to set the stage for change, but for the most part, it happens "behind our backs." This does not mean that we never need to choose consciously. We often do. Forming the intention to separate psychologically is an example of this. It is a choice. Observation and radical self-acceptance are also choices. Psychologically separating persons do not avoid these choices. They do not leave them to others, though sometimes their choice will be to follow the advice of another.

Being on the Wisdom path does not guarantee that we will always choose wisely, however. We are free to choose evil as well as good, excess over moderation. When such a faulty decision is made, we actually get off the Wisdom path, at least for that moment, and move again toward fusion. By and large persons on the Wisdom path generally choose in the direction of moderation. Moderation in all aspects of our existence supports the spirit, while excess supports fusion. Cardiologist Dean Ornish considers heart disease to be a disease of excess. Most animals know when they have had "enough" of anything. Only humans with their overweening egos often haven't a clue to what is enough. Hence our proclivity toward excess. Psychologically separating persons know what is enough and do not waste time in a compulsive search for "more."

E. Courage/compassion. Related powerfully to choice is courage. Courage refers not so much to superhuman heroics of the kind we are encouraged to emulate, but rather to those moments when we resist temptation, when we refuse to do something that our demonic fusion is telling us to choose. Courage is in daily decisions not to have a piece of cake if we are struggling to get to a healthy weight or to tell the truth when to lie would save us "trouble." These are the courageous acts of psychological separation, and it is here that true separation takes place, not in the grand gesture. Psychological separation also takes place, I should emphasize, in acts of compassion toward ourselves when our courage fails us and we regress, as we all do.

What about the relationship of compassion to courage? Benjamin Hoff writes:

> One of the most important terms of Taoism: Tz'u...can be translated as "caring" or "compassion" and...is based upon the character for heart. In the sixty-seventh chapter of the Tao Te Ching, Lao-Tse named it as his "first treasure," and then wrote, "from caring comes courage." We might add that from it also comes wisdom. It's rather significant, we think, that those who have no compassion have no wisdom. Knowledge, yes; cleverness,

maybe; wisdom, no. A clever mind is not a heart. Knowledge doesn't really care. Wisdom does. We also consider it significant that *cor*, the Latin word for "heart," is the basis for the word courage. Piglet put it this way: "She isn't clever, Kanga isn't, but she would be so anxious about Roo that she would do a Good Thing to Do without thinking about it."[2]

I think certitude is the most troublesome of human characteristics and compassion the most blessed.

F. Reliability/Trustworthiness/Perseverance. Psychologically separating persons can count on themselves, and others can count on them. Persons who have separated psychologically from parents are interested in co-creating the present with the world and their peers, not in re-creating the childhoods of their past by transforming their present into shadowy images of that past. They are trustworthy; they persevere. Others can count on them and *they can count on themselves as well.*

I have often heard people counseled to "trust themselves" or "trust their feelings." This has often seemed the wrong advice. "Love God and do as you please," a statement reputed to St. Augustine, seems more appropriate if we understand "love God" to refer to a sincere desire to conform to the Transcendent. If we are focused on God rather than parents, indeed we can trust ourselves and what we do. In fact, this is a very important aspect of radical self-acceptance. If we form the intention to let go and to be an independent adult, and take the steps necessary to move in that direction (observation, therapy, meditation, intimacy, for example), then the unfolding of our inner processes, the spirit aligned with Spirit, will flower.

Psychologically separating persons are capable of relatedness and love and can be counted on. They will be interested in knowing who others actually are and rejoice in their freedom. They will appreciate our acceptance of them and our confirmation of them, not needing it, but celebrating it. They love in companionate affiliation, if not more.

G. Independence/Maturity/Unfolding of potential/"Growing out." Consider the following dialogue between "Joe" (a clergyman) and me:

> Joe: I have to let her [mother] go....God and she are one...God and I are one....But she and I are *not* one....I don't want to let her go because I don't want to be fully me and fully responsible....God will not allow me to attach myself to him in an unhealthy way....It's so hard to separate...I see her body, her face.

Me: You know you're not going to live forever.

Joe: I feel I must protect her....It's my mission and purpose.

Me: Bullshit....You feel you'll be safe if your identity is taking care of her...but you won't be safe....What makes you safe is knowing you are you...and that won't save you from death either.... *Nothing* will!

The mature person is independent. He does not depend on another to make him safe; he does not depend on another to make him worthwhile; he does not, in delusion, depend on anyone to save him from death. He has separated psychologically from these deep beliefs; he takes care of himself. He sees life through his own eyes. While he learns from everyone, the most "humble" included, he has no guru. He knows he came into the world alone, will leave alone, and each day, if he permits himself to be aware, he will experience his aloneness. As a young patient told me, "After the day is over, when I go to sleep with my heart, it is by myself." The psychologically separating person is not overly troubled by this because he is central-to-self. Not drowning in fusion, he is in touch with the natural gratitude for existence and keeps going, even in mystery.

But psychologically separating persons are not isolates, and they are certainly not narcissists. They are comfortable alone; they can have great fun and enjoy. Some may even pursue vocations as monks or be quite solitary. Most, however, have many loving relationships. Typically they have happy marriages, are good parents, friends, and community members. But even by themselves *psychologically separating persons are related to others*. Their friends and lovers exist within them and are loved even in their absence. So even alone they are rarely lonely. Loneliness is having something or someone in between our relationship to self. When we are central-to-self, we need never be lonely because our loved ones live within us as psychologically separate entities and are a comfort even in their physical absence. We may miss them, even long for them, but we are not lonely.

Some of the strategies people employ to deny separation and aloneness include feeling responsible for others, feeling guilty, being fearful, being depressed, being angry, being sick, denying mortality by mistreating or neglecting the body, being "in need of improvement," refusing to work at life, compulsive and addictive behavior, work, not enjoying vacations, or getting injured, getting "in trouble," going crazy, worry, shame. *The psychologically separating person doesn't do these any more.*

Psychologically separating persons are not immobilized by rejection and take responsibility for health, economic security, sexual security, and self-concept. *They produce rather than achieve, create rather than repeat.* They take joy in presenting to the world what their spirits prompt them to manifest. They are adults.

Spontaneity, risk, openness, and receptivity are all functions of the extent to which we have left home. This is in contrast to the deep belief that "I am essentially unlovable but my family will accept me any way I am, so I will be loyal to them; others will never accept me as I am once they get to know me." The person who remains in the grip of that mad belief stays in the parent-child axis. And parent-child roles are interchangeable. Chronologically grown-up persons can stay in these roles forever, alternating back and forth, sometimes parent, sometimes child, never breaking out to become psychologically separated. Only independent adults can relate and love sexually and feel joy, not merely occasional safety. The price we pay for remaining in the parent-child axis is high. If we continue to aspire to be better children, we will be visited by chronic unhappiness.

Maturity is the realization that we are in charge of our life, and the commitment to separate psychologically. It doesn't matter how well we do it; that is, how "right" we are or what we accomplish. It is better to accomplish less by ourselves than to accomplish more under the aegis of someone or something else. *To insist on living our own life is maturity.* We can learn from others, be humble and open, but it is better to be ourselves than to be right.

We, too, have much to teach. We see the world in our unique way. We owe it to humankind and to the powers that gave us life to tell them what we think about life. Each of us has the right and the obligation to put our "two-cents" into the pot of human knowledge and experience however we are prompted to do it.

H. Radical self-acceptance. We have spoken at great length about this. The psychologically separating person daily works toward complete and radical acceptance of himself *just as he is*. He knows he is just fine. He has confidence that as he keeps focused and honest about his intention to separate out unto himself, does what his spirit prompts him to do, and observes his life with the aid of whatever tools he finds helpful at the time, he will change in whatever way is right for him. He will be just fine then, and more important, he knows he is just fine right now. My patient Mar-tin said it so well: "I see my problems for what they are, but I don't have to hold it against myself."

Values

A. Giving up perfectionism. Being concerned with the *outcome* of things becomes less important. The *actual engagement* in the activity becomes the important thing. David Reynolds, the proponent of Japanese Morita therapy in the United States, once inscribed a book for me, "Practice *is* Perfect!" The psychologically separating person knows that the ideal of perfection is based on an unseparated deep belief that she must be perfect or she won't get mother's love (and then she won't live forever). The psychologically separating person knows she does not *need* mother's or anyone's love to be all right. She is all right because she exists and she accepts herself. She knows she is enough. She is free.

B. Abandoning avarice. Psychologically separating persons understand that accumulating "stuff," whether wealth, lovers, diplomas on the wall, antiques, or whatever, will not make them all right. They are already all right. Rather, they know these things can *limit* their lives. The stronger our aspiration for "enough," the less satisfied we are with the "enough" that we already have. We miss out on all the peace and joy in the most elemental gifts of life. As with any false god, the desire for "more" has at its root the deep belief that *we* are not enough, that there is something missing. This is a tragic delusion. There is nothing missing, and if we chase the illusion of "more" of anything to make up for that supposed "lack," we miss our life. Sometimes it seems to me that most of society is in a hypnotic fugue state, racing unthinkingly toward "prosperity," incapable or unwilling to give the time of day to a neighbor. It is very sad.

Psychologically separating persons know they have enough and that they are enough. They are free.

C. Enjoyment and care of body. Psychologically separating folks are natural, lusty animals who live life with gusto. They are comfortable with all the functions of the body. They lack bodily shame. They eat, drink, and make love with passion and fullness. Yet, seemingly paradoxically, these things can be temporarily given up with little complaint. They enjoy what they do thoroughly, but everything is in perspective. If for some reason they cannot, that's all right too. There is much more in life to occupy them. Moderation is a key value; things are done with passion, but not to excess. Good health is valued, and psychologically separating persons follow health regimens of diet and exercise, rest and recreation, that make sense to them. They have separated from the attitudes toward body and health that they grew up with and have taken these matters into their own hands. They take care of themselves and attend to their bodies, listening, not obsessively but carefully, as one would to a child. They are free.

D. Emotional and spiritual "hygiene." It appears that all that is necessary to feel *bad* is memory and thought. But to feel *good* takes action. We can feel bad for the rest of our lives through one bad act; to feel good, we must do the right thing every day.

Self-neglect is possibly the worst thing we do to ourselves. This is true even of the apparently egregiously self-interested or selfish; it is perhaps truest of them. We abuse our bodies. We depend on the doctors as if we were little children. This is all unseparated-child behavior. So, too, with the spiritual and emotional. Even when we get help—therapy or spiritual guidance—we tend to think that occasional "work" will sustain itself over time. We need to find a way to take care of our well-being every day. Only such an alertness enables us to withstand the constant assault of the demons, which want us to regress, to re-fuse, not to grow out unto ourselves. So we must have a program of emotional and spiritual hygiene. We need to find ways to neutralize the unceasing propaganda to remain in mother-fusion, which comes both from within and from without. We must form the intention to do this and, if we are sincere, ways to care for ourselves will occur to us. Let me suggest a few that have been helpful to me:

• *Search for sources of nourishment.* These can be music, bubble baths, car-racing, whatever your heart desires that is not dangerous to you. It may be therapeutic processes, therapy, meditation, exercise, massage, Twelve Step programs. Groups are especially helpful. Dean Ornish has had great success in reversing heart disease through diet and stress reduction. He insists that each of his patients participate in a group. The value of groups in healing many other types of physical maladies has been widely demonstrated. And this is true also of spiritual and emotional maladies. We need to speak to one another; we need to express what is bottled up inside. So find a place where you can speak of your innermost thoughts and feelings and feel safe while you are at it. You must propagandize yourself or the manifestations of the demons—in advertising or memory or just the "values" of the time we live in—will do it for you. You will be wise to create an environment where your spirit can be allowed to grow in freedom. Going on requires constant renewal to the commitment to life. Find a way to do it! Ask for help. You needn't be alone in the struggle.

• *Bailing out.* Don't settle into proving yourself *right in the past.* It is important to say yes to life, to enter a carefully observed and evaluated situation with all the gusto and enthusiasm you can muster. But it is also important to bail out when it is patently clear that the situation, relationship, job, habit, vocation, belief system, loyalty, or whatever no longer supports your spirit. Many folks seem to spend their entire lives defending and "making right" either the errors of the past or those situations that no longer work. This is why older people can be boring. If they haven't been bailing out, they have all sorts of accumulated claptrap rattling around inside themselves, which they will unpack at a moment's notice and use as a substitute for wisdom or novelty. This is why wisdom is often found, paradoxically, in young people, who are not yet so cluttered. It is much better for the spirit to hang around with "young" people, regardless of their chronological age.

Psychologically separating persons live in the present; they peek gently and modestly into the future and rarely but always pleasantly into the past. They are fresh. They are capable of learning from all sources, from everyone. They are free.

• *Being your own best friend.* The psychologically separating person takes his physical, emotional, and spiritual welfare very seriously. This is not selfishness in the sense of disregarding another person. The psychologically separating person watches over himself, and while that may include avoiding people who are toxic to him, he also knows that loving and helping others is very good for him in every way. He is particularly mindful, though perhaps not always consciously focused on this, of his feelings about himself. He wants to love himself. He knows he is enough, and when that awareness slips away, as it tends to do, he brings himself back to it. When he notices a self-critical thought, he attends to it immediately and speaks lovingly to himself: "That was an abusive thought and I reject it."

Regardless of what we have been taught, we are meant to be happy, just as a rose is meant to be beautiful. We recognize and accept the pain and tragedy of life, but we know it is our nature to be happy and we work toward it. Psychologically separating persons are free.

Behavior

A. Expression vs. acting or acting out. In addition to thinking and feeling, and often instead of these things, humans tend to act. Actions are what we "do," but not all actions are the same, even though they may look that way. We may have sexual intercourse with another because we want to express our love for that person, or we may be attempting to distance ourselves from our inner experience, or we may just be passing the time of day. There are even more possibilities, and any particular act may have several motivations.

Psychologically separating persons tend to *express* rather than act. They are, of course, capable of mindless activities, of harmlessly going on "automatic pilot." They also perform the routine functions of life in an efficient manner without too much thought. But most of their acts are, in some manner, *expressions* of inner experience. Action is a behavior separated from essence; expression *grows naturally* from essence. Act is focused on result. Expression is truthfully unmindful of outcome.

Finally, there is minimal "acting out" in the life of the psychologically separating person. Acting out is behavior designed to medicate an unpleasant feeling or impulse and perhaps partially express that impulse at the same time. Psychologically separating persons are aware of their feelings and inner experiences and impulses, value that awareness, and have little need of symbolic expression. They may do stupid things, but they know about them and own them.

B. Achievement vs. productivity-creativity. Related to expressing rather than acting is the issue of the meaning of the acts to the actor. Just as they express rather than act out, psychologically separating persons are not so much interested in *achievement* as they are in *productiveness*. Achievement is for the approval of others; productiveness is the expression of self. To achieve is to master the accumulated wisdom of others; to produce is to serve as the conduit of our own discoveries. Psychological separation is to do work in the world—to be productive, to be absorbed with the nature of reality, to create. To achieve is to be the "good child" of the family, performing in order to get the approval of our parents or their surrogates. Productiveness stems not from an inspired call to action and punishment of guilt and shame waiting for us when we fail, but rather from a commitment to study our ongoing life in a way that attempts to have our behavior *our own*.

Productivity is generous; achievement is selfish. Psychologically separating persons produce, "lead forth" their inner experience in a creative way, and persevere, regardless of the immediate rewards. They do it because it is their calling, their vocation. Although reality generally rewards their efforts, this is not first on their minds. They are free.

C. Generosity. Psychologically separating persons know that they are enough and that they have enough of everything they need and will ever need. They are not worried about "running out" or of becoming depleted. "Cheap" persons, I suspect, have a deep belief that their parents were a gift to them and that, consequently, they have a debt to pay for all eternity. They experience themselves as always in debt, certainly not in a position to be generous. Being cheap is a way of staying fused with mother. The reality is that *we* are the gift. Our parents were the instruments of the Transcendent providing us with life. Perhaps we owe something here (gratitude is all that is actually asked), but our arrival into their lives probably was the most wonderful gift that they will ever receive. Talk about co-creating with the transcendent! And we are the outcome. We are the gift! When we grasp that truth, we realize that we have always been taken care of and always will be. All we have to do is to discover that truth, and then we will want to keep giving.

Generosity is our natural condition. Psychologically separating persons are naturally generous and experience joy in giving to others. They are not afraid. They need not hoard and protect their "limited" supplies. They know they have enough; they know they *are* enough; they know their love is self-regenerating. They encourage and praise others. They do not keep their positive evaluations of others to themselves. They never experience their gifts to others as a depletion of themselves. They know the truth of the St. Francis prayer, though they may never have heard of it or even think in those terms: "For it is in giving that we receive." They are not afraid. They are free.

Interpersonal Relationships

Structure of Personality

A. Adulthood. Psychologically separating persons constantly are working to remove themselves from the parent-child axis which, as we have seen, enables a person to switch roles continually and remain in the ambience of childhood. Psychologically separating persons have left childhood. They are good parents to dependent children and others, because they are truly adults, and only adults can be good parents, fostering the independence of their charges rather than ensnaring them in a web of mutual dependency. If they are lucky, they may have a wonderful adult relationship with the persons who birthed them and raised them. They can also be "parental" within a relationship when the nature of the relationship calls for it, and they certainly can be playful children, because they are not afraid of their inner impulses and emotions. Even then a psychologically separating person is a child of the moment, not the pseudo-child of a fused relationship which is not of the present but of the past.

B. **Presence and empathy.** Psychologically separating persons "come out to play." They give themselves permission to leave the psychic home of childhood and to engage the world. As they do that, they "show up" for the people they interact with. They are present. Presence involves being in touch with our own inner experience and having that readily available when interacting with others. This enables psychologically separating persons to communicate their *intimus* to the other, and it also is the instrument with which they are capable of experiencing the other. Thus, they can be empathic. They use their own inner availability to pick up on the inner experience of the other, and so the possibility of relatedness is there, at least from their side. They are not compelled to do this; they may pick and choose where they will exercise this capability, but it is readily available to them. It is part of the structure of their relatedness.

C. **Gratitude.** Psychologically separating persons experience gratitude for life. As the process of psychological separation continues, they know increasing gratitude for all the experiences in their life, even those that have been painful. They are capable of finding the value in every human relationship they have ever had and of being grateful for these.

I am not speaking here of a pollyanna-ish optimism that, at least in the stereotype, disregards harsh realities. And notice that I do not include gratitude in the section on values. Rather, gratitude is part of the actual structure of the psychologically separating person's being, something experienced, not merely held as a worthy point of view.

There is an interesting Japanese psychotherapy called Naikan, which basically involves providing an atmosphere in which the patient is able to focus on what he has received in his life from others. He spends most of his time in isolation, interrupted occasionally by his therapist (who is experienced as a harsh task master, at least initially) and told to concentrate on what a particular person has done for him in his life. Whenever I do an exercise similar to this I find incredible the amount that has been done for me by everyone in my life, present and past. And not just in my personal life. When I walk around Central Park, for example, and enjoy this beautiful oasis in the midst of urban stress and sometimes menace, I focus on the fact that a man no longer alive, a contemporary of no one in this park right now or even on the planet, had the foresight to design this place. Others recognized the wisdom of his design and agreed that it should be created. Others worked hard in the physical creation of it; still others paid for it out of their own labors. And here I am walking around and enjoying myself and not thinking of that reality at all. The opportunities to reflect on what people past and present are doing and have done for us are literally endless. I am much more inclined to dwell on what people have *not* done for me, but if I am honest, those deprivations pale in light of the infinite gifts I have been given, including life in this conscious form which, much as I complain, I cherish and dread losing.

There is no need for guilt about this, nor am I suggesting that we ignore our resentments and anger at our deprivations. I am just noticing the neglect of the reality of our enormous gifts. I have resentments that I cherish and it is very hard for me to relinquish them, much less find gratitude. But every time I do, I find great joy and happiness. Can we imagine a life where we are grateful for everyone? Where we have no resentments? We would be bursting with joy! Psychologically separating persons move in this direction, which is why they increasingly experience an inner atmosphere of joy.

Values

A. The uses of resentment and judgments. It is natural to have resentments and judgments. We all do. But the attitude of psychologically separating persons distinguishes them from fused persons. Resentments and judgments are used by psychologically separating persons largely for their epistemological value. In other words, the awareness and acceptance of these attitudes and the affects that accompany them are neither condemned nor wallowed in. Rather, they are studied for the information they can provide about reality and the persons involved. That is the only purpose of such attitudes. They are not valued as "real," and they are not permitted to run the psychologically separating person's life. They are just factual states to use and discard. When resentments and judgments cause damage to other persons or to themselves (and damage includes suffering or obsessing), psychologically separating persons rid themselves of such clutter as rapidly as they can and with whatever assistance is needed. They know that those consumed by resentments and judgments are not free.

B. Tolerance. Tolerance is highly regarded by psychologically separating persons. They accept, on increasingly deeper levels of their being, that "all [people] are created equal" and are entitled to "life, liberty, and the pursuit of happiness." They may not *like* a particular person, but they work toward rooting out any prejudice—prejudging based on superficial characteristics such as race or religion or ethnicity. They accept their humanity and their basic limitedness and accept that in others as well. They know that prejudice separates them from certain classes or groups of people and serves to maintain mother-fusion. While they may take right pleasure in their own group characteristics, they basically understand that those characteristics are subservient to their membership in the human family under the grace of the Creator of us all.

The deeper they appreciate these realities and the more independent they become in their journey on the Wisdom path, the more intolerable the concept of war becomes. War, for any reason, is the most primitive example of unseparated behavior and one in which we have not changed at all from earliest recorded history.

As psychologically separating persons discover on deeper and deeper levels of their beings that they and all others are afraid, they grow in compassion for themselves. Simultaneously they "see" in a pristine way that, aside from our unique spirits, we are all the same. All of us are afraid, limited by our very natures, damaged to one extent or another by the randomness of our genes and our forbears. There is nothing left but mercy. So with mercy in their hearts and the determination to rid themselves and all others they can of suffering, they grow in tolerance of all persons and in intolerance of the madness of racial prejudice and war.

Could it be that psychological separation is actually an evolutionary step that humankind has been in the process of since the very beginning? Could it be that psychoanalysis is the most recent development in that spiritual unfolding? And that an end to war and racism cannot be accomplished until more and more people get on the Wisdom path?

Behavior

A. Generosity, compassion, and tolerance. It is one thing to feel these things in our heart and to hold them as values, and it is another to form our life upon them. Psychologically separating persons act toward others in a generous way. They are compassionate and tolerant. And they are these things *whether they feel like it or not.* So in their behavior, psychologically separating persons go a step further than holding these values and even feeling them. They are determined to *act* kind and loving regardless of how they feel at the moment.

This is a good time to make another point about feelings. It is not so important what emotional state we are in. Feelings come and go. They are mostly to inform us about the nature of the world and ourselves. They should rarely, if ever, be the impetus toward interpersonal behavior. It is OK to feel whatever we feel. It is OK to hate. It is OK to feel resentment. In fact, it is harmful to us to deny these feelings.

It is also possible to behave lovingly when we feel resentful, and it is likewise possible to be generous, compassionate, and tolerant when we hate! It is hard to get these distinctions straight. In order to do "good" we believe we have to feel loving. If we hate, we believe that justifies hateful behavior. Psychologically separating persons behave in a loving way regardless of what they feel. This doesn't mean they never criticize or express their resentments or inform another about hurtful behavior. It just means they never behave in a way that is *designed* to hurt. They know it is in their own best interests and that of the universe to be kind. I've heard it said that happiness is a yearning to give; unhappiness, a yearning to get. Psychologically separating persons know that generosity, compassion, and tolerance make them very happy, and they wisely choose them instead of their ego.

B. Relatedness and giving up control. Psychologically separating persons are *present*, prepared to share their innermost self with others should they choose to do so. They relate easily to others. At the same time they avoid toxic people, people who "press their buttons" with no good reason. They seek out nourishing persons and relate to them.

They are ever vigilant lest they attempt to control others. While they are present to others, they rarely initiate guidance or evaluation of others' behavior, overtly or covertly. They acknowledge the sovereignty of others and respect it, just as they protect their own. They know that relatedness is the antithesis of control, and they fight the urge to control others, even "for their own good."

The best book I have ever found that discusses this subject was written not by a psychologist or philosopher but by a businessman, Harry Browne. His foray into human relatedness stands out as the epitome of common sense and wisdom. I have been reading this book for two decades now and always find something new and valuable in it.

> And so one day you may discover that you've achieved a new freedom, an emotional freedom that's greater than any you've known before—freedom from the urge to control others.
>
> When you have that freedom, you'll experience a wondrous sense of weightlessness, an absence of burdens, a freedom to let the world unfold as it will—adventurously, challengingly. You'll know that whatever happens isn't your problem because you no longer have the responsibility to see that others do what they should.[3]

C. Productivity/Efficiency. Psychologically separating persons act on the world in productive and efficient ways. They express their gifts for the sake of expressing them and offer them as a gift to the world even though they are not so dependent on the world's evaluation of them or their gifts. They express themselves because they must. Quite capable of leisure and even idleness and thoroughly enjoying frivolous moments, psychologically separating persons are efficient in sharing their inner experience with others and can work quite hard when it is called for. And they get joy in such work.

Relationship with the Transcendent

Structure of Personality

A. Humility. Humility does not mean "humiliation." It means "of the earth." "Remember, man, from dust thou art and unto dust thou shalt return," the priest intones on Ash Wednesday. Humility merely refers to our realization that we are what we are, nothing more—and nothing less!

Psychologically separating persons have abandoned grandiosity, have surrendered their egos to the ever-deepening realities they experience as they move relentlessly to higher consciousnesses. They love themselves madly and are charmed by their growing relationship with the Transcendent. They experience the Transcendent as "mystery outside of us and life within us." They accept this *magnum mysterium*; they do not deny it. They accept transcendent impulses—awe, the urge toward worship. They know this is part of human nature (Maslow's self-actualized individuals[4] and just about all scientists of the genius calibre are keenly aware of the Transcendent) and don't clandestinely hold to ego and mother-fusion by the surreptitious superstition of believing in the omnipotence of science. They are teachable. They have things in perspective. They are free.

B. Gratitude/serenity. As they now accept their spiritual nature, they have gratitude for life and for the world. They are at peace with life. Although not immune to pain and the tragedies of life, they are generally serene and, at times, downright joyous. They "wear life like a loose garment," as the saying goes. They increasingly experience their oneness with all living things and the Transcendent, the source of all life. They accept what life has to give them. They trust it.

Values

A. Equality of all persons. The psychologically separating person believes increasingly deeply that we are all part of something larger; that all persons are the expression of the source of life; that we are all, even mother, the children of mothers. Thus there can be no racism or war under any conditions. There is love of all humanity despite whatever feelings we may have about any particular person at any particular time.

B. The approval of death. This seems like a strange notion. Nobody likes the idea of death; self-preservation is the strongest of human instincts. Yet, as psychologically separating persons overcome ego, they become more trusting in the plan of the universe. As we have seen, much of the meaning of death for us has to do with a primitive belief that mother will save us from it and also that death is horrible because it will separate us from her. As we relinquish our fused relationship with mother, we see death in a more realistic fashion. We may still not be crazy about the notion, but we accept it as a reality, and we order and conduct our lives with that reality in front of us. We trust that the universe is our mother and that it works the way it is supposed to. Life will not be too much to bear, nor will death. Psychologically separating persons get the increasing sense that death will be easier to handle to the extent that they have lived their life fully and with devotion. Death is to be feared if we have not lived, if we have not separated. Death "hath no sting" to the extent that we become truly ourselves. In that sense it can even be approved of as part of the transcendent plan of the universe, to which we have surrendered.

Behavior

A. Forgiveness/gratitude. Imagine what life would be like if we had only gratitude and forgiveness for all the manifestations of the Transcendent, including all people who are or have been in our life. What freedom! What joy! Psychologically separating persons constantly move in that direction. All resentments are the detritus of ego, and to the extent that ego goes, resentment vanishes and in comes forgiveness. Forgiveness and gratitude may characterize much of our behavior, but it is possible for them to live side by side with our hatred and fear and all the residual affects that come from the unfinished business of our personality. Psychologically separating persons feel *all* these things, learn from them, accept themselves as having them, but are not controlled by them. Their commitment is to move in the direction of forgiveness and gratitude, because they know that's where the "winners" go. Winners are those who get gratitude for life and all they've been given by others, present and past; forgiveness for all who have harmed them; generosity toward the mystery of life and all living things; independence; radical self-acceptance and compassion and tolerance toward self and others; understanding and acceptance of the essential limitedness of mortal human beings; freedom to think their own thoughts, feel their own feelings, act and express their gifts, and co-create the universe with the Transcendent. They can feel negative feelings and even learn from them. But they refuse to be enslaved by them, for they have found out through personal experience that the big payoff in joy is in spiritual development.

B. Ethics/Golden Rule. Psychologically separating persons do unto others as they wish to be treated themselves. But in addition, they infuse their behavior with massive doses of generosity. They live and give without reservation and are joyous as a result. They are free.

Conclusion

When we read about an ideal, such as forgiving parents or being independent of such and such, it is tempting to want to leap right to that characteristic. "Arriving," however, is not a goal but rather a by-product. It is the commitment to the journey that is important, and if our ambition, avarice, or self-centeredness prompts us to skip the journey to get to the result, we will have lost out altogether. It is the gentle journey, step by step, observation by observation, failure by failure, self-acceptance by self-acceptance, loving by loving that counts. Then, often unbeknownst to us, we change "behind our backs."

To be separate is to know our aloneness. It is the most courageous and fully human thing a person can do. To be able to be alone, to engage the *magnum mysterium*, to reach out to others in companionate affiliation, to know love of Spirit and Universe and lover and child and parent and friend; to look with awe at this creation and celebrate it and our part in it, to co-create with the Transcendent our very world; to meet the ambiguity and yet go on, to suffer, yet love, to fail and still create, to struggle to overcome mother-fusion and then fall gently yet resolutely into the arms of the infinite, doing our work as best we can, letting ourselves know the magnificence of what a human is capable of—love, tolerance, patience, forgiveness, gratitude…and finally, to accept with magnanimity, grace, and gratitude the last mystery, the ultimate embrace of that which gave this all to us—this is what human life is, in its brilliance.

Notes

Chapter 2: Our Love of Loves

[1] *People* (February 26, 1990), 37.

[2] S. O'Casey, *Autobiographies* 1 (New York: Carroll and Graf, 1984), 5.

[3] M. Besdine, *The Unknown Michelangelo* (New York: Vanguard, 1986), 2.

[4] Ibid., 3.

[5] A. Robbins, *Unlimited Power* (New York: Simon & Schuster, 1986).

[6] Neurolinguistic programming is the esoteric name for a series of techniques designed to teach trainees to become aware of, and utilize more effectively in communication, their cognitive and behavioral patterns.

[7] L. H. Silverman, F. Lachmann, and R. Milich, *The Search for Oneness* (New York: International Universities Press, 1982).

[8] L. H. Silverman, F. Lachmann, and R. Milich, "Mommy and I Are One: Implications for Psychotherapy," *American Psychologist* 40, no. 12 (1985): 1296.

[9] V. Adams, *Psychology Today* (May 1982), 30–32.

[10] British psychiatrist Ann Dally, in discussing pathological parenting, says, "Occasionally the same kind of situation can be created by an unusually controlling or powerful father, but mother is much more often the cause because she is the one who usually has most to do with the child" (*Inventing Motherhood, the Consequences of an Ideal* [New York: Schocken Books, 1983]), 236.

[11] L. J. Kaplan, *Oneness and Separation: From Infant to Individual* (New York: Simon & Schuster, 1978).

[12] M. Mahler, F. Pine, and A. Berman, *The Psychological Birth of the Human Infant* (New York: Basic Books, 1967), 231.

Chapter 3: The Eternal Conspiracy

[1] Stephen Levine, *Who Dies? An Investigation of Conscious Living and Conscious Dying* (New York: Anchor Books, 1982).

[2] I am deeply grateful to Selma Turkel for her honesty, her courage, and her wisdom.

[3] Ernest Becker, *The Denial of Death* (New York: Macmillan Publishing Company, 1973).

[4] Ann Dally, *Inventing Motherhood, the Consequences of an Ideal* (New York: Schocken Books, 1983), 93. Dally also powerfully describes the results of disturbed

mothering. See, particularly, the chapters "Conditions of Power" and "Devious Mothers," 201–40.

Chapter 4: Fusion

[1] I prefer the term *psychological separation* to the commonly used term, *individuation*, because the latter implies a "state" that can be arrived at; psychological separation implies a *position relative* to the essential other. It is in such a relative position that, existentially, we always are.

[2] M. Klein, "Some Theoretical Conclusions Regarding the Emotional Life of the Infant," in *Envy and Gratitude and Other Works* (New York: Delta, 1977), 61.

[3] Ibid., 178.

[4] J. M. McMahon, "Discussion of S. Hymer's 'What's in a Name?'" *Dynamic Psychotherapy* 3, no. 2 (1985): 199–200.

[5] A concise yet excellent summary of Freudian theory can be found in Charles Brenner, *An Elementary Textbook of Psychoanalysis* (Garden City, NY: Doubleday Anchor Book, 1955).

Chapter 5: Psychological Separation

[1] I use the term *psychologically separating* to refer to a person who has the *intention* of becoming fully herself. Such a person I consider to be in the *process* of separating psychologically.

[2] Henry David Thoreau, *Walden* (New York: New American Library, 1960), 104–5.

[3] G. Cocks, *Psychotherapy in the Third Reich: The Göring Institute* (Oxford: Oxford University Press, 1980).

Chapter 6: The Nature of Psychological Change

[1] J. Strachey, "The Nature of the Therapeutic Action of Psycho-Analysis," in *The Evolution of Psychoanalytic Technique*, ed. M. Bergmann and F. Hartman (New York: Basic Books, 1976), 341.

[2] F. M. Alexander, *The Use of the Self* (Long Beach, Calif.: Centerline Press, 1985), 50–51.

[3] Ibid., 53.

[4] Strachey, 360.

[5] Figure 6–1 shows the person in relation to reality. This is true whether the reality is external or within.

Chapter 7: Spirituality and Psychology

[1] Stephen Mitchell, *The Enlightened Heart* (New York: Harper & Row, 1989), 3.

[2] Norris Clarke, S.J., *Theology Digest* 33, no. 4 (Winter 1986), 453.

[3] *Meditations of Julian of Norwich* (Santa Fe: Bear & Company, 1983), 105.

[4] Brother Lawrence of the Resurrection, *The Practice of the Presence of God*, trans. John J. Delaney (New York: Doubleday, 1977), 69–70.

[5] Courtesy of Dr. Kenneth Byrne. Jonathan Aitken, "The Tapes That Tricked Then Undid Nixon," *The Age* 20 (February 1993).

[6] Stephen Hawking, *A Brief History of Time* (New York: Bantam, 1988), 174–75.

[7] Michael Beldoch, *Readings* 3, no. 3 (September 1988): 21–23.

[8] Eric Hoffer, *The True Believer* (New York: Mentor, 1951).

[9] Robert Karen, "Shame," *The Atlantic Monthly*, February 1992, 40–70.

[10] E. Kurtz, *Shame and Guilt: Characteristics of the Dependency Cycle* (Minneapolis: Hazelden Press, 1981).

[11] Carl Rogers, *On Becoming a Person* (Boston: Houghton Mifflin, 1961).

[12] Kurtz, 53.

[13] Vaclav Havel, *Disturbing the Peace* (New York: Knopf, 1990), 11.

[14] Ibid., 12.

[15] Karen, 70.

[16] Bill Wilson, *The Language of the Heart—Bill W's Grapevine Writings* (New York: AA Grapevine, Inc., 1988), 236–38.

[17] H. M. Rizzuto, personal communication (1983).

[18] *All You Need Is Love*. Words and music by John Lennon and Paul McCartney. Copyright ©1967, Northern Songs Limited. All rights controlled and administered by Blackwood Music, Inc. under license from ATV Music (Maclen). All rights reserved. International copyright secured.

Chapter 8: Intimacy Among Friends and Lovers

[1] J. M. McMahon, "Marriage as a Developmental Stage: The Role of Transference in Intimacy and Growth," in *Man and Woman in Transition*, ed. D. Milman and G. Goldman (Dubuque, Iowa: Kendall Hunt, 1978), 109–10.

[2] Melanie Klein, *Envy and Gratitude and Other Works* (New York: Delta, 1977), 188.

[3] J. M. McMahon, "Intimacy Among Friends and Lovers," in *Intimacy*, ed. M. Fisher and G. Stricker (New York: Plenum Press, 1982), 293–304.

[4] Gabriel Marquez, *Love in the Time of Cholera* (New York: Penguin Books, 1989), 224.

[5] Murray Bowen, *The Family Therapy Networker* 3, no. 4 (1991).

[6] Type 2 communicators are notoriously cheap—they have difficulty giving anything of themselves for fear of being emptied out.

[7] Philip Roth, *My Life as a Man* (New York: Holt, Rinehart, & Winston, 1970).

[8] See the work of Carol Gilligan, *In a Different Voice* (Cambridge, Mass.: Harvard University Press, 1982).

[9] I am indebted to Linda Lande Brown for emphasizing this point to me.

Chapter 9: How Change Occurs

[1] Quentin Crisp, Live in Performance, "Sunday Tea with Quentin Crisp" (October 18, 1992).

[2] Stephen Levine, *Who Dies? An Investigation of Conscious Living and Conscious Dying* (New York: Anchor Books, 1982), 71.

[3] Joyce McDougall, *Plea for a Measure of Abnormality* (New York: International Universities Press, 1980), 12.

Chapter 11: Loving Yourself Madly

[1] Bill Wilson, *Twelve Steps and Twelve Traditions, A.A. Grapevine* (1986 <1952>), 124–25.

Chapter 12: Joy

[1] "Program Notes," Santa Fe Chamber Music Festival in Seattle, August 1991.

Appendix: The Person on the Wisdom Path

[1] The word *feelings* is sometimes confused because the phrase "I feel" is often used to mean "It is my opinion." When I use the word *feelings*, I am referring to emotions or affective states.

[2] Benjamin Hoff, *The Tao of Pooh* (New York: Penguin Books, 1983), 128.

[3] Harry Browne, *How I Found Freedom in an Unfree World* (New York: Macmillan, 1973), 377.

[4] A. Maslow, *Motivation and Personality* (New York: Harper and Bros., 1954), esp. chaps. 12, 13.

Glossary

Acting out. Behavior prompted by an out-of-awareness idea or emotion and which is designed to express something we are in conflict about or to relieve tension.

Affect. An emotional state.

Chronic affect. An emotional state characteristic of an earlier period in life which lingers into the present as a habitual or familiar feeling.

Contact. An emotional state of pleasant union with another as a result of mutual shared intimacies.

Demons. A symbolic word to describe the unconscious forces in each of us that work psychologically toward avoiding change.

Deep belief. Strong convictions, often out of awareness, developed at an earlier period, generally under duress, which profoundly influence our behavior in the present.

Ego. Inflated, grandiose, sense of self-worth based on fusion with mother.

Fusion. A psychological state of union with another so that independent thinking, feeling and behavior are compromised.

Guilt. A feeling of discomfort as a result of behavior considered by us as transgressive.

Intention. The clear focus on what we should like to do or become.

Intimacy. Something of a personal or private nature.

Intimus. That which is most within us; the deepest and most private thoughts and feelings.

Narcissism. Overweening self-centeredness.

Observation. The keen study of one's behavior, feelings and thoughts conducted with no evaluation or judgment or attempt to change.

Person. The end product at any moment of the self's struggle to resolve the conflict between spirit and demons.

Presence. The psychological state of readiness to reveal one's most personal and private thoughts, feeling and nature.

Radical Self-Acceptance. The complete and total acceptance and reception of one's self exactly as is with no demand to change.

Relatedness. The behavior which communicates one's intimacy to another and, in turn, receives the other's.

Self. The agency of the personality which negotiates the individual's tendency to stay the same (demons) with his impulse to grow (spirit).

Separation. The psychological and spiritual processes by which an individual struggles to disentangle his thoughts, feelings and behaviors from others, primarily parenting figures and contemporary re-creations of them, so that he feels, thinks, and acts largely from his own lights.

Shame. The emotional state of anguish elicited by the belief that one is not acceptable—in his very essence—to be a human being.

Spirit. The unique participation in the Transcendent Force of life which is characteristic of each of us from conception and which prompts us to move forward, understand the world through our own eyes, and express ourselves in our unique way.

Transcendent. That which transcends us all. The Living Force of the universe; the higher power, God.

Transference. Reacting to a person currently in our life with the feelings and attitudes and beliefs that were formerly directed to a significant person of our childhood.

Wisdom. The capacity and willingness to see the world through our own eyes as unique individuals, and the courage to express ourselves as we are called to do.

Works Cited

Adams, V. *Psychology Today* (May 1982), 30–32.

Aitken, J. "The Tapes That Tricked Then Undid Nixon." *The Age* (February 20, 1993).

Alexander, F. M. *The Use of the Self.* Long Beach, Calif.: Centerline Press, 1985; originally published New York: E. P. Dutton, 1932.

Becker, Ernest. *The Denial of Death.* New York: Macmillan, 1973.

Beldoch, M. "Review of 'A Godless Jew: Freud, Atheism, and the Making of Psychoanalysis.'" *Readings* 3, no. 3 (September 1988).

Besdine, M. *The Unknown Michelangelo.* New York: Vanguard, 1986.

Bowen, Murray. *The Family Therapy Networker* 3, no. 4 (1991).

Brenner, C. *An Elementary Textbook of Psychoanalysis.* New York: Doubleday Anchor Books, 1955.

Browne, H. *How I Found Freedom in an Unfree World.* New York: Macmillan, 1973.

Clarke, N. *Theology Digest* 33, no. 4 (Winter 1986).

Cocks, G. *Psychotherapy in the Third Reich: The Göring Institute.* New York: Oxford University Press, 1980.

Dally, A. *Inventing Motherhood, the Consequences of an Ideal.* New York: Schocken Books, 1983.

Gilligan, Carol. *In a Different Voice.* Cambridge, Mass.: Harvard University Press, 1982.

Havel, V. *Disturbing the Peace.* New York: Knopf, 1990.

Hawking, S. *A Brief History of Time.* Toronto and New York: Bantam, 1988.

Hoff, B. *The Tao of Pooh.* New York: Penguin Books, 1983.

Hoffer, E. *The True Believer.* New York: Mentor Books, 1951.

Hymer, S. "What's in a Name?" *Dynamic Psychotherapy* 3, no. 2 (1985): 199–200.

Julian of Norwich. *Meditations of Julian of Norwich.* Santa Fe: Bear & Company, 1983.

Kaplan, L. J. *Oneness and Separation: From Infant to Individual.* New York: Simon & Schuster, 1978.

Karen, Robert. "Shame." *Atlantic Monthly* (February 1992), 40–70.

Klein, M. "Some Theoretical Conclusions Regarding the Emotional Life of the Infant." In *Envy and Gratitude and Other Works.* New York: Delta, 1977.

Kurtz, E. *Shame and Guilt: Characteristics of the Dependency Cycle*. Minneapolis: Hazelden Press, 1981.

Lawrence, Bro., of the Resurrection. *The Practice of the Presence of God*. Trans. John J. Delaney. New York: Doubleday, 1977.

Lennon, John, and Paul McCartney. "All You Need Is Love." Northern Songs, Inc., 1967.

Levine, S. *Who Dies? An Investigation of Conscious Living and Conscious Dying*. New York: Anchor Books, 1982.

Mahler, M., F. Pine, and A. Berman. *The Psychological Birth of the Human Infant*. New York: Basic Books, 1967.

Marquez, Gabriel, *Love in the Time of Cholera*. New York: Penguin Books, 1989.

Maslow, A. *Motivation and Personality*. New York: Harper and Bros., 1954.

McDougall, Joyce. *Plea for a Measure of Abnormality*. New York: International Universities Press. 1980.

McMahon, J. M. "Marriage as a Developmental Stop: The Role of Transference in Intimacy and Growth." In *Man and Woman in Transition*. Ed. D. Milman and G. Goldman. Dubuque: Kendall Hunt, 1978.

———. "Intimacy Among Friends and Lovers." In *Intimacy*. Ed. M. Fisher and G. Stricker. New York: Plenum Press, 1982.

———. "Discussion of 'What's in a Name?' by Sharon M. Hymes." *Dynamic Psychotherapy* 3, no. 2 (1985).

Mitchell, S. *The Enlightened Heart*. New York: Harper & Row, 1989.

O'Casey, S. *Autobiographies 1*. New York: Carroll and Graf, 1984.

Reynolds, D. *Constructive Living*. Honolulu: University of Hawaii Press, 1984.

Rizzuto, H. M. Personal communication. 1983.

Robbins, A. *Unlimited Power*. New York: Simon and Schuster, 1986.

Rogers, C. *On Becoming a Person*. Boston: Houghton Mifflin, 1961.

Roth, Philip. *My Life as a Man*. New York: Holt, Rinehart, and Winston, 1970.

Silverman, L. H., F. Lachmann, and R. Milich. *The Search for Oneness*. New York: International Universities Press, 1982.

———. "Mommy and I Are One: Implications for Psychotherapy." *American Psychologist* 40, no. 2 (1985).

Strachey, J. "The Nature of the Therapeutic Action of Psychoanalysis." In *The Evolution of Psychoanalytic Technique*. Ed. M. Bergmann and F. Hartman. New York: Basic Books, 1976.

Thoreau, Henry David. *Walden*. New York: New American Library, 1960.

Wilson, W. *Twelve Steps and Twelve Traditions, A.A. Grapevine*. New York, 1986<1952>.

———. *The Language of the Heart—Bill W's Grapevine Writings*. New York: AA Grapevine, Inc., 1988.

Index

resentment, 239; uses of, 237–38. *See also* anger

responsibility, 78, 149–50, 223

Reynolds, David, 231

Rizzuto, Helen Morrissey, 130–31

Robbins, Anthony, 21

Rogers, Carl, 123–24, 167

romantic love, 34, 135

Roth, Philip, 158

schizophrenia, 77

science, 118–20, 125, 132

security, search for, 50–51, 54

Self, 24, 30. *See also* spirit

self, 24, 25, 53, 130; becoming oneself, 9, 32, 33, 54–55, 62, 87, 127, 219 (*see also* separation); beliefs about, 133; defined, 51; essential, 48 (*see also* spirit). *See also* ego; "I"; true self

self-acceptance, 165–66; intention of, 47, 54, 55, 204; and maturing into true self, 127; meaning of, 176–78; of one's flaws, 61; as separation, 81, 204

self-awareness, 24–25, 77–78

self-centeredness, 133, 193–95; of residual mother-fusion, 133, 193–95

self-communication, 114

self-connectedness, 150, 155, 156

self-criticism, 93–95, 176, 177, 206; saying no to, 95

self-determination, 113–14

self-esteem, low, 86, 139. *See also* shame

self-esteem regulation: separation and, 81, 82; taking responsibility for, 78

self-evaluation, separation as giving up, 202

self-identity, 40

self-justification, 139, 140

self-knowledge, 77–78

self-love, xii, 87, 88, 175–76, 178, 194; capacity for, 199, 207; fear of, 20; higher power and, 197; intention for, 205–7; not having enough, 205; self-

ishness *vs.*, 203; shame *vs.*, 190–91; strategies for achieving, 205, 207; unconditional, 94, 190, 210. *See also* narcissism

self-neglect, 232

self-relatedness, separation as requisite for, 9

self-revelation, 141, 142. *See also* intimacy

self-transcendence, 113, 114

self-worth, 132, 203

separating persons, 133–36, 148, 150–51, 223, 228–30; intimacy in, 152, 155–56

separation (psychological), 8–11, 23–25, 27–29, 243; and being central-to-self *vs.* central-to-other, 149, 156, 161, 223, 229; in boys *vs.* girls, 159–60; "call back" in, 32, 53; conditions facilitating, 40, 77; definition and meaning of, 42, 59, 62, 63, 77, 149, 202; dimensions of, 63, 223–24; efforts to deny, 229; fear and pain of, 35–36, 44–45, 54, 75, 153; and freedom, 62; humankind's journey toward, 130; and independent thinking, 66–69; love and, 62; mutual letting go in, 35; and psychic destiny, 62; and range of feelings, 73; as requisite for self-relatedness, 9; and the Transcendent, 52, 115–17, 212–13; as the unusual state, 60. *See also* individuation; *specific topics*

serenity, 241

sex, 67–68, 158, 159

sex differences, 159–60

sexual desire, 145

sexual union, 158

sexuality, 68, 160, 219–20

shame, 123, 127, 144, 183, 186, 188; and change process, 89; destructive effects of, 183, 189, 191; guilt *vs.*, 122, 123, 184–86; as healthy guidance, 186; institutionalization of, 189; neurotic/